Studies in Regional and Local History

General Editor Jane Whittle

Previous titles in this series
Founding Editor Nigel Goose

Volume 1: *A Hertfordshire demesne of Westminster Abbey: Profits, productivity and weather* by Derek Vincent Stern (edited and with an introduction by Christopher Thornton)

Volume 2: *From Hellgill to Bridge End: Aspects of economic and social change in the Upper Eden Valley, 1840–95* by Margaret Shepherd

Volume 3: *Cambridge and its Economic Region, 1450–1560* by John S. Lee

Volume 4: *Cultural Transition in the Chilterns and Essex Region, 350 AD to 650 AD* by John T. Baker

Volume 5: *A Pleasing Prospect: Society and culture in eighteenth-century Colchester* by Shani D'Cruze

Volume 6: *Agriculture and Rural Society after the Black Death: Common themes and regional variations* by Ben Dodds and Richard Britnell

Volume 7: *A Lost Frontier Revealed: Regional separation in the East Midlands* by Alan Fox

Volume 8: *Land and Family: Trends and local variations in the peasant land market on the Winchester bishopric estates, 1263–1415* by John Mullan and Richard Britnell

Volume 9: *Out of the Hay and into the Hops: Hop cultivation in Wealden Kent and hop marketing in Southwark, 1744–2000* by Celia Cordle

Volume 10: *A Prospering Society: Wiltshire in the later Middle Ages* by John Hare

Volume 11: *Bread and Ale for the Brethren: The provisioning of Norwich Cathedral Priory, 1260–1536* by Philip Slavin

Volume 12: *Poor Relief and Community in Hadleigh, Suffolk, 1547–1600* by Marjorie Keniston McIntosh

Volume 13: *Rethinking Ancient Woodland: The archaeology and history of woods in Norfolk* by Gerry Barnes and Tom Williamson

Volume 14: *Custom and Commercialisation in English Rural Society: Revisiting Tawney and Postan* edited by J.P. Bowen and A.T. Brown

Volume 15: *The World of the Small Farmer: Tenure, profit and politics in the early modern Somerset Levels* by Patricia Croot

Communities in Contrast

Doncaster and its rural hinterland,
c.1830–1870

Sarah Holland

University of Hertfordshire Press
Studies in Regional and Local History

Volume 16

First published in Great Britain in 2019 by
University of Hertfordshire Press
College Lane
Hatfield
Hertfordshire
AL10 9AB
UK

© Sarah Holland 2019

The right of Sarah Holland to be identified as the author of this work has been asserted by her in accordance with the Copyright, Designs and Patents Act 1988.

All rights reserved. No part of this book may be reproduced or utilised in any form or by any means, electronic or mechanical, including photocopying, recording or by any information storage and retrieval system, without permission in writing from the publisher.

British Library Cataloguing in Publication Data
A catalogue record for this book is available from the British Library

ISBN 978-1-912260-12-6 hardback
ISBN 978-1-912260-13-3 paperback

Design by Arthouse Publishing Solutions Ltd
Printed in Great Britain by Charlesworth Press, Wakefield

Contents

List of illustrations	vii
General Editor's preface	ix
Acknowledgements	xi
Abbreviations	xiii

1 Introduction — 1
- Contrasting communities: models of village typology — 3
- Chronological framework — 7
- The region — 8
- The village case studies — 9
- Studying the region — 13

2 Social hierarchies, power relations and agency in the countryside — 15
- Landownership and landowners — 16
- Landowner agency beyond the village — 21
- Leadership not landownership — 23
- External agents — 30
- Agricultural workers — 32
- Conclusion — 34

3 Rural economies — 35
- Agriculture — 37
- Micro-commerce and industry — 53
- Conclusion — 69

4 Living and working conditions — 71
- Wages — 73
- The employment of women in agriculture — 76
- Cottage accommodation and gardens — 79
- Conclusion — 85

5 Religion and education — 87
- Religion — 87
- Education — 100
- Conclusion — 110

6 Rural recreation — 111
- Doncaster — 118
- The countryside as a destination for leisure — 119
- Conclusion — 122

7 Conclusion — 123

Bibliography	127
Index	142

Illustrations

Figures
1.1	Map of the Doncaster district	10
2.1	Sprotbrough Hall	17
2.2	Agricultural labourer's smock, c.1880	33
3.1	Cattle market, Doncaster	39
3.2	a and b Doncaster Agricultural Society medal awarded for best sheep	48
3.3	Doncaster Corn Exchange	52
3.4	Proportion of trades, crafts and industries in the six case-study villages, 1837–77	53
3.5	Gravestone to George Nassau, Sprotbrough churchyard	58
4.1	Cottages at Rossington	81
5.1	St Michael's Church, Rossington	94
5.2	Carved fox heads, St Michael's Church, Rossington	98
5.3	Rossington school	102
6.1	Sprotbrough pub	114

Tables
1.1	Overview of landownership, acreage, land type and transport routes in the six case-study villages	11
2.1	The ownership and occupation of the land belonging to the main landowners in Braithwell	21
3.1	Arable crops grown in the six case-study villages, 1866	36
3.2	Livestock in the six case-study villages, 1866	38
3.3	Farm size in the six case-study villages, 1851	42
3.4	Attendance at the celebratory dinner to mark the opening of the new covered corn market by farmers from the six case-study villages	50
3.5	Ten essential trades and crafts businesses in the six case-study villages, 1861	57
3.6	Relationship between population size and the number of trades and crafts businesses in the six case-study villages, 1861	57
3.7	Relationship between population size and the range of different trades and crafts in the six case-study villages, 1861	57
4.1	Average weekly wages for agricultural workers, 1860–70	74
5.1	Provision of and attendance at Anglican churches in the six case-study villages, 1851	89
5.2	Provision of and attendance at non-conformist chapels in the six case-study villages, 1851	90

Grants for the publication of this book were very gratefully received from the Marc Fitch Fund and the Scouloudi Foundation in association with the Institute of Historical Research.

Studies in Regional and Local History

General Editor's preface

The novelty of the industrialisation and urbanisation experienced by northern England in the nineteenth century has led the experience of rural communities in the North during the same period to be largely overlooked. In fact, the great majority of studies of English villages, from the medieval period onwards, have been studies of southern England and the Midlands. It is a great pleasure therefore to introduce Sarah Holland's research on six villages in the Doncaster region (now the eastern part of South Yorkshire). It offers a powerful reminder that nineteenth-century northern England was not all smoking mills and factory workers, or even upland sheep farms: there were also large areas of highly productive lowland arable agriculture which existed in close proximity to the rapidly expanding industrial cities. The title of *Communities in Contrast* nods towards the founding influence on comparative village studies of Margaret Spufford's *Contrasting Communities* (1974), which focused on three villages in early modern Cambridgeshire. Spufford introduced a template for comparative studies which showed how villages in close geographical proximity could develop quite differently over time. She not only paid attention to underlying geology, agricultural systems and land tenure, but also examined the consequences of patterns of education and religious belief on the social life of the village. This is the approach adopted in here: Holland looks carefully at patterns of landownership, agricultural production, and forms of wage labour, but also at educational reform, religion and leisure activities within the villages studied, offering a rounded view of the constraints and opportunities of nineteenth-century rural life.

Communities in Contrast is also framed by the important debate about open and closed villages. The characterisation of villages as either open or closed first appeared in nineteenth-century poor law reports, but was developed into a model of social and geographical history by the work of Dennis Mills, published between 1959 and 1980. Closed villages were dominated by a single landowner. The landowner's ability to control development shaped the social structure and religious life of the village. To keep poor rates down few new houses were built and thus the population grew slowly, if at all, over time. As a result such villages lacked economic dynamism and remained solely agricultural communities. With a relatively small population and no opportunities to establish independent places of worship, the Anglican Church remained dominant. Open villages were not controlled by a single landowner. They were open to newcomers, allowing population growth which creating large sprawling communities. The large numbers of relatively poor inhabitants were balanced by mixed economies which offered more diverse opportunities of employment in crafts and industry as well as agriculture. Freedom from social control in such communities was marked by religious non-conformity, with a diversity of places of worship, and the proliferation of drinking houses. The open and closed model is a powerful and persistent one, not least because the shadow of these influences is still seen today across the broad swathe of lowland England that is dominated by nucleated villages, where 'chocolate box' (closed) villages of a selection of picturesque older houses clustered round the village church are interspersed with much more 'practical' (open) settlements where new housing estates sit alongside a wider range of housing types and a selection of small businesses. Yet it is also a model that has rightly been subjected to a great deal of criticism, and Sarah Holland is among these critics. There are two important strands to her critique. First, while the open/closed model suggests a binary division of villages into two types, what studies of rural England demonstrate is a continuum between two extremes. In other words, not all villages can be characterised as open or closed, and many combine elements of the two types. The six villages which form the focus of this study demonstrate this very well. Second, Mills placed a heavy emphasis on the type of landownership as the determining influence. Holland argues we need to look more carefully at agency, or the exercise of power, by particular individuals in particular circumstances. A village with a single absentee landowner who showed little interest in the community was not tightly controlled and might develop 'open' characteristics. On the other hand a particularly Anglican clergyman or large tenant, might fulfil the role taken by the landowner elsewhere and retain relatively tight control on the social fabric of the village. Where natural assets such as stone quarries offered profits other than agriculture, a landowner might promote the development of industry, and an industrial community, rather than a 'closed' agricultural village. Open villages varied in their openness, an elite of several large tenants might lead an impetus towards increased social control. In short, Holland's research demonstrates that while it is possible to generalise in broad terms about the types of villages, when communities are studied in sufficient detail to illuminate the particular personalities involved, the story that emerges is a much more complex and richer understanding to the past.

Jane Whittle
December 2018

Acknowledgements

Communities in Contrast would not exist without the invaluable contributions of a number of individuals and organisations, and I would like to extend my professional and personal gratitude to all those who have helped to shape my ideas and encourage them into print.

This book began life as my PhD thesis, undertaken at Sheffield Hallam University (SHU). My thanks go to Professor Peter Cain (SHU) and Dr Merv Lewis (SHU), who read and commented on drafts of the thesis, and to the examiners, Dr Matthew Roberts (SHU) and Professor John Chartres (University of Leeds). Special thanks, however, must go to Professor Nicola Verdon (SHU), who was not only my PhD supervisor but also a trusted academic colleague and mentor whose support and advice have been invaluable.

During the course of researching and writing this book I have presented the findings at various conferences, notably the British Agricultural History Society spring conference and EURHO Rural History. I am grateful to those who listened, asked questions and critically engaged with the material – and especially to those who discussed my work further afterwards or offered to read drafts of my work, not least Professor Alun Howkins, Professor David Hey and Professor Jeremy Burchardt. I am also grateful to colleagues and students at the University of Nottingham, especially Professor John Beckett and my third-year special subject groups (Rural Life in Victorian England). To the latter, and members of WEA history groups, I extend a special thank you for listening, engaging with the material and sharing their ideas about and enthusiasm for the subject.

Much of the archival research for the book took place in Doncaster's Archives and Local Studies Library, and my thanks go to the staff there for their friendly and helpful manner over the course of my studies. Particular mention goes to Dr Charles Kelham and Becky Andrews, for whom nothing was too much trouble. I would also like to thank Carolyn Dalton and Nicola Fox for the opportunity to curate *Life on the Land*, an exhibition exploring the six rural communities featured in this book, held at Cusworth Hall in summer 2016. My gratitude goes to Heritage Doncaster for granting permission to reproduce images in the book. I am also very grateful for the generous publication grants awarded to me by the Marc Fitch Fund and the Scouloudi Foundation in association with the Institute of Historical Research.

I am particularly grateful to the publishing team at the University of Hertfordshire Press, especially Jane Whittle (series editor), Jane Housham and Sarah Elvins for their dedication, painstaking attention to detail, insightful comments and professional service.

Friends and family have provided support and encouragement in varied ways and at different stages, from embarking upon the PhD to the completion of the book, and I hope that they will find something of interest here. You know who you are – thank you!

A special thank you goes to Louise, whose love and support has been invaluable during this process. She might have said 'What … you want me to read it AGAIN?' but always did so – and so much more beside. I could not have done it without you.

Finally, *Communities in Contrast* is dedicated to my late parents, Derek and Enid Mary Holland, who fuelled me with my passion for the past from a very young age.

They provided endless support and inspiration in the formative stages of the research, and although they were not here to enjoy the completion of the PhD or book, neither would have been possible without them.

Abbreviations

DA   Doncaster Archives
DONMG   Doncaster Museums and Galleries
TNA   The National Archives

Chapter 1

Introduction

During the mid-nineteenth century Doncaster's rural hinterland was characterised by contrasts between communities that transcended landownership. Rossington and Warmsworth, both estate villages near Doncaster, were two very different rural communities. The former demonstrated concentrated landownership (the whole estate was owned by one family), with low population density, large farms, an absence of industry and a programme of village rebuilding that included investment in agricultural infrastructure and well-appointed cottages. The latter, in contrast, had high population density and a large proportion of industrial employment, and endured complaints that the cottage accommodation was inadequate owing to poor ventilation and drainage and the use of kitchens as additional sleeping quarters, because many dwellings had only one bedroom – all characteristics that were more akin to multi-freeholder villages with multiple landowners rather than an estate village with only two landowners. As such, the contrasts between these villages cannot be explained by landownership alone, and yet models that purport to explain rural communities and village typology still tend to be defined by patterns of landownership. This book, concentrating on rural communities in the Doncaster district, seeks to reinterpret village differentiation, in the process offering new theoretical and geographical perspectives. It examines how and why rural communities in close proximity often developed differently, highlighting the nuances therein, and challenges existing models of village typology. The book demonstrates what a case study of a northern market town and its rural hinterland can tell us about village differentiation, exploring how and why rural communities developed in what was chiefly an industrial region during the mid-nineteenth century, and how the relationship between town and country affected rural communities.

The development of rural communities, and more specifically of English villages, has proved fertile ground for historians.[1] A rural community could be a spatial entity delineated by recognised and relatively static boundaries, such as the village or parish. It could, however, be more fluid, founded on shared resources, social and cultural institutions, connections forged through work and the relationships between people and places. As such, contrasting social and economic relationships within

---

1   A. Howkins, *Reshaping rural England: a social history 1850–1925* (London, 1991); B. Reay, *Microhistories: demography, society and culture in rural England, 1800–1930* (Cambridge, 2004); A. Howkins, 'Types of rural communities', in E.J.T. Collins (ed.), *The agrarian history of England and Wales*, Vol. VII, 1850–1914, Part 1 (Cambridge, 2000); J. Burchardt, 'Agricultural history, rural history, or countryside history?', *The Historical Journal*, 50/2 (2007), pp. 465–81; J.V. Beckett, 'Rethinking the English village', *The Local Historian*, 42/4 (2012), pp. 301–11; D. Hey, *The grass roots of English history: societies in England before the industrial revolution* (London, 2016); D.R. Mills, *Lord and peasant in nineteenth century Britain* (London, 1980).

and between rural communities can be investigated. The village itself occupies a distinctive position in the history of rural settlements, forming, along with the family unit and the farmstead, a 'base unit of rural society'.[2] Work on rural communities can broadly be categorised into village or parish case studies, thematic explorations of rural life, and theoretical frameworks, between which many parallels and interconnections can be drawn. This book draws upon the wide-ranging work of many historians for whom the village or 'rural community' in its broadest sense has been the foundation for the analysis of and engagement with fundamental issues within rural society.

Specifically how and why rural communities developed, often differently, in the nineteenth century has been the subject of extensive debate, with sociological models being constructed to explain differentiation. The 'open–closed' settlement model, developed by Dennis R. Mills between 1959 and 1980, is still at the heart of current thinking about village differentiation.[3] Yet, as Barry Reay argues, the fundamental weakness of the model is that few places actually correspond to it.[4] This book critically engages with the historiographical debates about village differentiation and village typology, arguing that existing models are restrictive in terms of understanding the nuances and complexities of rural life.

The extent to which rural communities were 'self-contained' was the subject of academic analysis in a volume edited by Christopher Dyer.[5] Self-contained communities are defined as being self-sufficient and self-perpetuating, with a strong sense of their own distinct identity and cut off from the outside world.[6] David Brown's chapter in Dyer's book, which focused specifically on the nineteenth century, acknowledged an erosion of the 'self-contained' community, but argued that elements of 'self-containedness' continued to exist within communities and that, to some extent, regional variation prevailed.[7] He identified four key indicators of the self-contained

---

2   Howkins, 'Types of rural communities', p. 1301.
3   D.R. Mills, 'The development of rural settlement around Lincoln, with special reference to the eighteenth and nineteenth centuries', *East Midland Geographer*, 11 (1959), pp. 3–15; D.R. Mills, 'The poor laws and the distribution of population c. 1600–1860, with special reference to Lincolnshire', *Transactions of the Institute of British Geographers*, 26 (1959), pp. 185–95; D.R. Mills, 'Landownership and rural population, with special reference to Leicestershire in the mid nineteenth century', PhD thesis (University of Leicester, 1963); D.R. Mills, 'English villages in the eighteenth and nineteenth centuries: a sociological approach', *Amateur Historian*, 6/8 (1965), pp. 271–8; D.R. Mills, 'The geographical effects of the laws of settlement in Nottinghamshire: an analysis of Francis Howell's report, 1848', in Mills (ed.), *English rural communities: the impact of a specialised economy* (London, 1978); Mills, *Lord and peasant*.
4   B. Reay, *Rural Englands: labouring lives in the nineteenth century* (Basingstoke, 2004), p. 14.
5   C. Dyer (ed.) *The self-contained village? The social history of rural communities, 1250–1890* (Hatfield, 2007).
6   Ibid.
7   D. Brown, 'The rise of industrial society and the end of the village, 1760–1900?', in Dyer (ed.), *The self-contained village?*, pp. 114–37.

community: formal legal independence, demographic separation, economic autonomy and cultural self-containedness – the latter two being the focus in this study of Doncaster. By comparing villages in the Doncaster district – communities that were in close proximity to one another and to the market town – the comparative ability of rural communities to be self-contained is demonstrated.

Historical and geographical context is vital to understanding village differentiation. John Beckett's work on rethinking the English village demonstrates the importance of historic determinants in the development of rural communities.[8] Three factors are identified by Beckett as crucial in establishing patterns of rural settlement: the economics of farming, the social value of the village, and the role of the church – each of which are examined here in the thematic sections of this book. A geographical perspective highlights that marked changes in the physical environment, and in geological and topographical conditions, can occur within relatively short distances, and acknowledges that these factors are powerful agents that can shape rural communities.[9] This approach was crucial for studying the rich geological tapestry of the Doncaster district.

Margaret Spufford's study of rural communities in Cambridgeshire during the sixteenth and seventeenth centuries placed great emphasis on the villagers beyond merely their economic situation.[10] My approach, while distinctive, has parallels with that of Spufford, whose work inspired the title of this book: both acknowledge great contrasts within a region, use case-study villages to examine themes, people and issues within a defined chronological framework, and engage with the lives of people who inhabited 'contrasting communities'.

Contrasting communities: models of village typology

The origins of the 'open–closed' model, and the subsequent debate about village differentiation, can be found in the ideas and terminology of the nineteenth-century poor law.[11] With responsibility for poor relief firmly rooted in parishes, landowners were anxious to reduce this expenditure by restricting settlement on their estates.[12] Parliamentary enquiries investigating the problems of the rural poor between the 1840s and 1870s sought to highlight the perceived consequences of such action. Consequently, landownership was blamed not only for controlling and restricting

---

8   Beckett, 'Rethinking the English village'.

9   M. Chisholm, *Rural settlement and land use* (London, 1970); B.K. Roberts, *Rural settlement in Britain* (London, 1977).

10 M. Spufford, *Contrasting communities: English villagers in the sixteenth and seventeenth centuries* (Cambridge, 1974).

11 An 'open' vestry was open to all resident ratepayers, while a 'select' vestry was restricted to an elected minority, generally dominated by large landowners. PP 1817, VI, *Report from the Select Committee on the Poor Laws*, pp. 22–3, 41, 49, 59, 62, 77, 110; PP 1834, III, *Poor law amendment bill*, pp. 30–31; PP 1843, XII, *Reports of Special Assistant Poor Law Commissioner on the employment of women and children in agriculture*, p. 237.

12 Mills, 'Landownership and rural population', p. 8.

population growth in 'close' parishes but also for intensifying the burden of the poor in already densely populated 'open' parishes.[13] The terms 'open' and 'close', or 'select', accordingly became emotionally charged, with responsibility for the rural poor assigned to landowners in what was increasingly regarded as a moral scandal.[14]

This was the foundation for Mills' interpretive and predictive model, in which three main arguments were incorporated. First, settlements were classified in accordance with landownership. Concentrated landownership equated to a small population, low population density, slow population change, low poor rates and quality, but limited, housing – all characteristics intertwined with the nineteenth-century poor law debates. The model went further, claiming that large capital-intensive farms, an absence of industry, minimal trades and crafts, few shops and public houses, strong Anglican control and deference in politics and social organisations were all key features of 'close' villages.[15] Conversely, 'open' villages had fragmented landownership and were characterised by large populations, high population density, rapid population increase, high poor rates, plentiful but poor-quality housing, small farms, rural industry, trades and crafts, non-conformity, radicalism and strong independence in politics and social organisations.[16] The second argument reasoned that the concentration of landownership was directly responsible for these different characteristics, with landowners motivated by social and economic considerations.[17] The third argument, again closely linked with the debates concerning the rural poor in the nineteenth century, claimed that a negative inter-dependency operated between villages, with 'close' villages not only dependent on 'open' villages for labour but also exacerbating the problems of overcrowding and poverty in them.[18]

The Mills model, as intimated above, remains the dominant framework for understanding different types of rural community. Numerous historical studies have applied it to villages and parishes, substantiating and developing the arguments

---

13 PP 1847, XI, *First report from the Select Committee on Settlement and Poor Removal*, pp. 28, 59; PP 1847, XI, *Second and third reports from the Select Committee on Settlement and Poor Removal*, pp. 25–8, 80–81; PP 1850, XXVII, *Reports to the Poor Law Board, on the laws of settlement, and removal of the poor*, pp. 41–2, 127–9, 132, 145, 168–71, 173, 187.

14 Howkins, 'Types of rural community', p. 1304; PP 1847, XI, *First report from the Select Committee on Settlement and Poor Removal*, pp. 28, 59; PP 1847, XI, *Second and third reports from the Select Committee on Settlement and Poor Removal*, pp. 25–8, 80–81; PP 1850, XXVII, *Reports to the Poor Law Board, on the laws of settlement, and removal of the poor*, pp. 41–2, 127–9, 132, 145, 168–71, 173, 187.

15 Mills, *Lord and Peasant*, pp. 28–31, 117, 120, 125–9, 133.

16 *Ibid.*, pp. 16, 28, 117–27; Mills, 'English villages', pp. 276–7.

17 Mills, *Lord and Peasant*, pp. 23–5, 78–9, 116.

18 PP 1847, XI, *First report from the Select Committee on Settlement and Poor Removal*, p. 28, 59; PP 1847, XI, *Second and third reports from the Select Committee on Settlement and Poor Removal*, pp. 25–8, 80–81; Mills, *Lord and Peasant*, pp. 119–20.

outlined by Mills.[19] Its enduring appeal is testimony to the fact that many consider it to be a useful starting point for explaining village differentiation;[20] indeed, the model was a springboard for my own research into contrasting rural communities. Alun Howkins reasoned that it was counter-productive to dismiss the 'open–close' classification 'if for no other reason than that contemporaries … used the category frequently', while Brian Short argued that 'the contrasts in rural settlement are clear in South East England', and that regional variation and change over time would still 'leave the parameters and variables essentially unchanged'.[21] Mills concluded that the 'open–closed' model retained its validity because it highlighted common distinctions between villages with similar landowning structures and was able to summarise a 'wide range of economic, demographic, social, religious and political data'.[22]

As noted, however, many historians have recognised the inherent weaknesses of the model. Sarah Banks, for example, has questioned its validity using evidence from the parish of Castle Acre in Norfolk. Despite concentrated landownership, it bore the classificatory hallmarks of an 'open' parish. It was populous, with high rates of population growth and poor-rate expenditure, and described as 'immoral, overpopulated with outsiders and as supplying labourers (often through the gang system) to neighbouring parishes'.[23] Lord Leicester of Holkham may have owned 97 per cent of the land but was an absentee landowner, whereas the remaining 3 per cent of landowners, who included 62 owner-occupiers and small tradespeople, exercised significant control because they were resident. Banks also argued that the application of the terms 'open' and 'close' by historians simply replicated the

---

19 B.A. Holderness, '"Open" and "close" parishes in England in the eighteenth and nineteenth centuries', *Agricultural History Review*, 20/2 (1972), pp. 126–39; D.R. Mills and B.M. Short, 'Social change and social conflict in nineteenth century England: the use of the open–closed village model', *The Journal of Peasant Studies*, 10/4 (1983), pp. 253–62; C. Rawding, 'Village type and employment structure: an analysis in the nineteenth century Lincolnshire Wolds', *Local Population Studies*, 53/2 (1994), p. 53; J. Obelkevich, *Religion and rural society, South Lindsey 1825–1875* (Oxford, 1976); A. Everitt, *The patterns of rural dissent: the nineteenth century* (Leicester, 1972); R. Wells and M. Reed (eds), *Class, conflict and protest in the English countryside 1700–1880* (London, 1990); K.D.M. Snell, 'Settlement, poor law and the rural historian: new approaches and opportunities', *Rural History*, 3/2 (1992), pp. 145–72.; K.D.M. Snell and P.S. Ell, *Rival Jerusalems: the geography of Victorian religion* (Cambridge, 2000); B. Khun Song, 'Parish typology and the operation of the poor laws in early nineteenth century Oxfordshire', *Agricultural History Review*, 50/2 (2002), pp. 203–24.

20 K. Tiller, *English local history: an introduction* (Stroud, 1992), p. 221; A.J.H. Jackson, 'The "open-closed" settlement model and the interdisciplinary formulations of Dennis Mills: conceptualising local rural change', *Rural History*, 23/2 (2012), pp. 121–36.

21 Howkins, *Reshaping rural England*, p. 25; B. Short, 'The evolution of contrasting communities within rural England', in B. Short (ed.), *The English rural community: image and analysis* (Cambridge, 1992), pp. 34, 39.

22 Mills, *Lord and Peasant*, pp. 24, 94, 116–17; Mills, 'English villages', p. 272.

23 S. Banks, 'Nineteenth century scandal or twentieth century model? A new look at "open" and "close" parishes', *Economic History Review*, 41/1 (1988), pp. 66–8.

confusion and inconsistencies surrounding their use in the nineteenth century.[24] In his work David Spencer reiterated the importance of detaching historical models from nineteenth-century terminology and the problematic landownership qualification. He proposed, instead, that communities should be interpreted within their spatial context, rather than in isolation.[25]

Thus delineating settlements exclusively by landownership, and the inferred agency of landowners, can be restrictive. While stark contrasts may be noted between villages with different landowning structures, more nuanced or subtle disparities and shared experiences that cannot be explained exclusively by landownership were characteristic of Doncaster's rural hinterland. Mills himself acknowledged that the 'distinction between open and closed was not always a sharp one', with residency and the number of landowners weakening the overall control exerted by landowners, and so advocated the use of a continuum.[26] He was acutely aware that in practice the model was unable to explain every aspect of village life or account for the extensive changes experienced during the mid-nineteenth century, and encouraged further research to test and refine it.[27] Howkins and Short also acknowledged the disparity between the extremes suggested by the model and the reality for most rural settlements, and supported the use of a continuum in interpreting the differences between 'open' and 'closed' communities.[28] Such a method is, however, under-developed in studies of village differentiation. In this book, the continuum is advocated as an effective tool for exploring contrasting rural communities rather than as a model for explaining village differentiation.

As a response to these critiques, this book firstly adopts the terms 'estate' and 'multi-freeholder' to refer to measurable patterns of landownership, rather than the increasingly nebulous 'open' and 'closed'. Secondly, landownership is interpreted as a form of human agency. It is not, therefore, a homogeneous or isolated determinant based on the amount of land owned or the residency of the landowner, but rather a fluid and variable concept. By deconstructing landownership and landowners it is possible to enhance our understanding of how the ownership of land affected the development of rural communities. Landownership is also placed within the context of actions and interactions with other agents, demonstrating the impact of proactive leadership over landownership. Thirdly, it is argued that inter-relationships between villages, and between the countryside and market towns, are vital in explaining how and why rural communities developed during the mid-nineteenth century. Current theories of village differentiation focus on indicators of change, agency and characteristics within the village, with connectivity between communities limited to

---

24 Ibid., p. 71.
25 D. Spencer, 'Reformulating the "closed" parish thesis: associations, interests, and interaction', *Journal of Historical Geography*, 26/11 (2000), pp. 85, 94–5.
26 Mills, *Lord and Peasant*, p. 93; D.R. Mills, 'Canwick (Lincolnshire) and Melbourn (Cambridgeshire) in comparative perspective within the open–closed village model', *Rural History*, 17/1 (2006), p. 5.
27 Mills, *Lord and Peasant*, pp. 24, 88–94, 116–17; Mills, 'English villages', p. 272; J.M. Wilson, *The imperial gazetteer of England and Wales* (6 vols, London, 1870).
28 Howkins, *Reshaping rural England*, pp. 25–6; Short, 'The evolution of contrasting communities', p. 37.

negative dependency and diminished capacity to be 'self-contained', or conceptual discussions of 'interactions'. External determinants and spheres of influence can reposition rural communities within the context of complex spatial dynamics and multiple connections and interactions between places and spaces. This book demonstrates the reciprocal relationships that operated between town and country, the shared experiences that transcended landownership and village type to forge collective identities, and the comparative ability of rural communities to be self-contained during the mid-nineteenth century.

An almost infinite combination of inter-connected factors influenced the development of rural communities and their ability to be self-contained. Accordingly, throughout this book the concept of spheres of influence is postulated as a fluid, flexible way to interpret village differentiation and thus preferable to the rigidity of theoretical models. Spheres of influence, both spatial and conceptual, represent the extent of influence a place, person or other agency has, or is subjected to, and the interactions between them. For example, a village is immediately affected by landownership – the people with direct influence over how and why the village develops – and land type. Beyond these, the parish, the immediate rural neighbours, the collective rural hinterland of the town, the market town itself, the county, the nation and even the world have the potential to affect the English village – particularly in terms of decision-making, the economy and trade networks. On a more conceptual level, spheres of influence could include agency, policy, supply-and-demand networks and attitudes and beliefs. Collectively, the application of spheres of influence embodies the complex inter-connections between these overlapping determinants and the contextual environments in which rural communities operated during the mid-nineteenth century. This serves to highlight the fact that nowhere operated in a vacuum and that many conceptual and spatial determinants were involved in the multi-dimensional interactions that took place between villages, town and country, impacting on all facets of rural life.

Chronological framework

The mid-nineteenth century, characterised by both continuity and momentous change, is a fertile period for investigating how and why rural communities developed.[29] This book focuses on the period between the late 1830s and the late 1870s. Dominated by an economic upswing juxtaposed between two downswings, changes included population growth, urbanisation, industrialisation and the introduction of new agricultural practices.[30] The pace and nature of this change was not consistent and varied considerably from place to place. Specifically rural and agrarian change took place against the backdrop of significant social and political reform, not the least of which were the fundamental changes to the Poor Law in 1834, which resulted in the

---

29　J.F.C. Harrison, *The early Victorians 1832–1851* (London, 1971); G. Best, *Mid-Victorian Britain 1851–1875* (London, 1971).

30　R. Lloyd-Jones and M.J. Lewis, *British industrial capitalism since the industrial revolution* (London, 1998), pp. 33–102.

perceived, although nuanced, impact on settlement development and the ensuing debates about village typology. Campaigns for and challenges to political reform manifested themselves in the countryside through protest, voting patterns and the emergence of election issues directly connected to land and agriculture. Social and moral investigations brought the experiences of villagers, agricultural workers and the rural poor to wider attention. The concepts of change and continuity are intrinsic to enhancing our knowledge and understanding of village typology. Questions of how and to what extent village life changed, and the implications of this for the study of village typology, can be addressed by focusing on a relatively narrow chronological period and assessing how rural communities reacted to key stimuli in Victorian society.

The region

The southern portion of the old West Riding of Yorkshire – what is now South Yorkshire – is renowned for its industry and urban settlements. Nevertheless, the region's history is interwoven with a rich tapestry of agricultural and rural communities. Doncaster was a country market town, and the district remained predominantly agricultural during the nineteenth century. The town's nucleus was the marketplace, which evolved in accordance with the demands of both urban and rural society.[31] Contemporaries noted the striking contrast between Doncaster and its industrial counterparts.[32] Dr T.F. Dibdin, on his tour of the northern counties in 1838, observed

> Of all the towns I have entered on the continent or in England, I am not sure that I was ever so impressed with the neatness, the breathing space, the residence-inviting aspect of any, as of the town of Doncaster. It is cheerful, commodious, and the streets are of delightful breadth. You need not fear suffocation, either from natural or artificial causes for no smoke is vomited from trailing column from manufacturing chimneys. The sky is blue, the sun is bright, the air is pure.[33]

The arrival of the Great Northern Railway in 1848, and the subsequent establishment of the Great Northern Railway Works in 1853, ushered in a period of change. Balby and Hexthorpe, villages on the immediate periphery of the town centre, were transformed into railway suburbs during the second half of the nineteenth century. West Laith Gate and Marshgate, both close to the railway, became nuclei for industrial development.[34]

---

31 S. Holland, 'The evolution of a northern corn market: Doncaster, 1843–1873', *Northern History*, 52/2 (2015); S. Holland, 'Doncaster and its environs: town and countryside – a reciprocal relationship?' in M. Hammond and B. Sloan (eds), *Rural–urban relationships in the nineteenth century: uneasy neighbours?* (Abingdon, 2016), pp. 77–89.

32 J. Hunter, *South Yorkshire: the history and topography of the Deanery of Doncaster*, Vol. 1 (London, 1828); W. White, *History, gazetteer and directory of the West Riding, 1837* (Sheffield, 1837).

33 T.F. Dibdin, *Bibliographical, antiquarian and picturesque tour in the northern countries of England and Scotland* (London, 1838), cited in D. Holland and E.M. Holland, *A Yorkshire town: the making of Doncaster* (iBook edition, 2012), p. 19.

34 Holland and Holland, *A Yorkshire town*, pp. 52–3.

The population of Doncaster and its suburbs grew considerably, from 12,967 in 1851 to 39,404 in 1901, and with it problems pertaining to public health.[35] Nevertheless, the majority of Doncaster's rural hinterland was not heavily industrialised until the development of large-scale collieries in the early twentieth century.[36] Agriculture remained an important, albeit evolving, economic force in the district as demand for agricultural produce increased as a result of the growth and commercialisation of Doncaster, and new market buildings were constructed to cater for the expanding supply-and-demand networks. This collectively stimulated a reciprocal relationship between the market town of Doncaster and the surrounding countryside.[37]

Studies of South Yorkshire's history, while encompassing the differentiation in the region, have adopted a broader chronological span or focused on the region's industrial development, aristocratic estates or individual rural communities.[38] As such, there is a dearth of comparative research on rural communities in close proximity to each other during the mid-nineteenth century. The Doncaster district is an important and interesting geographical area for research into village differentiation in this period owing to the variation in landownership, geology and soil type, and the inter-relationship between rural communities and between town and country: it offers an opportunity to understand how and why rural communities developed in a predominantly industrial region.

The village case studies

This book focuses on six villages: Sprotbrough, Warmsworth, Rossington, Fishlake, Stainforth and Braithwell (see Figure 1.1), chosen to represent the diversity of landownership and land type in the Doncaster district. Table 1.1 summarises the key characteristics of these villages.

Sprotbrough is located on the Upper Magnesian Limestone 3.5 miles south-west of Doncaster. The loam and lime soil was very fertile and well suited to arable farming, which was a natural inducement to the formation of a landed estate. The Copley family, to whom the estate passed through marriage in the sixteenth century, owned the village of Sprotbrough, the smaller satellite settlement of Newton and part of Cadeby

---

35 *Ibid.*, p. 27.
36 S. Holland and L.E. Robinson, 'The fluidity of the "farming ladder": the experience of the Duffin family, Yorkshire, 1870–1950', *Journal of Community and Family History*, 19/2 (2016), pp. 114–16; A.L. Barnett, *The railways of the South Yorkshire coalfield from 1880* (Bampton, 1984). Cadeby Colliery opened in 1893.
37 Holland, 'Evolution of a northern corn market'; Holland, 'Doncaster and its environs'.
38 S. Pollard and C. Holmes (eds), *Essays in the economic and social history of South Yorkshire* (Sheffield, 1976); D. Hey, *The making of South Yorkshire* (Newton Abbot, 1979); D. Holland, *Changing landscapes in South Yorkshire* (Doncaster, 1980); P.J. Nunn, 'The management of some South Yorkshire landed estates in the eighteenth and nineteenth centuries, linked with the central economic development of the area, 1700–1850', PhD thesis (University of Sheffield, 1985); D. Hey, *Yorkshire from AD 1000* (London, 1986); M. Jones, *The making of the South Yorkshire landscape* (Barnsley, 2000); D. Hey, *Medieval South Yorkshire* (Ashbourne, 2003).

Communities in Contrast

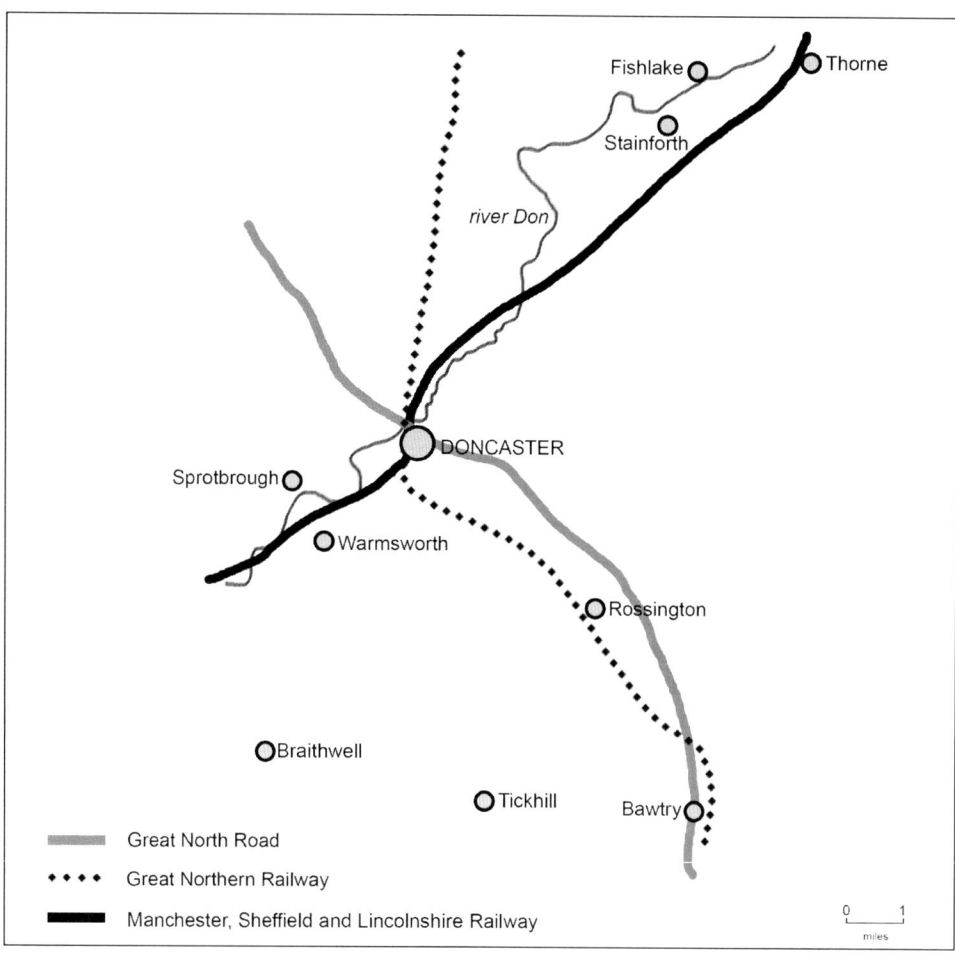

Figure 1.1 Map of the Doncaster district (hand-drawn by Sarah Elvins based on Bartholomew's ½-inch 1904 map).

(all within the parish of Sprotbrough).[39] Other landowners in the parish included Sir Fountayne Wilson (of High Melton Hall) at Cadeby and William Battie-Wrightson (of Cusworth Hall) at Cusworth (also within the parish of Sprotbrough). The Copleys resided in Sprotbrough Hall, built by Sir Godfrey Copley in 1685, which dominated the estate. The parish church was located in the heart of Sprotbrough village, while the river Don, running along the edge of the estate, provided a secondary focal point for settlement. Sir Joseph William Copley, lord of the manor between 1838 and 1883, resided in the hall with his wife Lady Charlotte and undertook a programme of rebuilding in the village that included new estate cottages, a school and a bridge over the river Don.

---

39 D. Holland (ed.), *Sprotbrough in history*, part two (Rotherham, 1969), pp. 19–25.

Introduction

Table 1.1
Overview of landownership, acreage, land type and transport routes in the six case-study villages

Villages	Acreage (township, 1877)	Landowners	Land type/geology	Transport routes
Estate				
Sprotbrough	2,701 acres	Copleys resident 12th century to 1926	Upper Magnesian Limestone	River Don
				South Yorkshire Railway
				Local roads
Warmsworth	1,074 acres	Battie-Wrightson absentee and resident	Lower Magnesian Limestone	River Don
		Aldam absentee and resident		South Yorkshire Railway
				Doncaster to Sheffield Turnpike Road
Rossington	3,051 acres	Prior to 1838 Doncaster Corporation absent	Bunter Sandstone	River Torne
		1838–1938 Brown resident		Great North Road
				Great Northern Railway
Multi-freeholder				
Fishlake	3,878 acres	59 landowners	Marshy lowland/ clay soil	River Don
				Local roads
Stainforth	3,483 acres	42 landowners	Marshy lowland/ clay soil	River Don
				Stainforth and Keadby Canal
				Manchester, Sheffield and Lincolnshire Railway and the North Eastern Railway
				Local roads
Braithwell	1,948 acres	23 landowners	Lower Magnesian Limestone	Local roads

Source: DA, P25/9/B1, Sprotbrough tithe apportionment and map, 1847; DA, P58/9/B1–2, Rossington tithe apportionment and map, 1838; DA, DD/BW/E11/41–42, Warmsworth tithe apportionment and map, 1838–1841; DA, P71/9/B1–2, Braithwell tithe apportionment and map, 1840; DA, DY/Wall/1–2, Hatfield tithe apportionment and map, 1843 (includes Fishlake and Stainforth); W. White, *History, gazetteer and directory of the West Riding, 1837*, Vol. 2 (Sheffield, 1837), pp. 165, 179–80, 188, 206–7, 200–1, 213; E.R. Kelly, *Post Office directory of the West Riding of Yorkshire, 1861* (London, 1861), pp. 206, 276, 328–9, 610, 811–12, 871; E.R. Kelly, *Post Office directory of the West Riding of Yorkshire, 1877* (London, 1877), pp. 217, 314, 385–7, 785–6, 1112, 1186.

Rossington, 4 miles south-east of Doncaster, is situated on Bunter sandstone overlaid with glacial sand and gravel and is characterised by predominantly sandy soil. By the mid-nineteenth century it was connected by road, rail and river. When Doncaster Corporation sold the estate in 1838 owing to debt it was purchased by an industrialist family, the Browns, from Leeds.[40] James Brown junior (1814–1877) inherited the estate in 1845 and, unlike his father, moved to Rossington. He undertook a programme of rebuilding that included the parish church, the school and some estate cottages. Two years after Brown junior's death the estate passed to a nephew, a Streatfield by name, who built an entirely new Victorian country house at Rossington in which to reside.

Warmsworth, located on the Lower Magnesian Limestone, is 2.5 miles from Doncaster, and was connected by road, river and railway. The soil required drainage, as it was difficult to work when wet owing to the high proportion of clay. Two landowning families owned Warmsworth: the Battie-Wrightsons, who owned 81 per cent of the land, and the Aldams, who owned the remaining 19 per cent – a legacy of earlier subdivision and consolidation of landholdings.[41] The parish church was some distance from the village by the eighteenth and nineteenth centuries, suggesting an earlier settlement nucleus close to the banks of the river Don. The Lower Magnesian Limestone was particularly good for construction, and the quarrying and lime-burning industries expanded during the mid-nineteenth century, with the satellite settlement of Levitt Hagg growing accordingly.

Braithwell, also located on the Lower Magnesian Limestone, is 6.5 miles south-south-west of Doncaster, and was not situated on main road, rail or river networks during the mid-nineteenth century. By the mid-nineteenth century there were 23 landowners, most of whom owned less than ten acres, and only five who owned over 100 acres.[42] Thomas Dyson, who occupied the manor house and owned 171 acres, was a practical agriculturalist and a proactive agent in the village. The divided landownership of Braithwell affected the physical layout of the village, which was focused upon more than one axis. The church and the manor house formed one cluster, while cottages and agricultural and industrial properties aligned along the main village street formed a second, with scattered farms beyond.

Fishlake is 8.5 miles north-east of Doncaster, and was connected by river, road and railway during the mid-nineteenth century. The parish was located on the marshy lowland, and the soil was predominantly heavy clay. Landownership was historically fragmented and, despite some post-enclosure consolidation, there were still 59 landowners during the mid-nineteenth century. The majority of these landowners owned only a small amount of land – between 1 and 60 acres – and land continued to change hands. The church, the manor house and the river all formed focal points for settlement development, in addition to the outlying hamlets. In addition to the Anglican church, there was a proliferation of non-conformist chapels in Fishlake and other settlements on the marshy lowlands around Doncaster.

---

40   DA, AB/7/3/63, Sale catalogue for the Rossington estate, 1838.
41   DA, DD/BW/E11/41–42, Warmsworth tithe apportionment and map, 1838–1841.
42   DA, P71/9/B1–2, Braithwell tithe apportionment and map, 1839–1840.

Introduction

Stainforth, located 7.5 miles north-east of Doncaster, was situated on the river Don at its confluence with the Stainforth and Keadby canal. The settlement extended along the canal, with farms beyond, and the soil was a combination of sand and clay. By the mid-nineteenth century there were 42 landowners in Stainforth, although many of them owned less than ten acres. Stainforth's history was intertwined with that of Hatfield parish, to which it belonged, and yet, because of the physical distance between the two settlements, Stainforth developed an independent identity.

Studying the region

This book spans the methodological boundaries of local history and micro-history, and applies them to a different and understudied geographical area.[43] This amalgamated approach both values the local in its own right and uses the local – in this case the Doncaster district and specifically the six villages described above – as a space in which to engage with complex historiographical issues and illuminate variants of wider trends. It enables an in-depth analysis of how and why rural communities in close proximity developed through the lives, livelihoods and experiences of their inhabitants, and the inter-relationships between people and places.

Not all villages are well represented in the archives, and well-documented landed estates are unrepresentative of the majority of rural communities. It is therefore necessary to reconstruct rural communities from fragmentary records. This presents methodological challenges for the study of how and why rural communities developed, and demonstrates the importance of comparative sources for explaining patterns of village differentiation. The survival rate of estate records for the Doncaster district is variable. Records for the Battie-Wrightson and Aldam families, who owned Warmsworth, exist. Although incomplete, they provide evidence for agriculture, industry and micro-commerce, tenants and tenancy agreements, and social life in mid-nineteenth-century Warmsworth. While the Rossington estate under Doncaster Corporation is documented

---

43   W.G. Hoskins, *Local history in England* (London, 1959); A. Everitt, *The community of Kent and the Great Rebellion, 1640–60* (Leicester, 1966); C. Phythian-Adams, *Rethinking English local history* (Leicester, 1987); A. Rodgers, *Approaches to local history* (London, 1977); Phythian-Adams, *Rethinking English local history*; Tiller, *English local history*; C. Phythian-Adams (ed.), *Societies, cultures, and kinship, 1580–1850: cultural provinces and English local history* (Leicester, 1996); J. Finberg, *Exploring villages* (Stroud, 1998); R.C. Richardson (ed.), *The changing face of English local history* (Aldershot, 2000); J.V. Beckett, *Writing local history* (Manchester, 2007); K. Tiller and D. Dymond, 'Local history at the crossroads', *The Local Historian*, 37/4 (2007), pp. 250–58; J.V. Beckett, 'Local history in its comparative international context', *The Local Historian*, 41/2 (2011), pp. 90–104; K. Wrightson, 'Villages, villagers and village studies', *Historical Journal*, 18/3 (1975), pp. 632–9; C. Phythian-Adams, 'Local history and national history: the quest for the peoples of England', *Rural History*, 2/1 (1991), p. 2; *ibid.*, pp. 3, 20; C. Phythian-Adams, 'Local history and societal history', *Local Population Studies* 51 (1993), p. 44; D. Hey, 'Reflections on the local and regional history of the north', *Northern History*, 50/2 (2013), pp. 155–69; S. Williams, *Poverty, gender and life cycle under the English poor law 1760–1834* (Woodbridge, 2011), p. 1; P. Hudson, 'Regional and local history: globalisation, post modernism, and the future', *Journal of Regional and Local Studies*, 20/1 (1999), pp. 16–18.

with farm surveys, committee meeting minutes and the 1838 sale catalogue, very few estate records survive from the period in which the estate was the property of the Brown family. Similarly, the Copley papers for Sprotbrough are frustratingly sparse for the mid-nineteenth century. The incomplete nature of these estate records poses potential limitations; yet it also creates opportunities. The vast array of documentary and statistical evidence produced in the mid-nineteenth century, available for most if not all villages, provides a valuable foundation for comparative analysis. This includes parliamentary reports, census reports and census enumerators' books, trade directories, Ordnance Survey maps, and newspapers, together facilitating a certain degree of consistency in analysis and complementing detailed farm and estate records where they exist.[44]

The book is divided into thematic chapters that explore different characteristics of rural communities. Chapter 2 examines the concepts of social hierarchies and agency and challenges the landownership-centric model of rural differentiation. It highlights the importance of differentiation between landowners and how leadership exercised by alternative agents, such as the clergy and farmers, could take precedence over landownership as a factor in development.

Chapter 3 explores differentiation in the rural economies of the Doncaster district by comparing crops and livestock, farm size, agricultural knowledge networks, market facilities, food-processing industries, trades and crafts, and industry, and demonstrates the relative roles of landownership, other agency, geology, and the reciprocal relationship between town and country.

Living and working conditions are the focus of chapter 4. The notion of higher wages and better living conditions in the north of England is deconstructed to reveal nuances not only between but also within rural communities, as well as the emergence of social hierarchies within the labouring population largely negotiated in the market place with whatever bargaining power they possessed.

The provision of and participation in religion and education in the rural communities are examined in chapter 5, demonstrating nuances within estate and multi-freeholder villages, the role of external stimuli, and the close alignment between attendance at church, chapel or school and agricultural employment.

Chapter 6 explores rural recreation, including the provision of and participation in leisure activities within villages, access to them in nearby villages and the market town, and the countryside as a leisure destination.

Finally, the conclusion revisits key questions about village differentiation and demonstrates how historical research into the Doncaster district contributes new theoretical and geographical perspectives on how and why rural communities developed.

---

44   D. Hey, *Journeys in family history: the National Archives guide to exploring your past – finding your ancestors* (Richmond, 2004); Tiller, *English local history*; M. Drake and R. Finnegan (eds), *Studying family and community history – 19th and 20th centuries, vol. 4: sources and methods: a handbook* (Cambridge, 1994); D. Mills and K. Schürer (eds), *Local communities in the Victorian census enumerators' books* (Oxford, 1996); D. Mills, *Rural community history from trade directories* (Aldenham, 2001).

Chapter 2

Social hierarchies, power relations and agency in the countryside

The Victorian countryside was undeniably hierarchical, with the ownership of land conferring power and agency. James Caird described a tripartite system, consisting of landowners, farmers and labourers, with expectations and constraints imposed on each social group.[1] Models of village typology are based on landownership, with landowners being credited with having absolute agency. This has perpetuated the idea, originally disseminated by nineteenth-century writers and in parliamentary reports, that landownership was pivotal in the development of rural communities.[2] Concurrently, agricultural labourers were perceived as passive and stereotyped as 'Hodge'.[3] Social hierarchies and agency are, however, far-reaching concepts that transcend landownership, and the development of rural communities during the nineteenth century were affected by various social and occupational groups and the power relations between them.

This chapter demonstrates the importance of differentiation within and between social groups. It also considers the concept of agency. Agency, the mechanism for change or decision-making, is a useful tool for examining rural society that encourages a human-centred approach. It manifested itself in the roles, responsibilities, actions and behaviour of people, and refers to active decision-making that affected their lives and the lives of others. This chapter will examine the inter-connections between agents and their agency; the scope of and limitations to their agency; the processes whereby the boundaries of agency were constantly renegotiated; and the role of towns in renegotiating social hierarchies, power relations and agency. Landowners were not a homogeneous group, and nor were they the only group in rural society to have agency. The chapter is concerned with those who lived and worked in the rural communities of the Doncaster district, as well as those who owned the land, and with external agents such as Doncaster Corporation. As such, it looks at their individual and collective agency.

---

1   J. Caird, *The landed interest and the supply of food* (London, 1878), pp. 56–64.
2   PP 1847, XI, *First to eighth report from the Select Committee on Settlement and Poor Removal*; PP 1850, XXVII, *Reports to the Poor Law Board, on the laws of settlement, and removal of the poor*; PP 1860, XVII, *Select Committee on the Irremovable Poor*; Mills, *Lord and peasant*, pp. 29, 79, 117; G.E. Mingay, *Land and society in England, 1750–1980* (London, 1994); F.M.L. Thompson, *English landed society in the nineteenth century* (London, 1963).
3   J. Dent, 'The present condition of the English agricultural labourer', *Journal of the Royal Agricultural Society of England*, 2nd series, 7/2 (1871), pp. 343–4; Caird, *Landed interest*, pp. 61–4; M. Freeman, *Social investigation and rural England, 1870–1914* (Woodbridge, 2003), p. 22.

Landownership and landowners

Doncaster and its environs were regarded as an attractive proposition for landowners during the nineteenth century. Its appeal lay in its distinctive economic and topographic composition, despite its location in a primarily industrial region. According to White's 1852 *Directory*:

> The absence of manufactories, the wealth of its Corporation, its cheap and abundant supply of provisions, and the fertility and salubrity of the surrounding country have combined to render Doncaster a favourite residence of genteel families.[4]

The Doncaster district was home to numerous small and medium-sized country estates belonging to both new and old gentry landowners.[5] The foundation of these estates and the geography of social hierarchies were shaped by almost a millennia of land acquisition, dispersal and purchase. The heterogeneous geological configuration of the West Riding of Yorkshire was particularly striking in Doncaster's rural hinterland, with stark contrasts discernible between the Magnesian uplands and the marshy lowlands. Parts of the Doncaster district were therefore more desirable than others, with a strong link between land type and patterns of landownership.[6] The concentration of landed estates corresponded with the fertile and well-drained soil of the Magnesian Limestone belt to the west of the town. Multi-freeholder settlements were prevalent on the marshy lowlands to the north-east of the town, where poorer-quality land was less suited to development or agricultural prosperity, and in need of reclamation and improvement. The relationship between landownership, land type and village type was subtler in the territory between these two extremes.

The landowners of Doncaster were not one homogeneous mass who acted and reacted in a predetermined and predictable fashion. Rather, they were individual agents, operating within a collective position of power and influence, but often exerting their agency very differently. Differentiation in landownership was determined by residency, wealth, approach to estate management, diversified interests, external determinants, the agency of others, and factors beyond landowners' immediate control. Attempts to explain village differentiation as solely the result of the concentration of landownership are therefore formulaic, founded on nineteenth-century expectations rather than the reality of differentiated landownership.[7] Landowners required sufficient knowledge and impetus in order to fulfil their expected roles, knowing both how to manage their estates responsibly and efficiently and what decisions to take and when to invest, as well as having the capital to do so. Some landowners were inevitably

---

4 W. White, *Gazetteer and general directory of Sheffield, 1852* (Sheffield, 1852).
5 These included Aldam of Frickley and Warmsworth, Battie-Wrightson of Cusworth, Childers of Cantley, Cooke of Wheatley, Copley of Sprotbrough, Cooke-Yarborough of Campsmount, Davies-Cooke of Owston, Halifax of Hickleton, Montagu of High Melton, Thellusson of Brodsworth, and Warde of Hooton Pagnell.
6 Holland, *Changing landscapes*, p. 1.
7 Caird, *Landed interest*, pp. 57–9.

Social hierarchies, power relations and agency in the countryside

Figure 2.1 Sprotbrough Hall, unknown artist (Heritage Doncaster, DONMG: 1986.983).

more proactive, and some estates better managed, whether due to wealth, ability or inclination.[8] By examining the landownership and landowners of the six case-study villages in more detail, a nuanced understanding of landownership is derived and these elements of differentiation can be understood in practice.

At Sprotbrough, the Copley family represented longevity in landownership. The estate, which had been granted to the Fitzwilliams in the twelfth century, passed to the Copleys through marriage in the sixteenth century. Such continuity conferred a custodial responsibility on each generation. Sir Joseph William Copley (1804–1883), lord of the manor between 1838 and 1883, resided at Sprotbrough Hall (Figure 2.1) with his wife Lady Charlotte.[9] Their fortunes were intimately linked with the estate, with income largely derived from the land and rents. Copley appeared motivated by a combination of paternalism, a desire for social control and a commitment to the estate. His proactive stance manifested itself in a partial rebuilding programme during the mid-nineteenth century, which included new estate cottages, a school and a bridge over the river Don; in rent abatements for his tenants in times of economic distress; and in the control of education, religion and recreation. Nevertheless, despite being a resident landowner, partial responsibility was devolved to a land agent, who oversaw the estate and performed day-to-day management. This somewhat dissipated their otherwise absolute power and, through the employment of a tenant farmer, Thomas Wood, as land agent, extended the agency of farmers.

---

8   J. Caird, *English agriculture in 1850–51* (London, 1852), pp. 145, 222; J.V. Beckett, 'Agricultural landownership and estate management', in E.J.T. Collins (ed.), *The agrarian history of England and Wales*, Vol. VII, 1850–1914, Part 1 (Cambridge, 2000), pp. 730–34.

9   Holland, *Sprotbrough in history*, pp. 19–25.

The dual ownership of Warmsworth – the result of subdivision and consolidation of earlier landholdings – weakened the unequivocal agency of the respective landowners. Although the Battie-Wrightson family owned 81 per cent of the land, they were absentee landowners by the mid-nineteenth century. William Battie-Wrightson (1789–1879) inherited the family estates in 1827 and lived at Cusworth Hall, rather than their smaller residence at Warmsworth. While the family maintained an interest in their land at Warmsworth, it was often secondary to their agricultural and industrial concerns elsewhere in the country, and to William's work as a politician and in public office; and their interest was largely from a business perspective, focusing on the limestone quarries at Levitt Hagg. In William's absence, Thomas Wood, the same agent employed by the Copleys at Sprotbrough, was employed as a land agent to oversee the day-to-day management of their land at Warmsworth, while between the 1830s and 1860s Richard Heber Wrightson, William's brother, lived in Warmsworth. Nevertheless, the absence of Battie-Wrightson created opportunities for the Aldam family, who owned only 19 per cent of the land but were resident, to become active agents.

The Aldam family, cloth merchants from Leeds, owned land in the Doncaster area during the nineteenth century. William Aldam junior (1813–90) was given the Frickley estate in 1844 as a wedding gift, but also assumed some responsibility for the land at Warmsworth on account of his father's ill health. Aldam (junior) was a politician, businessman and active participant in a number of charitable societies, and yet retained a direct and active interest in the management of the agricultural land owned by the family. He was a hands-on agriculturalist, who applied management skills acquired from business to the land. His personal diaries, kept between 1848 and 1890, and his notebooks and farm memoranda books, demonstrate his direct involvement with and diligence in agricultural and estate management. Examples include records of the occasions on which he personally went into the fields to examine crops, with references made to wheat, turnips, swede, beans and mangolds, and to inspect farm buildings and authorise necessary maintenance and improvements. He also noted the division of cattle to avoid infection with cattle plague and showed an interest in investing in new machinery.[10] The brevity of entries is often frustrating, merely noting, for example, that he found workers 'dibbling beans in Warmsworth Field' or mentioning a meeting with a machine-maker at which he registered his interest in threshing machines, but making no record of the outcome.[11] While often no more than observational comments, they are, however, testimony that Aldam was sufficiently interested in such matters to keep a record of them.

---

10 DA, DD/WA/D1/1, Diary of William Aldam, 19 June and 5 August 1848; *ibid.*, 19 June, 5 August, 20 November 1848; DA, DD/WA/D1/2, Diary of William Aldam, June–December 1849; DD/WA/D1/3, Diary of William Aldam, June–August 1850; DD/WA/D1/5, Diary of William Aldam, 12 April 1853; DA, DD/WA/D1/7, Diary of William Aldam, 12 June, 27 June, 22 August 1855; DD/WA/E7/5, Farm memoranda and cattle book, 1864–1883, pp. 1–3; DD/WA/E5/4, Notebook of William Aldam, 1860s, pp. 15, 20; DD/WA/E6/1, Rental book, 1860, pp. 63–5.

11 DA, DD/WA/D1/2, Diary of William Aldam, 14 February 1849; DD/WA/D1/7, Diary of William Aldam, 19 December 1855.

An issue that Aldam engaged with more extensively in his diaries was that of drainage, on account of the soil on his estates being difficult to work owing to the high proportion of clay. In June 1848, when many fields in Warmsworth and Frickley were under water, he made frequent reference to the destructive effects of heavy rain. He consulted articles about drainage in the *Journal of the Royal Agricultural Society of England* and commented on them in his diaries, before calculating the cost of draining several fields, drawing up plans accordingly and embarking upon a programme of drainage work.[12] Just over a year after the heavy rains struck, Aldam recorded in his diary on 30 September 1849 that 15 men were employed consistently in drainage, and then again in December that nearly 20 men had been draining. Drainage continued to be mentioned in his diaries throughout the 1850s and 1860s. Through direct observation and intervention, Aldam's agency manifested itself in expedient improvements to his land, crops and drainage.

Aldam's interest in the estate was not exclusively economic, extending to the people on his land and societal concerns. His diaries and notebooks noted meetings with existing and prospective tenants, and at the end of 1858 he stated that he had become better acquainted with the Warmsworth estate during that year.[13] The Aldams built and supported the village school and were actively involved in the village Feast.[14] They were also patrons of the Warmsworth Cottagers' Show and offered small premiums, prizes deemed to be useful to the cottagers, at least twice a year for the best specimens of flowers and vegetables.[15] Aldam's active role within the village, encompassing the land, agriculture, education and leisure, demonstrates the importance of residency and the attitude of landowners when scholars attempt to differentiate between them.

The purchase of the Rossington estate, which Doncaster Corporation sold in 1838, by James Brown (1786–1845), an industrialist from Leeds, was indicative of the increasing investment in country estates by merchants and manufacturers during the nineteenth century. Their business acumen no doubt influenced their choice of estate, as Doncaster Corporation had already begun to invest in agricultural infrastructure from the late eighteenth century. Initially the Brown family continued to reside at Harehills, near Leeds, although they took an active interest in their new estate from the outset, including rebuilding the parish church in 1844. James Brown junior exhibited the hallmarks of a resident landowner with proactive agency when he inherited the estate in 1845 and moved to Rossington. His actions included enlarging the size of the estate's farms and improving the agricultural infrastructure through the development of model farms. He also undertook further estate rebuilding, including the school and

---

12 DA, DD/WA/D1/1, Diary of William Aldam, 17 June 1848; DA, DD/WA/D1/1, Diary of William Aldam, 16 and 17 October 1848; DA, DD/WA/D1/2, Diary of William Aldam, 13 February 1849, 23 May 1849, 28 May 1849, 30 September 1849, November and December 1849; DD/WA/D1/43, Diary of William Aldam, August 1850; DA, DD/WA/D1/5, Diary of William Aldam, April and May 1853; DD/WA/D1/14, Diary of William Aldam, February 1862.
13 DA, DD/WA/D1/10, Diary of William Aldam, 1858.
14 Warmsworth Feast is discussed in chapter 6 of this book.
15 See chapter 6 for more about the society and these shows.

some cottages, and combined attentiveness to both estate aesthetics and the needs of his tenants. Brown again demonstrates the importance not only of residency and wealth but also of managing the estate directly, which enabled him to successfully synthesise existing patterns of agricultural management and practices with his own ideas and investment.

The ownership of land remained a platform from which to exert influence and agency in multi-freeholder communities. The scope of agency was often diminished, however, owing to the number of landowners and the smaller acreages owned. Of 61 landowners at Fishlake, the majority, who included farmers, tradespeople and craftspeople, owned between 10 and 60 acres. Similarly, at Stainforth there were 42 landowners of whom 67 per cent owned less than ten acres. Braithwell had 23 landowners, and again the majority each owned less than ten acres. However, the largest proportion of land at Braithwell was owned by only three landowners, who each owned in excess of 150 acres (Table 2.1); a further seven landowners owned between 50 and 150 acres each, and the remainder was made up of small freeholders.[16] Thomas Dyson, who owned and occupied 171 acres of land at Braithwell, and farmed a further 124 acres of land belonging to the earl of Scarborough, was a proactive resident landowner in the village. However, as an owner-occupier, Dyson blurred the distinction between landowner and farmer. He was noted as having 'some of the best portions of the soil' and as taking an active role in agricultural matters,[17] providing leadership in agricultural improvement as secretary of the Braithwell Ploughing Club, in advocating the reform of hiring practices and via the Doncaster Agricultural Society and Doncaster Farmers' Club.[18] He also attended protectionist meetings in Doncaster, where he actively participated in discussions throughout the campaign to repeal the Corn Laws between 1839 and 1846.[19] In the absence of concentrated landownership, large freeholders such as Dyson could provide leadership within defined spheres such as agriculture, illuminating the way in which the agency of landowners and farmers could be combined in the figure of the owner-occupier.

Landowners in the Doncaster district were predominately male, with the exception of Mary Amory at Braithwell (see Table 2.1) and some other women who owned relatively small portions of land in multi-freeholder villages. This, however, conceals the agency of women within the landowning classes, which is evident in the work

---

16   DA, P71/9/B1–2, Braithwell tithe apportionment and map, 1839–1840; C.W. Hatfield, *Hints for pedestrians* (Doncaster, 1850), p. 271.

17   Hatfield, *Hints for pedestrians*, p. 271.

18   *Doncaster Gazette*, 15 May 1840, p. 5; *Doncaster Gazette*, 10 July 1840, p. 5; *Doncaster Gazette*, 6 May 1842, p. 5; *Doncaster Chronicle*, 8 July 1842, p. 5; *Doncaster Gazette*, 30 May 1843, p. 5; *Doncaster Gazette*, 15 November 1844, p. 5; *Doncaster Chronicle*, 22 November 1844, p. 7; *Doncaster Chronicle*, 24 October 1845, p. 5; *Doncaster Gazette*, 10 October 1845, p. 6; *Doncaster Chronicle*, 31 July 1846, p. 5; *Doncaster Chronicle*, 16 October 1846, p. 7; *Doncaster Chronicle*, 23 October 1846, p. 5; *Doncaster Chronicle*, 16 November 1846, p. 7; *Doncaster Chronicle*, 24 September 1847, p. 7; *Doncaster Chronicle*, 26 November 1847, p. 7; *Doncaster Chronicle*, 13 April 1849, p. 5; *Doncaster Chronicle*, 4 July 1851, p. 5; *Doncaster Chronicle*, 14 November 1856, p. 5.

19   *Doncaster Gazette*, 29 March 1839, p. 4; *Doncaster Gazette*, 13 February 1846, p. 5.

Table 2.1
The ownership and occupation of the land belonging to the main landowners in Braithwell

Landowner	Amount of land	Occupancy	Other information
Mary Amory	335 acres	Occupies 291 acres herself Sublets to 5 other tenants	Tenants include William Atkinson, farmer of 23 acres in 1851
Thomas Dyson	171 acres	Occupies land himself	Land farmed increased to 295 acres by 1851
Edward Fox	159 acres	Occupies none of the land himself Sublets to 6 tenants	Tenants include Charles Kay, a farmer of 35 acres in 1851 and of 79 acres in 1861

Source: DA, Braithwell tithe apportionment and map, P71/9/B1–2, 1839–1840.

undertaken by the wives, sisters and daughters of landowners.[20] While little evidence survives to indicate that women assumed an active role in the running of the landed estates discussed here, they were proactive and influential in the spheres of education, religion and recreation. For example, Lady Copley was noted for her interest in the education of female children at Sprotbrough, while Miss Aldam 'diligently attended' to the education of children in Warmsworth.[21]

Landowner agency beyond the village

The pivotal role of landowners with regard to the development of rural communities has largely been constructed from within the spatial confines of the estates they owned. Their agency, in fact, extended beyond the immediate territory they owned and presided over, creating dynamic spheres of influence. The collective agency of landowners was signified by politics, public office and membership of district-wide and regional societies, in which they made decisions and influenced policies that affected most if not all rural communities. This still did not equate to homogeneity, however, and collective action was littered with disagreement and debate.

Political agency was a particularly significant external sphere of influence on the Victorian countryside. Land and political power were traditionally synonymous; and, even as the dynamics of this relationship changed, the political sphere was still very much dominated by landowners during the mid-nineteenth century. Through political representation, landowners could exert their influence far beyond the confines of their estates. Political agency could be a double-edged sword, however, because it necessitated a process of negotiation between candidate, constituents and party that inhibited absolute agency. The constituencies represented by landowners were often physically and economically distanced from the rural communities where they

---

20 P. Horn, *Ladies of the manor: wives and daughters in country-house society 1830–1918* (Stroud, 1991); B. McDonagh, *Elite women and the agricultural landscape, 1700–1830* (Abingdon, 2017).

21 *Doncaster Chronicle*, 14 November 1839, p. 6; E.R. Kelly, *Post Office directory of the West Riding of Yorkshire, 1877* (London, 1877).

owned land. William Battie-Wrightson, a Whig, was elected MP for Hull in 1830 and MP for Northallerton in 1835; James Brown, a Liberal, was elected MP for Malton in 1857; and William Aldam, a Liberal, was elected MP for Leeds in 1841.[22] Issues fought in parliament resonated in town and country, albeit from different perspectives. Landowners were often adept at balancing the divergent views of their constituents and tenants, as evidenced during the campaign to repeal the Corn Laws and the work of William Aldam.

The Corn Laws, and their repeal in 1846, formed arguably the most controversial agricultural policy in Victorian England.[23] Introduced in 1815, against the backdrop of European wars and the political dominance of landowners, their primary objective was to protect agriculture through the taxation of foreign imports. However, the Corn Laws were attributed with increasing food prices and intensifying hardship among the working class, as well as impeding free trade. Opposition quickly mounted, until the campaign became one of class struggle orchestrated by the industrial middle class in the name of the working class. The Anti-Corn Law League, founded in Manchester in 1839, received support from manufacturing interests who placed landowners at the heart of the problem.[24] Yet the issue of repeal was complex and divided landowner opinion, so that landowners with diversified interests, such as William Aldam junior, often supported repeal.[25]

Aldam was first and foremost a businessman, although he had acquired an astute awareness of agricultural affairs from his father. During the campaign to repeal the Corn Laws he inherited the Frickley estate and assumed greater responsibility for Warmsworth. He stood for election as a Liberal candidate for the Borough of Leeds in 1841, largely on a platform of free trade.[26] A recurring theme of his campaign was that free trade would benefit agriculture and manufacturing alike, and that to succeed industry needed agriculture to be prosperous.[27] After being elected in 1841 he continued to campaign for free trade, but correspondence suggests that at times this proved contentious. He appeared reluctant to attend a free-trade meeting in Manchester in 1843 on behalf of the Leeds Borough, as requested by the Leeds Anti-Corn Law Committee. A letter from Edward Baines junior, sent a few days after

---

22 *The assembled commons, or parliamentary biographer* (London, 1838); D.G. Paz, 'William Aldam, backbench MP for Leeds 1841–1847: national issues versus local interests', *Transactions of the Thoresby Society*, 2nd series, 8 (1998); DA, DD/WA/P/36–55, Parliamentary papers including speeches and House of Commons papers [William Aldam], 1841–1843.
23 A. Howe, *Free trade and liberal England 1846–1946* (Oxford, 1997), p. 1; C. Schonhardt-Bailey, *From the corn laws to free trade: interests, ideas and institutions in historical perspective* (Cambridge, MA, 2006), introduction.
24 Howe, *Free trade*, p. 24.
25 Mingay, *Land and society*, pp. 48, 63; C. Schonhardt-Bailey, 'Specific factors, capital markets, portfolio diversification, and free trade: domestic determinants of the repeal of the corn laws', *World Politics*, 43 (1991), pp. 545–69.
26 DA, DD/WA/P/1, 1841, Leeds parliamentary election handbills and other publicity.
27 *Ibid.*; DA, DD/WA/P/25–26, Speeches delivered by Aldam, 1843. DA, DD/WA/P/16, Draft speech on the Corn Laws, 1841; DA, DD/WA/P/19, Speech delivered in Leeds, 1841.

the initial request (to which there had been no reply), implored Aldam to attend the Manchester meeting. Baines stated, 'I find the feeling very strong', referring to the Leeds Committee, and astutely reminded Aldam that 'you cannot stay away from Manchester without attracting the notice both of friends and opponents: the former will mourn, and the latter will triumph.'[28] Aldam was defensive in his reply to Baines, writing that it was 'in no part the duty of a member of the legislative to take an active part in the agitation of questions not of parliament', although he did in the end attend the meeting in question.[29] During the same year, over 3,200 of his constituents signed a petition requesting him to demand an immediate repeal of the corn laws, a clear message of their expectations.[30] Aldam struggled at times to balance his own personal interests with those of his constituents and his father's tenants. The letters make it clear that he had reservations about aligning himself with a single-issue pressure group, especially as he had other political concerns and objectives. Nevertheless, between 1841 and 1843 he wrote and delivered a number of passionate speeches on the subject of free trade in which he sought to demonstrate not only its benefits but also the harmful effects protection had had on agriculture.[31] Throughout the duration of the campaign there is little evidence to suggest that his inheritance of the Frickley estate had outwardly affected his attitude to free trade. He continued to vote in favour of the repeal in 1844 and 1845, although, notably, he did not vote in 1846.[32] Aldam's experience exemplifies how external determinants and spheres of influence, such as politics, both extended and inhibited the agency of landowners.

Leadership not landownership

Agency extended beyond landownership, with other agents – notably the clergy, farmers and land agents – exerting leadership and influence both in and beyond rural communities. The clergy, another key component of the rural elite, had opportunities to be active agents in both estate and multi-freeholder villages, although in practice this was dependent on the individual incumbents, and, where applicable, their relationship with resident landowners. This could manifest itself as a form of collaborative agency in conjunction with a resident landowner, or as a replacement for a dominant landowner, and represented the concerns of the Church of England, which embraced the wider community, rather than just the interests of one landowning family.

The Revd C.E. Thomas, the incumbent of Warmsworth, sought to reform hiring practices and living accommodation for agricultural workers. His pioneering work, part of wider Church of England reforms, was carried out within the village but had ramifications far beyond the locale. Thomas not only opposed hiring fairs

---

28 DA, DD/WA/P/12, 1843, Letters regarding the Corn Laws.
29 *Ibid.*
30 Paz, 'William Aldam', p. 36; DA, DD/WA/P/5, 1843, petition to W Aldam (Leeds) opposing corn laws.
31 DA, DD/WA/P/16, DD/WA/P/19, DD/WA/P/24–29, speeches on the corn laws.
32 P.A. Pickering and A. Tyrrell, *The people's bread: a history of the Anti-Corn Law League* (London, 2000), p. 266.

and discouraged parents from taking their children to be hired at the statute fairs but also offered a practical alternative for both farmers and farm servants alike by matching labour supply and work opportunities.[33] By gathering the names of young people wanting to become farm servants and circulating them among farmers and at tradespeople's shops in Doncaster Thomas successfully secured places for young people from Warmsworth and neighbouring villages before the local statute fairs. This practice received the support of the local clergy and was cited in the work of the Revd J. Skinner, who sought to reform hiring practices in East Yorkshire.[34] His agency thus extended beyond his parish and was a catalyst for change in the Doncaster district and further afield.[35]

The Revd Ornsby, incumbent of Fishlake parish, was in many respects a surrogate landowner. During his 36-year incumbency (1850–86) he sought to revive the fortunes of the Anglican church, successfully rebuilding two churches within the parish and increasing church attendance. His interest in the rural communities of the parish extended beyond religion and morality, although arguably both still underpinned the majority of his actions. Ornsby devoted time to all facets of rural life, including education, recreation, the labouring population and the poor. He supported the village school and organised a number of community events. His socially and morally motivated actions contributed to a sense of community, creating focal points for people to gather beyond church or chapel. This was important in a rural community without one dominant landowner, as landownership actively affected a village's sense of community. It also reflected the incumbent's quest to revive the Anglican church amidst the growth of non-conformity.

Farmers could also exert influence and agency, and as they were an extremely heterogeneous group in the nineteenth century this further demonstrates the importance of differentiation within social groups. Their agency depended on whether they were owner-occupiers or tenants, the size of their holding and the extent of their additional roles and responsibilities. The agency of tenant farmers was closely interlinked with that of landowners. Tenant farmers provided the working capital and stock, and were often expected to take risks and improve the land, enhancing the fixed capital (the land and buildings) of the landlord. Judiciously worded tenancy agreements and application books kept on behalf of Battie-Wrightson reveal the way in which landowners could assess the suitability of their tenants and guarantee the upkeep and careful management of individual farms, and show that some landowners recognised the potential agency of tenant farmers. Application books for tenancies on Battie-Wrightson's North Yorkshire estates contain detailed information about prospective tenants, including land they had previously farmed, marital status,

---

33 PP 1867–8, XVII, *First report of the Commission on the Employment of Children, Young Persons, and Women in Agriculture 1867*, p. 402.

34 Revd. J. Skinner, *Facts and opinions concerning statute hirings, respectively addressed to the landowner, clergy, farmers and tradespeople of the East Riding* (London, 1861), p. 18; *Doncaster Chronicle*, 15 November 1861, p. 6.

35 The Doncaster statute fairs are discussed further in chapter 4 of this book.

age, previous employment and even information about their families.[36] This was indicative of Battie-Wrightson's careful selection processes, applied across all his estates. The importance of ability, inclination and capital were emphasised in the tenancy agreements in order to safeguard the farming infrastructure. For example, an agreement stated that John Wood, tenant of a 125-acre farm in Warmsworth, was responsible for the upkeep and repair of the property and land and, as was expected of all tenants, should 'manage and cultivate the lands according to the best course of husbandry'.[37] This carefully managed relationship placed limitations and demands on the agency of both parties.

The renewal of tenancies was indicative of the value of 'good' tenants and their potential agency, demonstrating the landowners' reluctance to lose specialist knowledge, business contacts and even electoral support.[38] Landowners often offered incentives and cultivated loyalty accordingly by, for example, making rent reductions during periods of economic depression or uncertainty. Sir J.W. Copley offered his Sprotbrough tenants rent abatements of 15 per cent in 1846, when the norm in England was only 10 per cent.[39] For others, the annual rent dinner was perceived as an effective way to cultivate loyalty. William Aldam attended the rent dinners at Warmsworth whenever possible, and emphasised his desire to meet with his tenants.[40] Landowners could also use longer leases to facilitate continuity and investment, although this proved controversial during the nineteenth century, as it could enable inefficiency and inertia to fester.[41] Few tenancy agreements or leases survive for the Doncaster district, but those that do indicate that an annual tenure system was in operation. These often incorporated a guarantee that the lease would be renewed if both parties were in agreement.[42]

Continuity was a characteristic of tenant farmers in the Doncaster district. Between 1837 and 1877, 25–50 per cent of farms in the three estate villages continued to be occupied by the same person or family, indicating the relatively slow turnover of farmers in parts of England during the mid-nineteenth century.[43] Continuity was strongest on large farms. The Innocents, Jennings, Walkers and Wainwrights of Rossington, the Crawshaws and Walkers at Warmsworth, and the Hickmans and Woods at Sprotbrough are all examples of families with larger farms (between 140 and 350 acres) that remained in their hands for prolonged periods of time (at least 40–50 years). This suggests that, even where annual tenure was practised, leases were renewed if tenants had effectively demonstrated their abilities and aptitude.

---

36 DA, DD/BW/E14/91, Application book for farm tenancies, 1874–1879.
37 DA, DD/BW/E11/109, Tenancy agreement between Battie-Wrightson and John Wood, 24 January 1837.
38 Beckett, 'Agricultural landownership and estate management', p. 742; D.R. Stead, 'The mobility of English tenant farmers, c. 1700–1850', *Agricultural History Review*, 51/2 (2003), p. 174.
39 *Doncaster Gazette*, 22 May 1846, p. 3.
40 DA, DD/WA/D1/1–28, Diaries of William Aldam.
41 Mingay, 'The Farmer', in Collins (ed.), *Agrarian History*, p. 793.
42 For example, DA, DD/BW/E11/109, Tenancy agreement between Battie-Wrightson and John Wood, 24 January 1837.
43 Stead, 'The mobility of English tenant farmers', p. 188.

This continuity in the Doncaster district was facilitated through the practice of transferring tenant farms to family members, which was not uncommon in England during this period. Between 1837 and 1877 just under a fifth of all farm tenancies in the three estate villages were reassigned to family members after the death or retirement of the original tenant. Predominantly, sons and other male relatives were the recipients of these farms. Women were to some extent inhibited from becoming farmers, especially as agricultural societies tended to be dominated by men and middle-class women were withdrawing into the domestic sphere. Nevertheless, female relatives – especially widows – were not precluded from becoming tenant farmers.[44] In Rossington and Warmsworth women continued to occupy and run farms after the death of their husbands. Elizabeth Innocent occupied a 260-acre farm on the Rossington estate after her husband died. The 1841 and 1851 census enumerators' books indicate her position as head of the household, while her son, George, who lived with her, had the occupational designation of agricultural labourer. Four male farm servants provided further labour on the farm. After her death her son took over the tenancy and running of the farm. Similarly, between 1837 and 1841 Elizabeth Crawshaw occupied and ran the 200-acre farm at Warmsworth that had previously been tenanted by her husband and would subsequently be taken over by her son, Edward, who had been resident on the farm during this time. These examples suggest that the presence of an adult male on female-headed farms was particularly desirable. Permitting a widow to tenant a farm was a convenient way in which to ensure the continuity of family occupancy, albeit as a temporary measure until a male relative inherited.[45] The practice of collecting information about the whole family in tenancy application books, as employed by Battie-Wrightson, was testimony to the way in which women and children were seen as an integral part of the farm economy.

Continuity of tenancy increased opportunities for farmers to exercise their agency. In addition to cultivating crops, rearing livestock and investing in farming stock, long-standing tenant farmers could shape agricultural practices through their participation in agricultural societies and farmers' clubs. For instance, Thomas Wood, land agent and tenant farmer, and Mr Hickson and Mr Vickers, both large tenant farmers on the Sprotbrough estate, were active members of the Sprotbrough Farmers' Club, bringing their practical experience to club meetings. Vickers, a committee member, was also elected a member of the Royal Agricultural Society of England in 1849.[46] Farmers across the district also had the opportunity to contribute to knowledge networks, and thus exhibit their agency, through their participation in the Doncaster Agricultural Society.[47]

---

44 N. Verdon, 'The "lady farmer": gender, widowhood and farming in Victorian England', in R. Hoyle (ed.), *The farmer in England, 1650–1980* (Farnham, 2013), pp. 241–62.

45 Verdon, 'The "lady farmer"', p. 262.

46 S. Holland, 'Contrasting rural communities: the experience of South Yorkshire in the mid nineteenth century', PhD thesis (Sheffield Hallam University, 2013).

47 Knowledge networks, agricultural societies and farmers' clubs are discussed further in chapter 3 of this book.

Social hierarchies, power relations and agency in the countryside

The nineteenth century witnessed the politicisation of farmers. In addition to the enlarged franchise after the 1832 Reform Act, electoral issues were significant in repositioning farmers as active political agents. Tenant farmers were traditionally perceived as being susceptible to landlord influence and exhibiting deferential behaviour,[48] with Mills, for example, arguing that landed estates were the basis for 'political coercion and patronage'.[49] A re-evaluation of the rural electorate, however, suggests that voting patterns were fluid and constantly reconstructed.[50] Divisive political issues, such as the repeal of the Corn Laws, had a notable effect in politicising the rural electorate to an unprecedented extent.[51] Doncaster was an important forum for debate, where farmers from both estate and multi-freeholder villages could engage with political ideas, and as such the town was significant in facilitating independence in rural politics.

Both the Anti-Corn Law League and the pro-Corn Law movement were represented at Doncaster. In 1839 the Doncaster Anti-Corn Law Association (ACLA), one of 223 ACLAs in England, was founded with several landowners from the Doncaster district among the leading figures of the organisation.[52] They engaged in debates with their opponents, such as one in 1840 held at the theatre in Doncaster in which Dr Holland, of the pro-Corn Law faction, and Mr Acland, of the National Anti-Corn Law League, represented their relative causes. Reports in local newspapers evoked the melodrama of proceedings and the verbal sparring that ensued.[53] As with other events organised by the Anti-Corn Law League, this one was carefully choreographed,[54] enabling them to present a convincing and persuasive case and gradually gain the upper hand.

Concurrently, a group of local landowners, clergy and large tenant farmers formed a pro-Corn Law group in Doncaster, known as the Anti-League, to counter the Anti-Corn Law agitation.[55] A public meeting was held in the town in 1839 in order to register opposition to the proposed repeal,[56] the *Doncaster Gazette* reporting that it was 'one

---

48 Mills, *Lord and peasant*, p. 117; D.C. Moore, *The politics of deference* (New York, 1976).
49 Mills, *Lord and peasant*, p. 31.
50 P. Salmon, *Electoral reform at work: local politics and national parties, 1832–1841* (Woodbridge, 2002); D. Eastwood, 'Contesting the politics of deference: the rural electorate, 1820–1860', in J. Lawrence and M. Taylor (eds), *Party, state and society: electoral behaviour since 1820* (Aldershot, 1997), pp. 27–8.
51 J.R. Fisher, 'The limits of deference: agricultural communities in a mid nineteenth century election campaign', *Journal of British Studies*, 21 (1981), pp. 90–91; Eastwood, 'Contesting the politics of deference', pp. 33–4.
52 Pickering and Tyrrell, *The people's bread*, p. 254; *Doncaster Gazette*, 19 April 1839, p. 5; *Doncaster Gazette*, 17 May 1839, p. 4; *Doncaster Gazette*, 1 November 1839, p. 5; *Doncaster Gazette*, 28 February 1840, pp. 6–7; *Doncaster Chronicle*, 29 February 1840, p. 5; *Doncaster Gazette*, 28 February 1840, pp. 6–7; *Doncaster Chronicle*, 29 February 1840, p. 5; DA, DD/WA/P/12, Letters regarding the Corn Laws, 1843.
53 *Doncaster Gazette*, 6 November 1840, pp. 4–5.
54 Pickering and Tyrrell, *The people's bread*, p. 192.
55 *Doncaster Gazette*, 19 April 1839, p. 5.
56 *Doncaster Gazette*, 22 February 1839, p. 6; *Doncaster Chronicle*, 23 February 1839, p. 1.

of the most numerously attended agricultural meetings we ever witnessed' and that the town hall was 'densely crowded'.[57] Representation was made by local farmers, as well as by land agents, farmers and industrialists. The over-riding message was the potentially detrimental effects of repealing the Corn Laws on the English farmer. Following this meeting, a petition against the repeal secured the signatures of 56 people from the estate villages of Sprotbrough, Cadeby and Melton and 83 from the multi-freeholder village of Stainforth – many of whom were farmers.[58]

The 1841 election campaign was fought between Denison and Wortley, the Conservative and pro-Corn Law candidates, on the one hand, and Milton and Morpeth, the Liberal and anti-Corn Law candidates, on the other. The links between the Conservative Party and the countryside had deep roots:[59] when Denison spoke at a pro-Corn Law meeting in Doncaster in 1840 he expressed alarm at how the Anti-Corn Law campaign was being conducted and especially the ways in which he felt its supporters were misrepresenting farmers and landowners. He also suggested that repeal would be 'equally unjust towards the farmer and prejudiced to the country at large'.[60] He went on to argue that continued protection was in the interests of landowners and farmers, concluding 'I am firmly convinced it [repeal] would be the most dangerous experiment the country had ever made; that it has never made one equally dangerous; and I hope and believe the experiment will never be tried.'[61] The repeated use of 'experiment', with no reference to agriculture or the economy prior to the Corn Laws, suggests this was a deliberate rhetorical flourish on the part of Denison, although it is worth noting that in the early 1840s there were genuine fears and uncertainty about what would happen to agriculture if the corn laws were repealed.

The pro- and anti-corn law candidates received support from both estate and multi-freeholder villages. The voting behaviour of farmers in the 1841 election for the West Riding of Yorkshire suggests that the issue of repeal stimulated the political independence of farmers, and that debates in Doncaster played an important role in bestowing them with greater agency. In the absence of a secret ballot, details of those who voted and who they voted for were listed in poll books and in some cases were reprinted for sale. Votes for Denison and Wortley came from all the farmers in the estate village of Sprotbrough, but also from the majority of farmers in the multi-freeholder villages of Fishlake and Braithwell.[62] The farmers of the estate village of Rossington and the multi-freeholder village of Stainforth were divided between those who supported repeal and those who favoured continued protectionism.[63] Only at

---

57 *Doncaster Gazette*, 22 February 1839, p. 6.
58 *Doncaster Gazette*, 29 March 1839, p. 4.
59 A. Flynn et al., 'The political power of farmers: an English perspective', *Rural History*, 7/1 (1996), p. 16.
60 *Doncaster Chronicle*, 29 February 1840, p. 7.
61 *Doncaster Gazette*, 19 April 1839, p. 5.
62 *West Riding election: the poll for the 2 knights of the shire for the West Riding of Yorkshire* (Wakefield, 1841), pp. 177–8, 188, 522–3.
63 Ibid., pp. 186, 189–90.

Warmsworth, where William Aldam was resident landowner and a Liberal MP who supported free trade, was there overwhelming support among the farmers for the Liberal, anti-Corn Law candidates.

After the repeal of the Corn Laws in 1846 voting in the six case-study villages reverted to more traditional patterns, as evidenced by the 1848 election. Farmers in the estate villages voted overwhelmingly for Denison, the Conservative candidate. The only exception was George Blagden, who in addition to farming a small amount of land was joint proprietor of the quarries at Warmsworth. In the three multi-freeholder villages voting behaviour was more varied, with farmers voting for both the Conservative and Liberal candidate in similar proportions. Whereas farmers in the estate villages appeared to have been more politicised during the campaign for repeal, farmers in the multi-freeholder villages became more politicised in the aftermath.[64] The role of political issues and the way in which Doncaster acted as a forum for political debate was important in bestowing agency on farmers, demonstrating how external spheres of influence impacted on rural communities.

Tenant farmers could further extend their agency if appointed to the position of land agent on a landed estate. Land agents occupied a pivotal role in estate management.[65] From a landowners' perspective it was important to ensure the calibre of the land agent. James Caird argued that 'The selection of a properly qualified [land] agent or steward is, on every large estate, a matter of the utmost importance.'[66] The ability to farm did not, in Caird's opinion, equip anyone to manage farmland. He was particularly critical of the employment of tenant farmers as land agents, which he argued equated to poor management skills on behalf of the landowner.[67] Nevertheless, experience and familiarity with the land were valuable assets that favoured the employment of farmers as land agents, especially on medium-sized estates of between 1,000 and 3,000 acres.[68] As such, the agency of a small group of farmers was increased, as, despite acting on behalf of their respective landowners, some power was inevitably delegated to them.

Thomas Wood, the land agent for Battie-Wrightson from the 1830s and for Sir J.W. Copley from the 1850s, was also a tenant farmer.[69] Wood had not undertaken any official training, which was not uncommon at this date, when most agents were

---

64 *Ibid.*, p. 105.
65 Beckett, 'Agricultural landownership and estate management', pp. 731–3; S.A. Webster, 'Estate improvement and the professionalisation of land agents on the Egremont estates in Sussex and Yorkshire, 1770–1835', *Rural History*, 18/1 (2007), pp. 47–69; S.A. Webster, 'Agents and professionalism: improvement on the Egremont estates c.1770 to c.1860', PhD thesis (University of Nottingham, 2010), pp. 26–8.
66 Caird, *English agriculture* (1852), p. 493.
67 *Ibid.*
68 Beckett, 'Agricultural landownership and estate management', pp. 732–3.
69 TNA, HO 107/2346, CEB Sprotbrough 1851; RG 9/3516, CEB Sprotbrough 1861; RG 10/4716, CEB Sprotbrough 1871; E.R. Kelly, *Post Office directory of the West Riding of Yorkshire, 1867* (London, 1867).

not properly qualified and training was rare.[70] His aptitude was determined by his familiarity with the practicalities of farming on the Magnesian Limestone soils: he occupied 160 acres of farmland on his own account and was a leading member of the Sprotbrough Farmers' Club. Wood successfully combined farming with the day-to-day management and accounting duties that he performed on behalf of the two landowners. He used his practical experience to shape estate management and to inform meetings of the local farmers' club. For example, having grown a large white globe turnip that weighed 12 pounds and had a circumference of 31 inches, he contributed to a club meeting about the cultivation of turnips on the Magnesian Limestone and provided insights into his agricultural exploits.[71] The local press noted that Wood had been successful in fulfilling the wishes of Sir J.W. Copley through his 'praise worthy endeavours'. Wood's financial acumen and administrative abilities are evidenced through the cash books kept on behalf of Battie-Wrightson between 1837 and 1872, which consistently balanced and were astutely organised.[72] His competency was born of local knowledge and experience, which was applied to the two estates and met the requirements of the landowners accordingly.

His agency was further enhanced by his physical presence within the community. The land agent's house, a large brick property with intricate architectural detailing, was located at the heart of the village and in close proximity to the church. The addition of a room to accommodate tenants on rent day and reports that Wood showed 'kind feeling' towards his neighbours were testimony to the way in which the land agent had been physically and socially integrated into the village.

External agents

Agency in the Victorian countryside also originated externally. Doncaster Corporation, the local press and knowledge networks such as the agricultural societies and farmers' clubs were powerful external agents influencing rural communities in the Doncaster district. While all transcended the landownership of specific rural communities, landowners often held influential positions within many of them, which extended their own power beyond the village. This also had the potential to affect the relative self-containedness of rural communities, with agents beyond the village influencing decisions that affected villagers.

Doncaster Corporation was an influential agent affecting the rural hinterland surrounding the town, especially through the reciprocal relationships forged between

---

70 Royal Agricultural College Archives, Cirencester, RAC/16/27/1, Student register, 1863–1883; RAC/16/004/2, Class and prize lists, 1859–1870. Admission lists for students attending the Agricultural College at Cirencester do not survive prior to 1880, but Thomas Wood does not appear in the printed student registers 1844–1897 or in the handwritten student lists from 1848.
71 *Doncaster Chronicle*, 12 September 1845, p. 5; *Doncaster Chronicle*, 1 February 1850, p. 3.
72 DA, DD/BW/A/36, Copy cash book of Thomas Wood, January 1845–December 1857; DD/BW/E3/14, Cash book of Thomas Wood, February 1839–June 1847; DD/BW/E3/15, Cash book of Thomas Wood, January 1865–December 1872. DA, DD/BW/E3/14, Cash BOOK of Thomas Wood, February 1839–June 1847; DD/BW/E3/15, Cash book of Thomas Wood, January 1865–December 1872.

town and country. Its proactive role in initiating and investing in the redevelopment of the market infrastructure between the 1840s and 1870s, including building and rebuilding the corn market and market hall, was indicative of this reciprocal relationship.[73] A recurring theme was the assertion that the market improvements would be advantageous to the town and its immediate neighbourhood in terms of the local economy.[74] The improvements also reflected the agriculture of the district, responding to the needs of local agriculturalists as well as those of urban consumers and those from further afield.[75] The committee frequently talked of their agricultural friends and the bond of friendship or union between agriculturalists and the town of Doncaster.[76] This relationship was, however, largely managed by the town, and increasingly in the interests of the town rather than the countryside, as discussed further in chapter 3.

The local press also provided agency that penetrated the countryside, whether offering its opinion on the roles and responsibilities of different social groups or providing advice and information about agricultural matters. The *Doncaster Chronicle* and *Doncaster Gazette* both emphasised the responsibilities of the landowning class with regard to agriculture and the labouring population, although they largely praised the rural elites in their reports.[77] They also commented on the actions of Doncaster Corporation and the development of the market infrastructure. Again, the reports were to a large extent positive, increasingly reflecting a burgeoning civic pride felt throughout the town. However, some reports were more balanced, including concerns or complaints raised by agriculturalists when they arose. This was especially apparent in reports about the new covered corn market in Doncaster: the majority focused on the practical advantages it brought to buyers and sellers, and yet some highlighted concerns about the tender process and the expense being accrued by the Doncaster Corporation.[78]

Both Doncaster Corporation and the local press supported the agricultural societies in the district, especially the work of the Doncaster Agricultural Society (DAS). The Corporation supported the formation of the DAS in the 1840s and provided the impetus for the reformation of the society in the 1870s. The *Doncaster Chronicle* encouraged farmers in the district not only to subscribe to the society but also to actively participate in its work and exhibit at the shows, as this was considered an integral part of agricultural improvement.[79]

---

73 Holland, 'Doncaster and its environs', pp. 77–89. The market infrastructure is discussed further in chapter 3 of this book.
74 DA, AB/2/6//21/3, Council minutes, 11 March 1840.
75 Holland, 'Doncaster and its environs', pp. 79–80; DA, AB/2/2/3, Council minutes, 9 May 1843.
76 Holland, 'Doncaster and its environs', pp. 80–81.
77 Reports from the *Doncaster Chronicle* and *Doncaster Gazette*, and other regional newspapers, are used throughout the book and provide evidence of the points made here, including reference to agricultural matters in chapter 3 and other aspects of rural life in chapters 4 to 6.
78 *Doncaster Chronicle*, 12 May 1843, p. 6; *Doncaster Chronicle*, 2 June 1843, p. 5; 9 June 1843, p. 3; *Doncaster Gazette*, 5 May 1844; *Doncaster Gazette*, 17 May 1844, p. 5; *Doncaster Chronicle*, 14 June 1844, p. 5.
79 *Doncaster Chronicle*, 6 May 1842, p. 5; *Doncaster Chronicle*, 1 October 1847, p. 8; *Doncaster Chronicle*, 31 March 1871, p. 5.

Agricultural workers[80]

The Hodge stereotype perpetuated the notion of the passivity of the labouring population. The infamous perception of the labourer as 'unimaginative, ill-clothed, ill-educated, ill-paid, ignorant of all that is taking place beyond his own village, dissatisfied with his position and yet without energy or effort to improve it', as set out by J. Dent in his discussion of agricultural labourers in the *Journal of the Royal Agricultural Society* in 1871, suggests that the position of the labourer was fixed and devoid of agency.[81] Historical studies have gradually revealed the complexities of the nineteenth-century agricultural labourer, including their agency and proactive stance. Such work has largely focused on collective action through unions and on labourers in southern and eastern counties, where conditions were worse and wages were lower than in the north of England.[82] Agricultural workers in the Doncaster district exercised considerable collective agency in the wider labour market. They formed a large occupational group and occupied a pivotal role in the fortunes of estates and farms. Their very presence gave them agency. As the chairman of a local agricultural society argued, 'the labouring classes were a class of the community neither landlords nor farmers could possibly do without'.[83] In an effort to preserve their own interests, landowners and farmers were effectively engaged in the careful management of human resources.

Agricultural workers should not simply be positioned in relation to landowners and/or farmers, as a deferential or reactionary group whose identity was shaped by their relationship to those who had greater power and wealth. Behind the iconic agricultural labourers' smock (see Figure 2.2) lay a complex group of agricultural workers, with collective and individual identities. In the Doncaster district labourers could be more assertive on account of the close proximity of rural communities to industry, resulting in increased competition for labour. Their labour was a commodity in demand, for which they increasingly commanded higher wages. This process was particularly notable with regards to the hiring of farm servants, whose bargaining power was facilitated by the public nature of the statute fairs and was most effective when demand exceeded supply. Attempts to reform hiring practices were met with resistance from labourers in the Doncaster district, who were reluctant to be 'driven' inside and suspicious that a restructuring of hiring practices would jeopardise their day of leisure and undermine

---

80 Different types of agricultural worker, including how they were hired, are discussed in further detail in chapter 4.
81 Dent, 'The present condition', pp. 343–4; Freeman, *Social investigation and rural England*, p. 22.
82 J.P.D. Dunbabin, 'The "revolt of the field": the agricultural labourers' movement in the 1870s', *Past and Present*, 26/1 (1963); A. Howkins, *Poor labouring men: rural radicalism in Norfolk, 1870–1923* (London, 1985); Howkins, *Reshaping rural England*; Reay, *Rural Englands*; B. Reay, *The last rising of the agricultural labourers: rural life and protest in nineteenth-century England* (London, 2010); C. Griffin, *Protest, politics and work in rural England* (Basingstoke, 2014).
83 *Doncaster Chronicle*, 23 October 1846, p. 5.

Social hierarchies, power relations and agency in the countryside

Figure 2.2 Agricultural labourer's smock, *c.*1880 (Heritage Doncaster, DONMG: 1912.40).

their collective bargaining power by removing the process to the private domain.[84] This suggests that agricultural workers were to some extent conscious of their agency. The process also created social hierarchies within the labouring population, with the more skilled and experienced farm servants able to command higher wages and obtain work, while unskilled, younger, inexperienced workers, although undeterred in asking for higher wages, failed to secure work.

Conclusion

Social hierarchies are an important factor in understanding agency and power relations in the Victorian countryside. Landowners had the potential to exert great influence, whether for better or worse, through the ownership of land and the power this bestowed on them. Yet, as the landowners of the Doncaster district demonstrate, this agency and influence could manifest itself in different ways. The four key landowning families in the three estate villages, for instance, adopted different approaches and strategies to estate and agricultural management. Differentiation in landownership makes the deconstruction of landowners crucial to an understanding of rural communities. The nuances and disparities in landownership and agency underpin differentiation in rural communities. Landowners in the Doncaster district did exert influence and affect the development of rural communities – economically, socially and physically – but not all power resided with landowners and they were not the only agents of change. In both estate and multi-freeholder villages other social groups had the power to exert influence and to negotiate with landowners over certain aspects of rural society, undermining the causal relationship between landownership and rural agency advocated by many contemporaries and historians alike. External institutions, such as Doncaster Corporation, local agricultural societies and political movements, also offered alternative forums of power and channels for demonstrating agency. Moreover, the power and agency of each social group and individuals within them were fluid, determined by internal and external factors and spheres of influence, with each constituent constantly acting and reacting in response to other stimuli. Power relations, and opportunities to exhibit or exert agency, converged on the market town of Doncaster, where relative power and agency could be renegotiated. The evidence of social hierarchies, power relations and agency discussed in this chapter underpins the remainder of this book, and is explored in greater depth in some of the thematic chapters.

---

84 *Doncaster Chronicle*, 15 November 1861, p. 5; S. Holland, 'Farm service and hiring practices in mid-nineteenth-century England: the Doncaster region in the West Riding of Yorkshire', in J. Whittle (ed.), *Servants in rural Europe 1400–1900* (Woodbridge, 2017), pp. 199–200.

Chapter 3

Rural economies

White's *Directory of the West Riding* noted in 1837 that 'Doncaster has never been a manufacturing town'[1] – in spite of good communications, its position in an industrialised county and the presence of small-scale industry and manufacturers. Doncaster was originally located on two important trade arteries – the Great North Road and the river Don. The nearby towns of Rotherham and Sheffield had large iron and steel works, while the textile industry dominated the West Riding towns of Leeds, Huddersfield and Halifax. Doncaster's economic and social transformation began with the arrival of the Great Northern Railway in 1849, White's directory of 1852 being quick to note that the town's 'commercial facilities have lately been much increased by the opening of the Great Northern and South Yorkshire Railways'.[2] The establishment of Great Northern Railway engineering works in the town in 1853 encroached upon the rural communities of Balby and Hexthorpe, both bordering the town, and stimulated further industrial and commercial development in the town during the late 1860s and early 1870s. Yet very few rural communities in the Doncaster district were transformed by industrialisation at this date, and the coal mines that would eventually transform and dominate the district were a feature of the late nineteenth and early twentieth century. Doncaster and its rural hinterland remained predominantly agricultural during the mid-nineteenth century. This chapter explores the extent of variation in the rural economies of the Doncaster district and their relationship with the market town, focusing on agriculture, micro-commerce and industry.

Differentiation in rural economies has largely been attributed to landownership. Accordingly, in the Mills model, estate villages are associated with agriculture, domestic service, a small selection of trades and crafts and little or no industry, whereas multi-freeholder villages have more complex economies, often combining agriculture and industry and with a greater range of trades and crafts.[3] The balance between economic activities, their management and development and their scale and scope was more complex, however, and often transcended landownership. The co-existence of agriculture and micro-commerce with some small-scale industry was characteristic of the rural economies of the Doncaster district. Although village economies often differed in accordance with patterns of landownership, the extent of variation between estate and multi-freeholder villages was in fact not always very marked. Moreover, there were nuanced differences between villages with similar patterns of landownership. Differentiation in the rural economies of the Doncaster district was also linked to geology, the balance of power within communities, the level of agency exercised by particular individuals and the inter-relationship between

---

1 White, *History, gazetteer and directory of the West Riding of Yorkshire, 1837*, p. 267.
2 White, *Gazetteer and general directory of Sheffield, 1852*, p. 432.
3 Mills, *Lord and peasant*, p. 117.

Table 3.1
Arable crops grown in the six case-study villages, 1866

	Estate villages				Multi-freeholder villages	
Village	Sprotbrough	Warmsworth	Rossington		Fishlake	Stainforth
Geology	Upper magnesian limestone	Lower magnesian limestone	Sandstone		Marshy lowland with clay soil	Marshy lowland with clay soil
Wheat	451.25 (38.3%)	171.75 (33.2%)	363.5 (26.9%)		593 (38.1%)	319.5 (34.5%)
Barley	245.5 (20.8%)	118 (22.8%)	347.25 (25.7%)		217 (14%)	148.25 (16%)
Oats	24 (2%)	15 (2.9%)	110.5 (8.2%)		173.25 (11.1%)	117.25 (12.7%)
Rye	1 (0.1%)	-	46 (3.4%)		7 (0.5%)	7.25 (0.8%)
Beans	36 (3.1%)	13 (2.5%)	7 (0.5%)		241.75 (15.6%)	28.25 (3.1%)
Peas	23 (2%)	11 (2.2%)	-		51.5 (3.3%)	19.5 (2.1%)
Turnips and swedes	276.5 (23.5%)	108.5 (20.9%)	388 (28.7%)		147.75 (9.5%)	141.5 (15.3%)
Potatoes	59 (5%)	10 (1.9%)	28 (2.1%)		50 (3.2%)	65.75 (7.1%)
Mangolds	8.25 (0.7%)	5 (1%)	14 (1%)		1.75 (0.1%)	1.25 (0.1%)
Carrots	-	1.5 (0.3%)	5 (0.4%)		-	0.5 (0.1%)
Cabbage	14.5 (1.2%)	18 (3.5%)	27 (2%)		11.5 (0.7%)	34.5 (3.7%)
Hops	-	-	-		-	-
Other	38.75 (3.3%)	45.5 (8.8%)	14.25 (1.1%)		60 (3.9%)	41.5 (4.5%)
Total cultivated acreage	1177.75	517.25	1350.5		1554.5	925

Source: TNA, MAF 68/82. The agricultural returns (crops) for the West Riding of Yorkshire, 1866, pp. 1114, 1115, 1130.

different rural communities and between town and country. These matters are now discussed in more detail in relation to agriculture, micro-commerce and industry.

Agriculture

Agriculture underpinned the rural economies of the Doncaster district throughout the mid-nineteenth century. Urbanisation and population growth increased demand for, and stimulated, agricultural production.[4] To a large extent similar crops were grown in the different villages, albeit in differing quantities and partly in accordance with land type. Table 3.1 shows the range of crops cultivated in all the villages examined here, excluding Braithwell.[5] Crops grown were largely determined, ultimately, by geology, although the connection between soils and agriculture was undermined in the course of the nineteenth century by the development of farming practices that allowed farmers to be less governed by soil type.[6] Geology was emphasised in the prize essays published in the *Journal of the Royal Agricultural Society of England* between 1845 and 1869, including that of John H. Charnock. Charnock's 1848 report on agriculture in the West Riding provides a valuable insight into farming practices at the time. He highlighted the great variety in soil types as 'too numerous to detail' and explained the relative merits and practical advantages of different geological areas for farming.[7] Charnock's observations are particularly relevant here as a number of the geological areas he identified intersected in the Doncaster region.

The fertile, well-drained soils of the Magnesian Limestone to the west of Doncaster were particularly suited to arable farming. According to Charnock, the usual rotation on this geology was 'the four-course of turnips, barley, seeds, and wheat, varying the grain crops occasionally, and substituting red clover for seeds. Peas are also grown on the deeper portions of this soil, and are a judicious and profitable adjunct in the rotation.'[8] This is reflected in the principal crops grown at Sprotbrough and Warmsworth – wheat, together with a combination of turnips, other cereal crops, peas and beans. Wheat, however, occupied a large proportion of cultivated land in all the case-study villages. The nineteenth-century farming press argued that the application of artificial manures meant there was hardly any land where wheat could not be grown.[9] Large

---

4   E.J.T. Collins, 'Introduction', in E.J.T. Collins (ed.), *The agrarian history of England and Wales*, Vol. VII, 1850–1914, Part 1 (Cambridge, 2000), p. 2; E.A. Wrigley, *Continuity, chance and change: the character of the industrial revolution in England* (Cambridge, 1988), pp. 18–19; C. Hallas, 'The northern region', in E.J.T. Collins (ed.), *The agrarian history of England and Wales*, Vol. VII, 1850–1914, Part 1 (Cambridge, 2000), pp. 402–4.

5   No crop returns exist for Braithwell.

6   M. Overton, *Agricultural revolution in England: the transformation of the agrarian economy 1500–1850* (Cambridge, 1996), p. 195; B.A. Holderness, 'Farming regions', in E.J.T. Collins (ed.), *The agrarian history of England and Wales*, Vol. VII, 1850–1914, Part 1 (Cambridge, 2000), pp. 362–4.

7   J.H. Charnock, 'On the farming of the West Riding of Yorkshire: prize report', *Journal of the Royal Agricultural Society of England*, 9/21 (1848), p. 284.

8   *Ibid.*, p. 296.

9   *The Farmers' Magazine*, 18, second series (July–December 1848), p. 447.

Table 3.2
Livestock in the six case-study villages, 1866

	Sprotbrough	Warmsworth	Rossington	Fishlake	Stainforth	Braithwell
Milk cows	35	44	58	136	72	58
Other cattle 2 years and older	25	20	71	143	57	24
Other cattle under 2 years	46	57	104	186	53	85
Sheep 1 year and older	801	289	1260	274	155	498
Sheep under 1 year old	243	106	315	541	56	237
Pigs	143	84	170	348	114	151

Source: TNA, MAF 68/81, The agricultural returns (livestock) for the West Riding of Yorkshire, 1866.

quantities of wheat were grown on the lowlands at Fishlake and Stainforth, where lime was applied to the heavy clay soil to facilitate this.[10] Nevertheless, Charnock noted that, despite some good cultivation on the poorer soils, it was the exception and there was wide scope for improvement in farming practices and techniques.[11]

Charnock described cultivation on the sandstone as 'generally very good'. Here the usual rotation where the soils were lighter was 'the ordinary four-course turnip culture', and he noted 'the great facility which these sandy soils offer for the easy and rapid spread of twitch or couch grass, making the turnip crop every fourth year essential for the periodical eradication of this weed'.[12] Turnips were grown extensively through the Doncaster district, although in larger quantities on the sandy land. Rossington was noted for its preference for turnip cultivation at the beginning of the nineteenth century.[13] The light, well-drained soils were ideal to take advantage of newly developed varieties of root crops from the eighteenth century onwards.[14] Increased cultivation of turnips in the district was connected to urban expansion and population growth. Turnips were not only a cleansing crop that improved the fertility of the land but also a fodder crop used to fatten livestock. The district-wide failure of the turnip crop in 1858 impacted on both town and country, demonstrating how the fortunes of agriculture and the urban population were intertwined. Animals could not be over-wintered and the November fair was inundated with stock that were either sold

---

10 TNA, MAF 68/82, The agricultural returns (crops), 1866; Kelly, *Post Office directory, 1877*, pp. 314, 385.
11 Charnock, 'On the farming of the West Riding', p. 299.
12 *Ibid.*
13 E. Miller, *The history and antiquities of Doncaster and its vicinity* (1804, reprint Howden, 1984), p. 236.
14 S. Wade-Martins, *Farmers, landlords and landscapes: rural Britain 1720–1870* (Macclesfield, 2004), p. 27.

Rural economies

Figure 3.1 Cattle Market, Doncaster, Lionel Crawshaw (Heritage Doncaster, DONMG: 1916.16).

cheaply or not at all, which in turn affected the supply of meat in subsequent months.[15] Charnock also noted, regarding the sandstone, that 'where the soil possesses more stamina' longer rotations were practised and the barley was of a quality 'much esteemed by the better class of maltsters, and realizes the highest market value'. This was true of Rossington, where barley accounted for the second largest acreage of arable crops cultivated on the estate.

Charnock's discussion of livestock similarly highlighted variation within the county. This was also demonstrated on a smaller scale within the Doncaster district and indeed between rural communities in close proximity with one another (Table 3.2). Dairying, rearing and fattening were all taking place in the case-study villages to varying extents. The 1866 agricultural return highlights the prevalence of dairy farming in Fishlake, while Rossington had a relatively high proportion of cattle compared with other estate villages. The vibrancy of the cattle market at Doncaster (Figure 3.1) was testimony to the importance of livestock to the rural economies of

---

15   *Doncaster Gazette*, 19 November 1858, p. 5.

the Doncaster district. Charnock nevertheless argued that, compared with the East and North Ridings of Yorkshire, less attention had been given to the stock and breed of cattle in the West Riding and that there were 'a great variety of cross breeds of a most incongruous character'; however, there were 'some few breeders of shorthorns, whose stock is deserving of note'.[16] Reports of the Doncaster Agricultural Society Shows provide evidence of notable cattle breeders, including James Brown, a landowner of Rossington, who exhibited and won prizes accordingly. In 1873 he won a £10 prize in the category for best 'Alderney, Jersey or Guernsey cows or heifers in calf or milk'.[17] This corresponded with Charnock's observation:

> It has for some years too been the practice of the resident landowners, and the better class of farmers, to keep in their herds one or more Channel Island cows; and the fashion has also prevailed to some extent amongst the wealthier manufacturers, who, having their residences in the suburbs of towns, have deemed their domestic arrangements incomplete without an Alderney cow or two.[18]

This trend combined the fashionable desire of rural elites for specialist and pedigree breeds with the latest recommendations in livestock breeding.[19] The Alderney cow was especially commended for the 'richness of its milk, and the excellence of the butter made from it', and was valued accordingly.[20]

According to Charnock, more attention had been given to the breeds of sheep farmed in the West Riding, particularly in the turnip-growing districts.[21] Sheep were often grazed on the lighter sandy soils in conjunction with arable farming, as was the case at Rossington, where a total of 1,260 sheep one year or older and 315 sheep under one year was recorded in 1866.[22] Thus, the differentiation in crops and livestock within the rural communities of the district appears to have been largely determined by geology and soil type, rather than landholding structure or farm size.

Farm size and high farming

In the nineteenth century there was an expectation that landowners would improve, innovate in and influence agriculture. James Caird, the agriculturalist and agricultural writer, asserted that landowners were 'capitalists to whom the

---

16 Charnock, 'On the farming of the West Riding', pp. 300–301.
17 *Doncaster Gazette*, 27 June 1873, p. 8.
18 Charnock, 'On the farming of the West Riding', pp. 300–301.
19 J.R. Walton, 'Pedigree and the national cattle herd c. 1750–1950', *Agricultural History Review*, 34/2 (1986), pp. 149–70.
20 'The Alderney Cow', *The Saturday Magazine*, 7/198, 1 August 1835.
21 Charnock, 'On the farming of the West Riding', p. 300.
22 P. Brassley, 'Arable systems' in in E.J.T. Collins (ed.), *The agrarian history of England and Wales*, Vol. VII, 1850–1914, Part 1 (Cambridge, 2000), p. 463; B.A. Holderness, 'Intensive livestock keeping' in E.J.T. Collins (ed.), *The agrarian history of England and Wales*, Vol. VII, 1850–1914, Part 1 (Cambridge, 2000), p. 484; Caird, *English agriculture*, p. 294.

land belongs' and as such were responsible for the good management of landed estates.[23] Historians such as G.E. Mingay have emphasised the causal role of landowners in agricultural practices, arguing 'the most obvious of landowner influence lay in the sphere of agriculture' because of their 'near monopoly of farmland'.[24] However, expectation and opportunity did not always equate to practice, with some landowners lacking the knowledge, skills, capital or inclination to meet the expectations placed upon them.[25]

In models of village typology, farm size, the pursuit of so called 'high farming' (from the 1840s) and capital investment were the agricultural characteristics most affected by landownership. Mills argued that farm size was greater in estate than in multi-freeholder villages, with landowners favouring large farms as they were more likely to attract tenants with capital and ability.[26] However, there was little consensus among nineteenth-century agriculturalists and writers regarding what constituted a large or a small farm, or the impact farm size had on agriculture.[27] Calculating and determining farm size presents its own challenges. Occupiers of land were instructed to include the acreage they farmed in the census returns from 1851, although this data is sometimes inaccurate or incomplete, with smaller farmers in particular often failing to answer this question.[28] Nevertheless, a comparison of available records suggests that evidence of farm size in the census enumerators' books (CEBs) for the Doncaster district was reasonably accurate. For example, there is considerable consistency between the acreages returned in the CEBs and those recorded for some villages in tithe apportionment documents and field books.[29]

Charnock argued that the average farm size in the West Riding of Yorkshire was small as a result of the proximity of manufacturing, with those closest to industry being perhaps only 80 to 100 acres. Farm size accordingly increased in the more rural parts of the region, to between 100 and 200 acres, and in some instances up to 500 acres.[30] The 1851 census report provides statistical evidence to support this claim, with small farms dominating the county.[31] Farms in the Doncaster district varied in size despite their comparative proximity to the market town and neighbouring industrial centres; they tended to be larger in the estate villages, with

---

23 Caird, *Landed interest*, pp. 56–7.
24 Mingay, *Land and society*, pp. 34–6.
25 Beckett, 'Agricultural landownership and estate management', pp. 30–31.
26 Mills, *Lord and Peasant*, pp. 29, 117; Mills, 'Landownership and rural population', pp. 4, 165.
27 J.V. Beckett, 'The debate over farm sizes in eighteenth and nineteenth century England', *Agricultural History*, 57/3 (1983), pp. 308–13, 323; D. Low, *On landed property and the economy of estates* (London, 1844), p. 38; Caird, *English agriculture*, pp. 85–6; J.L. Morton, *The resources of estates* (London, 1858), pp. 19, 117–19.
28 D. Mills, 'Trouble with farms at the census office: an evaluation of farm statistics from the censuses of 1851–1881 in England and Wales', *Agricultural History Review*, 47/1 (1999), pp. 64–5; Beckett, 'Debate over farm sizes', pp. 208–10.
29 Holland, 'Contrasting rural communities', pp. 68–70.
30 Charnock, 'On the farming of the West Riding', p. 301.
31 PP 1852–53, LXXXVIII, *Census of Great Britain, 1851*, p. lxxxi.

Table 3.3
Farm size in the six case-study villages, 1851

Village	Number of farms	Number of farms of different acreages				
		0–99 acres	100–299 acres	300–499 acres	Over 500 acres	Acreage not specified
Sprotbrough	4		2	1		1
Warmsworth	6	3	2	1		
Rossington	9		6	2		1
Braithwell	17	12	4	1		
Fishlake	16	12	3			1
Stainforth (readjusted using tithe award)	16	9	4			3
Total	68	36	21	5		6

Source: TNA, HO107/2346, CEB Sprotbrough 1851; TNA, HO 107/2346, CEB Warmsworth 1851; TNA, HO 107/2348, CEB Rossington 1851; TNA, HO 107/2346, CEB Braithwell 1851; TNA, HO 107/2349, CEB Fishlake and Stainforth 1851; DA, DY/Wall/1–2, Hatfield tithe apportionment and map, 1843 (includes Stainforth).

a few in excess of 300 acres, while the majority in multi-freeholder villages were less than 100 acres. Nevertheless, even within individual villages and parishes there was a wide range of farm sizes (Table 3.3), a pattern that can be seen in 1861 and 1871 as well.

Farm size, together with sufficient capital investment, was considered a prerequisite for 'high farming'. Despite being a notoriously ambiguous concept, high farming was characterised by capital-intensive practices, innovation and the application of new knowledge. It was perceived as making agriculture more efficient, innovative and productive, although its success in economic terms has since been questioned.[32] High farming necessitated both permanent improvements, such as drainage, reclamation and new farm buildings equipped with machinery, and changes in the ordinary management of farms relating to, for example, the application of manure and fertilisers, types of crop and crop rotations, and livestock breeds, and thus depended on the active involvement of both landowner and tenant farmer. Historians such as Chambers and Mingay argued that farms smaller than 200 to 300 acres, such as many of those in the Doncaster district, were unsuited to these processes.[33] Capital investment, including farm buildings, drainage and

---

32 J. Caird, *High farming, under liberal covenants, the best substitute for protection* (Edinburgh, 1849), pp. 5–7; J.D. Chambers and G.E. Mingay, *The agricultural revolution 1750–1880* (London, 1966), pp. 170–98; Overton, *Agricultural revolution in England*, pp. 193–5, 206; M. Overton, 'Re-establishing the English agricultural revolution', *Agricultural History Review*, 44/1 (1996), pp. 1–20; P.J. Perry, 'High farming in Victorian Britain: the financial foundations', *Agricultural History*, 52/3 (1978), p. 365.

33 Chambers and Mingay, *The agricultural revolution*, pp. 172–4.

machinery, and experimentation or innovation were certainly greater in estate villages and on larger farms.[34]

The association between concentrated landownership, farm size and capital investment was most pronounced at Rossington. Farm size there was increasing from at least the late eighteenth century, when Doncaster Corporation, who owned the estate until 1838, began to amalgamate landholdings and rebuild farm buildings. The Corporation continued to make recommendations regarding farms during the early nineteenth century.[35] In 1833 the outbuildings of Rossington Grange Farm were found to be dilapidated, and the Rossington Committee of Doncaster Corporation made recommendations for their improvement.[36] The 1838 sale catalogue for the estate provides evidence of improvements made in response to those recommendations. It described the farm as being 'well arranged and in the most perfect condition'.[37] It was laid out around more than one yard, and had an extensive double barn, stables for eight horses, a cattle shed, a calf houses for six calves, a feeding house for 12 beasts with a granary and dovecote above it, piggery and poultry houses, a spacious barn with a threshing machine, stabling for three horses, and a slaughter house. Model farms such as this were laid out in accordance with the latest ideas about design and equipped with the latest machinery and tools, and were places where experimental agriculture could take place.[38] By 1838 Rossington Grange Farm was 284 acres, making it one of the largest farms on the Rossington estate at this date. This correlation between farm size and improvements to infrastructure was replicated throughout the estate, with both medium-sized and large farms being well equipped and carefully laid out by the time of the sale of the Rossington estate in 1838.[39] Mount Pleasant Farm, also on the Rossington estate, was similarly enlarged, rebuilt and reorganised during this period.[40]

Farm size at Rossington continued to increase between 1838 and the 1870s under the ownership of the Brown family, who further amalgamated landholdings.[41] The Browns also brought both commercial wealth and business ideas, and invested in the agricultural buildings accordingly, which suggests that they were aware of

---

34 Mills, *Lord and peasant*, p. 29; Overton, *Agricultural revolution in England*, pp. 193–4; J.V. Beckett, 'Landowners and estate management', in G.E. Mingay (ed.), *The agrarian history of England and Wales*, Vol. VI, 1750–1850 (Cambridge, 1989), p. 570.

35 DA, AB/2/2/4/2 and AB/2/2/4/3, Rossington committee meeting minutes in the Corporation Committee Orders and Papers, 1808–1840.

36 *Ibid.*, 21 May 1833.

37 DA, AB/7/3/63, Sale catalogue for the Rossington estate 1838, p. 21.

38 H. Stephens and R.S. Burn, *The book of farm buildings, their arrangement and construction* (London, 1861); S. Wade-Martins, *The English model farm: building the agricultural ideal* (Macclesfield, 2002), pp. 93–4; S. MacDonald, 'Model farms', in G.E. Mingay (ed.), *The Victorian countryside*, Vol. 1 (London, 1981), pp. 214–26; Mingay, *Land and society*, pp. 36–40.

39 DA, AB/7/3/63, Sale catalogue for the Rossington estate, 1838, pp. 8, 9, 10, 11, 12, 16, 17, 22.

40 DA, AB/2/2/4/2, Rossington committee meeting minutes, 29 June 1826 and 22 November 1826; DA, AB/7/3/63, Sale catalogue for the Rossington estate 1838, p. 9.

41 DA, DY/DAW/9/29, Sale catalogue for the Rossington estate 1938.

the importance of an adequate infrastructure to facilitate and stimulate innovation and agricultural development.[42] J.B. Denton drew parallels between agriculture and industry in terms of the need to have suitable buildings in order to be efficient in his *Farm homesteads of England* (1863), a comparison that no doubt resonated with the Brown family.[43]

With tenants and tenancies an important part of the agricultural economy, the patterns of change and continuity at Rossington after 1838 are particularly interesting. A change of landowner rarely destabilised the entire tenantry[44] and, based on the 1826 survey of the estate – which commented on the state of management and the farming abilities of tenants – and the 1841 Census Enumerators' Book, the turnover of farmers was not especially great. Seven out of 12 farms continued to be occupied by the same person. Farms tenanted by the Butterill, Piggott, Ellis, Bradford, Innocent and Hudson families were all described in the 1826 survey as being in a very good state of management. It is unsurprising that their tenancies continued under the Browns. It is less clear why tenants whose farms or farming abilities were found wanting in the 1826 survey continued, however, while some who tenanted well-managed farms did not. In some instances the survey may have triggered an improvement, or the change of tenants may have taken place prior to the sale of the estate.

In addition to the stationary machinery that model farms were equipped with, the increasing portability of agricultural machinery meant that smaller farmers could begin to take advantage of it. Mr Hanson of Hurst Farm, Rossington, owned a steam traction engine and threshing machine, and travelled from farm to farm in the locality threshing corn for farmers for a fee.[45] William Bradmore and Herbert Johnson, residents of Stainforth, were also proprietors of steam threshing machines and similarly operated in the neighbouring countryside.[46] This was mutually beneficial, as it provided farmers with access to new machinery without large-scale capital investment and entrepreneurs with opportunities to create a profitable business. The latest stationary and portable steam engines, grinding, threshing and sawing machines, and other implements and machinery for agricultural and general purposes were displayed in the showroom of Messrs Marshall, Sons and Co. Ltd in West Laith Gate, Doncaster and at agricultural shows in the district.[47]

Underpinning agricultural advancements was the acknowledgement that knowledge, ability and skill were as crucial as wealth in successfully implementing

---

42 R. Brigden, 'Farm buildings', in E.J.T. Collins (ed.), *The agrarian history of England and Wales*, Vol. VII, 1850–1914, Part 1 (Cambridge, 2000), pp. 497–504; R. Brigden, 'Equipment and motive power', in E.J.T. Collins (ed.), *The agrarian history of England and Wales*, Vol. VII, 1850–1914, Part 1 (Cambridge, 2000), pp. 505–13; Wade-Martins, *Farmers, landlords and landscape*, p. 88.

43 J.B. Denton, *The farm homesteads of England: a collection of plans of English homesteads existing in different parts of the country* (London, 1864), preface.

44 Stead, 'The mobility of English tenant farmers', pp. 176, 186–7.

45 *The Farmers' Magazine*, 27, 3rd series (January–June 1865), p. 358.

46 TNA, RG 9/3524, CEB Stainforth 1861.

47 Holland and Holland, *A Yorkshire town*, p. 71; *Sheffield Daily Telegraph*, 18 June 1874, p. 4.

new practices.[48] Charnock attributed agricultural improvements in the West Riding more to experience and the confidence to experiment than mechanisation alone:

> Many of the most valuable implements we now possess, and suggestions of the greatest benefit, have emanated from men whose knowledge of the mere practical routine of farming operations has been comparatively limited; but who, nevertheless, from observation and subsequent experiments, have been enabled to throw much true light on the subject generally, and to perfect many of the very best appliances which the agriculture of this day possesses.[49]

The generation and dissemination of agricultural knowledge was an important aspect of farming in the Doncaster district, as elsewhere. Opportunities to acquire the latest knowledge and share practical experience were possible in some villages, both estate and multi-freeholder, as well as in the town itself. Farmers' clubs and agricultural societies formed important knowledge networks. Such organisations were a vehicle for individual and collective agency in the sphere of agriculture. The emphasis was on cultivating agricultural knowledge through practical experience and the sharing of ideas, which was supported by local landowners, other members of the rural elite and practical agriculturalists.

Sprotbrough Farmers' Club was founded in 1848 with support from the landowner Sir J.W. Copley. Such clubs, increasingly popular from the 1840s, were a response to a desire for agricultural knowledge within farming communities.[50] At Sprotbrough, the club's management structure and rules were orientated towards the rural elites – the landowners, clergy and leading farmers – who dominated decision-making processes and financial arrangements, with a view to maintaining overall control.[51] Copley was the president, while William Battie-Wrightson (landowner of neighbouring Warmsworth and Cusworth) and the Revd J.G. Fardell (incumbent at Sprotbrough) were vice presidents; the committee was comprised of leading tenant farmers on the Sprotbrough estate. The committee could invite gentlemen of the Doncaster district to become honorary members, whereas regular members of the club were not allowed to introduce friends. Members also had to be elected, pay an annual subscription of 10s, and occupy at least 50 acres of land – unless they were farm bailiffs or 'learning farming'.[52]

---

48   N. Goddard, 'Agricultural institutions: societies, associations and the press', in E.J.T. Collins (ed.), *The agrarian history of England and Wales*, Vol. VII, 1850–1914, Part 1 (Cambridge, 2000), pp. 650–52, 684; N. Goddard, 'Agricultural societies', in G.E. Mingay (ed.), *The Victorian countryside*, Vol. 1, p. 246; S. Holland, 'Knowledge networks in mid nineteenth century England: a case study of the Doncaster district, South Yorkshire, England', in Y. Segers and L. Van Molle (eds), *Knowledge networks in rural Europe since 1700* (forthcoming).

49   Charnock, 'On the farming of the West Riding', pp. 304–5.

50   Goddard, 'Agricultural institutions', p. 650; N. Goddard, *Harvests of change: the Royal Agricultural Society of England, 1838–1988* (London, 1988), pp. 1, 77; Wade-Martins, *Farmers, landlords and landscapes*, pp. 13, 88.

51   Durham University Library Special Collections, G18/2/193, Miscellaneous box of papers relating to Miss Copley, rules of the Sprotbrough Farmers' Club, 1848.

52   *Ibid.*

The geographical scope of Sprotbrough Farmers' Club encompassed a five-mile radius. Villages within this catchment area were predominantly situated on the Upper or Lower Magnesian Limestone, enabling club meetings to concentrate on agricultural practices relevant to the geological area. As wheat and turnips were among the principal crops grown, discussions about these crops were particularly pertinent. For example, a meeting held in the club's first year focused on the growing of wheat and the advantages of thick and thin sowing.[53] In the following year, 1849, the club discussed the application of different manures, arguing that good farmyard manure was superior in the improvement of the soil and the most profitable form of cultivation. Club meetings encouraged local farmers to speak from experience. Richard Hickson, a tenant farmer at Sprotbrough occupying 270 acres and employing 13 labourers, spoke of his preference for mixed manures – a combination of manure from the stables, yard and cowshed – applied in a fermented state. Other farmers from Sprotbrough and neighbouring Cadeby and Scawsby also spoke, and the meeting concluded that 'with a view to the permanent improvement and most profitable cultivation of the soil ... good farmyard manure is superior to anything else' in its fermented state.[54] Although the meeting identified the importance of applying bones to the land, it still recommended that natural farmyard manure be used in combination with it.[55] Subsequent meetings discussed a range of agricultural matters and in each instance reference was made to geology and the practical experience of local farmers in order to determine which technique or idea to adopt or advocate.[56]

The advancement of agricultural knowledge was not restricted to estate villages. Braithwell Farmers' Club, established in 1843, hosted ploughing matches, evening lectures and meetings to discuss agricultural matters.[57] In the absence of a dominant resident landowner, a large owner-occupier farmer, Thomas Dyson, provided the impetus for the club, and its success was attributed to Dyson's 'unwearied exertions' in proactively supporting the club and ensuring that it engaged with the concerns of the Victorian countryside. This also meant that the club had a different structure to that of Sprotbrough and was slightly more 'open' in scope. Although membership of the club was still relatively limited, smaller farmers could join and the activities they hosted actively engaged labourers. Farmers had the 'opportunity of interchanging opinions and experience on various tillages and modes of managements and spreading those opinions for the general benefit of their class', while labourers were encouraged to increase their efficiency and skill set.[58]

The clubs' annual ploughing matches tested the skills of the labourers, and were considered particularly effective in stimulating greater agricultural efficiency. The objective of ploughing competitions was to plough the most land in a certain length of time or a set amount of land in the quickest time. Speed and scale were not the only

---

53 *The Farmers' Magazine*, 18, 2nd series (July–December 1848), p. 447.
54 *Doncaster Gazette*, 19 January 1849, p. 3; *Doncaster Gazette*, 9 February 1849, p. 5.
55 *Doncaster Gazette*, 19 January 1849, p. 3.
56 *Doncaster Gazette*, 16 March 1849, p. 3; *Doncaster Gazette*, 9 August 1850, p. 3.
57 *Doncaster Chronicle*, 22 November 1844, p. 7, 17 October 1845, p. 5; 24 October 1845, p. 5.
58 *Doncaster Chronicle*, 23 October 1846 p. 5.

criteria taken into consideration, as the ploughing had to be neat and accurate. The *Doncaster Chronicle* describes how labouring men were brought together to test their abilities against one another, 'without which they would never have attained to the degree of perfection they arrived at'. Prizes were awarded to those who ploughed the designated land in the best manner within a specified timeframe, which was argued to have stimulated 'spirited competition'.[59] A report of the 1844 annual ploughing match in Braithwell listed the competitors and those awarded prizes or highly commended for their efforts. Of the prize-winning labourers, six worked for farmers in Braithwell, including Thomas Dyson and Mr Thompson, and for other farmers from Micklebring, Stainton and Edlington.[60] The ability to plough land efficiently was of greater immediate importance than capital-intensive practices and innovations to the smaller farmers of Braithwell. Nevertheless, ploughing matches met with some resistance within the district. Complaints from farmers related to the pride induced by prize-giving, which they argued led to demands for higher wages and to intemperance and disorderly behaviour. Dyson countered this by arguing that the benefits outweighed any problems and urging labourers to set a good example by refraining from drunken or disorderly behaviour.[61]

Many rural communities in the district did not have their own farmers' clubs, but opportunities for the exchange of agricultural knowledge also existed in the market towns of Doncaster and Thorne. Town-based organisations intersected with local, regional and national knowledge networks, emphasising the importance of the relationship between town and country for rural communities in the district. The Doncaster Agricultural Society (DAS), first established in 1845 and re-established in 1872, held regular meetings and staged shows in the town. It also stimulated connectivity between the village farmers' clubs and the larger town- and region-based societies, facilitating the exchange of opinion 'for landowner, occupier and labourer alike'.[62] Local landowners occupied prominent positions on the DAS's committee, motivated in part by the prestige and agency it bestowed upon them.[63] Rural elites also provided the motivation and impetus for the re-establishment of the DAS in 1872, with £1100 subscribed for this purpose.[64]

The local farmers that the DAS successfully engaged were predominantly larger tenants and owner-occupiers, in spite of measures aimed at enabling smaller farmers to participate, such as lower subscription rates and show entrance fees. From the case-study villages, Thomas Dyson and Mr Thompson of Braithwell, Mr Webster, Mr

---

59   *Doncaster Chronicle*, 23 October 1846, p. 5.
60   *Doncaster Chronicle*, 22 November 1844, p. 5.
61   *Ibid.*, p. 7; *Doncaster Chronicle*, 16 October 1846, p. 7; *Doncaster Chronicle*, 23 October 1846, p. 5.
62   N. Goddard, 'Agricultural institutions', p. 686.
63   *Doncaster Chronicle*, 2 May 1845, p. 8; *Doncaster Chronicle*, 3 July 1846, p. 5; *Doncaster Chronicle*, 21 August 1846, p. 1; *Doncaster Chronicle*, 4 July 1851, p. 5; *Doncaster Chronicle*, 2 March 1855, p. 5; *The Farmer's Magazine*, 17, 1860, p. 477; *Doncaster Gazette*, 10 October 1845, p. 6; *Doncaster Gazette*, 27 June 1873, p. 8; *Doncaster Gazette*, 12 November 1875, p. 5; DA, DD/BW/E11/126, Miscellaneous papers, Doncaster Agricultural Society leaflets.
64   *Sheffield Independent*, 28 June 1872, p. 4.

Communities in Contrast

Figure 3.2a and Figure 3.2b Doncaster Agricultural Society medal awarded for best sheep (Heritage Doncaster, DONMG: 1912.40).

Hickson and Thomas Wood of Sprotbrough, Mr Piggott and Mr Walker of Rossington, T.J. Bladworth of Stainforth and J. and E. Walker and W. Wood of Warmsworth all actively participated in meetings of the Society and thus facilitated the exchange of knowledge, ideas and experience between town and country.[65]

The nature of meetings, the research undertaken and the prizes awarded show that the DAS was closely aligned to the agriculture of the district. The society offered nuanced perspectives when evaluating new ideas and techniques that took into consideration geological variations. For example, the use of bones as manure was considered beneficial on the limestone and lighter soils in the district, rather than on the heavy clay soils.[66] This recommendation agreed with the aforementioned findings of the Sprotbrough Farmers' Club, further highlighting the DAS's understanding of local geology and agriculture. Medals awarded by the DAS also reflect both the type of farming in the Doncaster district and the pride taken in livestock. For example, a medal was awarded to Mr J. Allison for the best sheep exhibited (Figures 3.2a and 3.2b).[67] Accordingly, the DAS assisted in forging interconnections between rural communities on the basis of shared characteristics such as land type.[68]

---

65 *Doncaster Chronicle*, 25 September 1846, p. 4; *Doncaster Chronicle*, 15 February 1850, p. 5.
66 *Journal of the Royal Agricultural Society of England*, 2, 1841, 320; *The Farmer's Magazine*, 5 (July–December 1836), p. 419; *New York Farmer and American Gardener's Magazine*, 10, 1837, p. 278.
67 Doncaster Museum, DONMG: ZH528, Doncaster Agricultural Society medal awarded to Mr J. Allison.
68 Holland, 'Knowledge networks'.

Market towns

Doncaster occupied a pivotal position in the local rural economy, facilitating the marketing of agricultural produce.[69] Through improvements to the market facilities during the mid-nineteenth century Doncaster Corporation increased its agency in agricultural matters and the economies of rural communities in the district. The improvements addressed not only the requirements of agriculturalists and consumers but also the commercial and civic ambitions of the town. Doncaster was aware of and sought to emulate the investment in market buildings of nearby towns such as Sheffield, Wakefield and Leeds, in the hope of attracting buyers and sellers and reaping the commercial benefits. By investing in architecturally grand yet practical market buildings, urban centres became increasingly competitive.[70]

The process of redeveloping Doncaster market was characteristic of a reciprocal relationship between town and country, balancing the demands of both spheres, although the process was managed and directed by Doncaster Corporation.[71] In 1843 the Corporation initiated a large-scale clearance of streets and houses around the marketplace at Doncaster in preparation for the construction of a new covered corn market.[72] This was imperative not only as wheat was grown extensively throughout the district and elsewhere in the county but also because nearby Leeds already had a purpose-built corn exchange, opened in 1826.[73] Doncaster's corn market, opened in October 1844, combined 'ornament with utility', according to the *Doncaster Gazette*, and thus fulfilled the civic ambitions of the Corporation while also responding to the needs of agriculturalists.[74] Of particular importance to both buyers and sellers of corn were the three key design elements of space, light and shelter, all of which were incorporated into the new building.[75]

Local agriculturalists held a dinner in honour of the mayor and Doncaster Corporation, which was considered to be testimony to 'the comfort and convenience

---

69 Holland, 'The evolution of a northern corn market', pp. 233–49; Holland, 'Knowledge networks'.
70 L. Miskell, '"Putting on a show": the Royal Agricultural Society of England and the market town, c.1840–1876', *Agricultural History Review*, 60/1 (2012), pp. 37–59.
71 Holland, 'Doncaster and its environs', pp. 77–89.
72 DA, AB/2/6/21/4, Council and Committee Records of Doncaster Corporation, finance committee including markets, 1843–1847; DA, AB/2/6/21/5, Council and Committee Records of Doncaster Corporation, finance committee including markets, 1847–1853. See also Holland, 'The evolution of a northern corn market', pp. 233–49.
73 E. Parsons, *The civil, ecclesiastical, literary, commercial and miscellaneous history of Leeds, Halifax, Huddersfield, Bradford, Wakefield, Dewsbury, Otley, and the manufacturing district of Yorkshire*, Vol. I (Leeds, 1834), p. 147; D. Fraser, *A history of modern Leeds* (Manchester, 1980), p. 183; S. Wrathmell, *Leeds* (London, 2005), p. 68.
74 *Doncaster Gazette*, 1 September 1843, p. 5; *The Farmer's Magazine*, 2nd series, 8 (July–December 1843), p. 63; *Doncaster Gazette*, 21 June 1844, p. 5; DA, AB/2/2/19/4, Council and Committee Records of Doncaster Corporation, finance committee including markets, 1843–1847, 10 June 1844; *Doncaster Chronicle*, 18 October 1844, p. 5.
75 *Doncaster Gazette*, 5 May 1844, p. 5; *Doncaster Gazette*, 17 May 1844, p. 5.

Table 3.4
Attendance at the celebratory dinner to mark the opening of the new covered corn market by farmers from the six case-study villages

Farmer (and farm)	Village	Approximate size of farm in acres
E. Walker	Warmsworth	348
T. Dyson (Manor House)	Braithwell	300
R. Jennings (Shooter's Hill)	Rossington	300
R. Hickson	Sprotbrough	270
G. Innocent	Rossington	250
J. Thompson	Braithwell	200
J. Walker (Rossington Grange)	Rossington	200
W. Walker (Rossington Bridge)	Rossington	200
W. Pigott	Rossington	160
T. Wood	Sprotbrough	160
G. Blagden	Warmsworth	50

Source: Doncaster Chronicle, 18 October 1844, p. 5; DA, P25/9/B1, Sprotbrough tithe apportionment and map, 1847; DA, P58/9/B1–2, Rossington tithe apportionment and map, 1838; DA, DD/BW/E11/41–42, Warmsworth tithe apportionment and map, 1841; DA, P71/9/B1–2, Braithwell tithe apportionment and map, 1840; TNA, HO 107/2346, CEB Sprotbrough 1851; TNA, HO 107/2346, CEB Warmsworth 1851; TNA, HO 107/2348, CEB Rossington 1851; TNA, HO 107/2346, CEB Braithwell 1851; TNA, HO 107/2349, CEB Fishlake and Stainforth 1851.

afforded them by the erection of a new corn exchange'.[76] Two-thirds of farmers from the case-study villages who subscribed to and attended this event (Table 3.4) owned or occupied 200 acres or more, and all except one occupied in excess of 150 acres. Given that the majority of farms in the Doncaster district were smaller than 150 acres, this suggests a correlation between the size of farm and attendance at this social function.[77] Those farming larger acreages, who were engaged with capitalist farming, relied upon market facilities to maximise their returns. As such, the attendance of these farmers at the dinner was underpinned by a proactive interest in and attitude to agricultural matters and core marketing activities beyond the village. This included being prominent figures in the foundation of the Doncaster Agricultural Society in 1845. Their attendance at the dinner was evidence of not only their wealth but also their desire to be at the forefront of shaping the evolving relationship with the town. This display of agency, acting and reacting in response to external stimuli, fostered a reciprocal relationship between town and country.

Civic ambitions and the agriculture of the district were both reflected as Doncaster Corporation continued to develop the market infrastructure of the town. New market

---

76 *Doncaster Chronicle*, 18 October 1844, p. 5.
77 *Ibid.*

buildings were constructed between 1845 and 1849, including shambles for meat, butter and poultry, a fruit market and a general market hall.[78] The *Doncaster Gazette* heralded them as 'an honour to the town, not only by their appearance, but by their immense usefulness and accommodation'.[79] The agency of Doncaster Corporation, and more specifically of members of the market committee, was evidenced by their recommendations, actions and decisions in this matter. The committee was anxious that the new market hall should be aesthetically complementary to the townscape and a credit to the Corporation, and accordingly inspected several recently erected market buildings in other towns.[80] Practical considerations were not overlooked, with the inclusion of a weighing machine and indoor provision for selling meat and butter in the new market hall, and the addition of wool and cattle markets in 1863, reflecting the extent to which livestock and dairy herds were a feature of local agriculture.[81] The continued enlargement and improvement of market facilities in Doncaster benefited local farmers while also stimulating relationships that extended beyond county boundaries, bringing competition as well as additional trade. For example, the Great Northern and South Yorkshire railways brought large quantities of wool from further afield to the new wool market.[82]

The mid-nineteenth-century market improvements culminated in 1873 with a new corn exchange (Figure 3.3), replacing the original enclosed corn market that had been constructed only 30 years earlier. Doncaster Corporation had begun to discuss the possibility of enlarging the covered corn market in 1861.[83] However, during the early 1860s the neighbouring towns of Wakefield (1862) and Leeds (1864) rebuilt their corn halls. The Corporation were once again facing a potential threat from nearby competitors, and plans to simply enlarge the existing covered corn market at Doncaster were soon superseded by the decision to build a completely new corn exchange. This exchange was undoubtedly symbolic of Doncaster Corporation's civic aspirations, through both its architecture and its ambitious scale.[84] The mayor emphasised this in his speech at the official opening, when he described it as one

---

78 *Doncaster Gazette*, 28 February 1845, p. 5; DA, AB/2/2/19/4, 17 February 1845, 4 December 1845, 16 January 1846, 10 July 1846, 23 July 1846; DA, DZMD/569, 1847, Order of procession for the laying of the first stone, 24 May 1847; *Doncaster Gazette*, 2 February 1849, p. 5.

79 *Doncaster Gazette*, 2 February 1849, p. 5.

80 DA, AB/2/2/19/4, Council and Committee Records of Doncaster Corporation, Finance Committee including Markets, 1843–1847, 23 June 1845, 28 January 1846.

81 *Doncaster Gazette*, 18 May 1849, p. 5; *Doncaster Gazette*, 25 May 1849, p. 5; *Doncaster Gazette*, 1 June 1849, p. 5; *Doncaster Gazette*, 8 June 1849, p. 5; *Doncaster Chronicle*, 30 January 1863, p. 5; *Doncaster Gazette*, 11 April 1863, p. 5; *Doncaster Chronicle*, 18 April 1873, p. 8; *Doncaster Chronicle*, 29 May 1863, p. 4; *Doncaster Chronicle*, 5 June 1863, p. 5; *Doncaster Chronicle*, 12 June 1863, p. 5; *Doncaster Chronicle*, 26 June 1863, p. 8.

82 *Doncaster Chronicle*, 5 June 1863, p. 5; *Doncaster Chronicle*, 12 June 1863, p. 5; *Doncaster Chronicle*, 26 June 1863, p. 8.

83 DA, AB/2/6/21/5, Council minutes, 25 October 1861; 14 May 1862; 13 August 1862; 22 October 1862.

84 *Doncaster Gazette*, 11 April 1873, p. 5; *Doncaster Chronicle*, 18 April 1873, p. 8.

Figure 3.3 Doncaster Corn Exchange (author's own picture).

of the 'grandest and most comfortable corn exchanges' in the country.[85] The new corn exchange was designed to be more than just a place to sell and buy corn, having space designated as well for concerts and performances.[86] It constituted an important civic space while still fulfilling a practical function. Local agriculturalists once again held a dinner in honour of the Corporation and this new building,[87] and local farmers, including Mr Bennett of Sprotbrough, occupied dedicated stands in the new exchange.[88] The mayor also drew attention to how the railway network connected local farmers with factors, millers and consumers further afield.

The market improvements embodied the agency of Doncaster Corporation, which stimulated the inter-relationships between town and country and affected rural economies in the Doncaster district. The way in which landowners and farmers engaged with and supported the Corporation's actions is symptomatic of the collective agency of rural and urban elites in Victorian society. Moreover, Doncaster represented an important sphere of influence over the surrounding countryside, acting as a forum for political debate and a hub for agricultural trade and knowledge.

---

85 *Doncaster Gazette*, 9 May 1873, p. 6.
86 *Doncaster Gazette*, 11 April 1873, p. 5; *Doncaster Gazette*, 9 May 1873, p. 6; *Doncaster Chronicle*, 9 May 1873, p. 6.
87 *Doncaster Gazette*, 11 April 1873, p. 5.
88 *Ibid.*

Rural economies

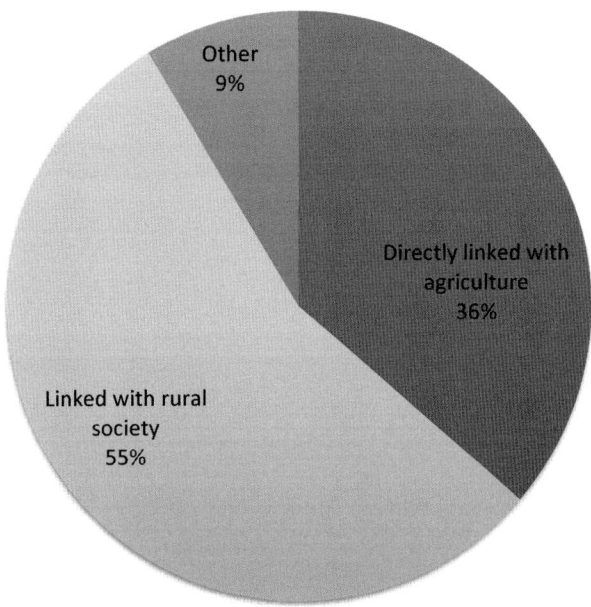

Figure 3.4 Proportion of trades, crafts and industries in the six case-study villages, 1837–77 (W. White, *History, gazetteer and directory of the West Riding* (Sheffield, 1837); E.R. Kelly, *Post Office directory of the West Riding of Yorkshire, 1861* (London, 1861); E.R. Kelly, *Post Office directory of the West Riding of Yorkshire, 1877* (London, 1877)).

Micro-commerce and industry

Micro-commerce – commercial enterprises operating on a small scale within highly developed supply-and-demand networks – and industry are juxtaposed with agriculture in models of village typology. Mills argued that industry, crafts and trades were associated with fragmented landownership and multi-freeholder communities, which made estate villages economically dependent on them, and as such industry and micro-commerce are perceived as separate from agriculture in rural economies. Existing models, however, underestimate the interconnectivity between micro-commerce, industry and agriculture in many rural communities, both estate and multi-freeholder, whereby all are vital cogs in the rural economy. In the Doncaster district the majority of industry and trades and crafts in rural communities complemented agriculture and/or the needs of the rural population (Figure 3.4). In the six case-study villages 81.5 per cent of businesses listed in trade directories between 1837 and 1877 were directly related to agriculture or to the needs of rural society, including food-processing businesses, clothing and retail businesses, blacksmiths, wheelwrights and agricultural engineers. The remaining 18.5 per cent were location specific, dependent upon topography, geology or occupational skills, and included quarries, brick and tile yards, boat-yards and sail-makers. An analysis of industry and micro-commerce provides insights into the close relationship between landownership, geology, agriculture and the needs of rural communities and urban society in an industrialising county, as well as the vitality of rural society and the interconnectivity between the countryside, the market town of Doncaster and surrounding urban areas.

Food-processing industries

The relationship between crops grown, food processing and consumption was still relatively intimate during the mid-nineteenth century.[89] Prior to 1860, English corn mills processed primarily home-grown corn, and the majority of wheat was processed and consumed close to where it was grown.[90] As wheat was one of the principal crops grown in the Doncaster district, it is not surprising that milling was the main rural industry. It took place in four of the six case-study villages in 1837 and in three in 1861 and 1877, and included both estate and multi-freeholder communities. The mills were small-scale operations responding to local demand, and in some instances wheat was grown and milled by the same family. For example, in 1837 the miller of Braithwell, William Thompson, was brother of a local farmer, John Thompson, while Robert Ward junior, miller at Fishlake, was the son of a farmer.[91]

Patterns of corn milling in the district during the mid- to late nineteenth century were predetermined by historic factors. Farmers from neighbouring villages used the manorial mill at Sprotbrough to grind their corn from 1279, and this continued in the nineteenth century.[92] Up to 15 entries per month were made in the account books for cereals ground at Sprotbrough Mill on behalf of Battie-Wrightson (landowner at Cusworth and Warmsworth), at an annual expenditure of approximately £30.[93] The demand from landowners and farmers from other villages, as well as from within Sprotbrough, ensured that this mill was operational until the early twentieth century. Its continuity was indicative of its significance in the locality and provides evidence of important economic relationships between rural communities in close proximity to one another.[94]

Fishlake and Stainforth both had multiple mills until the 1860s, after which the number diminished. At Fishlake one windmill was converted to steam power in the 1850s, a process that, although requiring considerable investment, increased efficiency. Another windmill was rendered inoperative for a long time after high winds caused considerable damage in 1860.[95] Gradually, Hanley's flourmill in Doncaster began to centralise trade, although for a long time much of the grain it processed was brought by barge from Hull. Changes in technology and imported grain stimulated the transition from small processors to large and the move to urban processing during

---

89 Various authors, 'Food processing industries', in E.J.T. Collins (ed.), *The Agrarian History of England and Wales*, Vol. VII, 1850–1914, Part 2 (Cambridge, 2000), pp. 1060–61; B.A. Holderness, 'Agriculture and industrialization in the Victorian economy', in G.E. Mingay (ed.), *The Victorian countryside*, Vol. 1 (London, 1981) p. 188.
90 R. Perren, 'Milling', in E.J.T. Collins (ed.), *The agrarian history of England and Wales*, Vol. VII, 1850–1914, Part 2 (Cambridge, 2000), pp. 1062–4.
91 White, *History, gazetteer and directory of the West Riding, 1837*, pp. 165, 180–81.
92 Holland, *Sprotbrough in history*, p. 45.
93 DA, DD/BW/B/149–153, Account books for cereals ground at the Sprotbrough Mill, 1853, 1858, 1860 x 2, 1862.
94 J. Tann, 'Corn milling', in G.E. Mingay (ed.), *The agrarian history of England and Wales*, Vol. VI, 1750–1850 (Cambridge, 1989), p. 400.
95 *Doncaster Chronicle*, 1 June 1860, p. 5.

the second half of the nineteenth century.[96] Yet in many instances corn mills in the Doncaster district continued to prosper until the early twentieth century. Although the number of corn mills in the three multi-freeholder villages decreased, they each still had at least one. With large quantities of wheat grown in the rural communities around Doncaster, there was sufficient trade for at least some rural corn mills to thrive. This meant that villages in the district without a corn mill remained dependent on mills in other rural communities rather than urban mills during the nineteenth century.

There were fewer maltsters and maltings than corn mills in the six case-study villages, in spite of barley being grown in all of them. The only maltsters listed in trade directories for the six villages in the mid-nineteenth century were in the multi-freeholder villages of Fishlake and Braithwell. Again, a close relationship is evident between malting and farming. Charles and George Kay of Braithwell and Thomas and Joseph Birks and Thomas Wilkinson of Fishlake were all listed as both farmers and maltsters in 1837.[97] There were similar links with retail. By 1861, George Kay of Braithwell was farmer, maltster and innkeeper of the Red Lion, while William Mason, also of Braithwell, was maltster and publican of the Butcher's Arms in 1837 and 1852.[98]

By 1877, both Fishlake and Braithwell were devoid of maltsters. This corresponded with a notable decline in the number of small brewers and village maltings in England from the 1860s and the rise of the large-scale brewing industry.[99] The demise of village maltsters in the Doncaster district was concurrent with the development of larger maltings and breweries in the area. For example, Milnthorp's maltings in Barnby Dun (established in the 1860s and expanded thereafter) and Darley's Brewery at Thorne provided competition for the village maltster and brewer. Darley's Brewery, founded by William Marsdin Darley (1827–92) in the 1850s, was less than five miles from Stainforth and Fishlake. Evidence from the account books of Darley's Brewery in Thorne certainly shows some local farmers and innkeepers trading with them. For example, in 1872 the brewery purchased barley from farmers at Fishlake and Stainforth, and in 1874 Abraham Coates, innkeeper of the Old Anchor Inn at Fishlake, purchased beer from Darley's.[100] The records are fragmentary, however, and as such it is impossible to reconstruct the changing supply-and-demand networks. Nevertheless, while the link between agriculture and the food-processing industries remained paramount, the nature of this relationship evolved during the mid-nineteenth century. Competition from large-scale maltings and brewers, located either in towns or on the periphery of villages, began to diminish local customary trade. The location and incidence of corn mills and

---

96   Various, 'Food processing industries', p. 1060.
97   White, *History, gazetteer and directory, 1837*, Vol. 2, pp. 165, 180.
98   E.R. Kelly, *Post Office directory of the West Riding of Yorkshire, 1861* (London, 1861), p. 206; White, *History, gazetteer and directory, 1837*, Vol. 2, p. 165; White, *Gazetteer and general directory of Sheffield, 1852*, p. 427; Kelly, *Post Office directory, 1861*, p. 206; TNA, RG 9/3513, CEB Braithwell 1861.
99   E.M. Sigsworth, *The brewing trade in the industrial revolution: the case of Yorkshire* (York, 1967); J. Brown, 'Malting', in E.J.T. Collins (ed.), *The agrarian history of England and Wales*, Vol. VII, 1850–1914, Part 2 (Cambridge, 2000), pp. 1076–7.
100 DA, DY/DAR/1, Ledger for the Darley brewery, 1863–1891.

maltings serves as a reminder that positioning estate and multi-freeholder parishes as diametrically opposed in the matter of the rural economy is fallacious; the evolving relationship between rural and urban, and between agriculture and industry, is vital to understanding rural economies.

Trades and crafts

The agricultural and wider rural community stimulated demand for a variety of trades and crafts, so fostering self-sufficiency within rural communities.[101] Economic autonomy was one of the four key indicators of the self-contained community identified by David Brown, and variation in the number and range of trades and crafts could be indicative of the comparative ability of rural communities to be self-contained. The relative independence of and the role of interconnectivity between rural communities are important to understanding both how and why rural communities developed and their scope to be self-sufficient. Table 3.5 suggests that both the quantity and the variety of trades and crafts businesses, based on the ten essential businesses identified by both Crompton and Mills, were greater in the multi-freeholder villages around Doncaster than in the estate villages. Mills argued that estate villages were home to only limited trades and crafts, making them dependent on the wider range available in multi-freeholder villages. This, he reasoned, was a one-way dependency that stemmed from limitations and deficiencies within estate villages and allowed multi-freeholder villages to serve as economic nuclei for surrounding communities.[102] However, differentiation in trades and crafts was not linked solely to landownership; population size was also a factor. Accordingly, Chartres and Turnbull used population thresholds to determine the optimum size of community necessary to support different businesses.[103] Tables 3.6 and 3.7 show the relationship between population size and the quantity and range of trades and crafts in villages in the Doncaster district, and the disparities between villages with similar and different landowning structures. For example, Stainforth had both the largest population and the most trades and crafts businesses in 1861, whereas Sprotbrough and Warmsworth had the smallest populations and the fewest trades and crafts. Rossington and Braithwell had different landowning

---

101 C.A. Crompton, 'Changes in rural service occupations during the nineteenth century: an evaluation of two sources for Hertfordshire, England', *Rural History*, 6/2 (1995), p. 193; C. Hallas, 'Craft occupations in the late nineteenth century: some local considerations', *Local Population Studies*, 44 (1990), p. 18.

102 Mills, *Lord and peasant*, pp. 120–23; Mills, *Rural community history*, pp. 66–70; Mills, 'Landownership and rural population', pp. 4–5; Rawding, 'Village type', pp. 60–61; Crompton, 'Changes in rural service occupations', p. 198.

103 J.A. Chartres and G.L. Turnbull, 'Country craftsmen', in G.E. Mingay (ed.), *The Victorian countryside* (London, 1981), pp. 320–21; J.A. Chartres, 'County tradesmen', in G.E. Mingay (ed.), *The Victorian countryside*, Vol. 1 (London, 1981) pp. 301–4; M.J.D. Edgar, 'Occupational diversity in seven rural parishes in Dorset, 1851', *Local Population Studies*, 52 (1994), p. 54; Rawding, 'Village type', pp. 60–61.

Table 3.5
Ten essential trades and crafts businesses in the six case-study villages, 1861

Trades and crafts	Sprotbrough	Warmsworth	Rossington	Fishlake	Stainforth	Braithwell
Shoemaker	1	1	2	3	5	1
Carpenter or wheelwright	0	1	1	3	4	2
Tailor	0	1	2	4	2	2
Blacksmith	1	1	1	3	2	1
Shopkeeper	2	1	3	3	8	2
Mason	0	1	0	0	0	1
Bricklayer	0	0	0	1	1	0
Publican	1	1	0	3	4	2
Butcher	1	1	1	1	3	0
Baker	0	0	0	0	0	0

Source: E.R. Kelly, *Post Office directory of the West Riding of Yorkshire, 1861* (London, 1861), pp. 206, 276, 328–9, 610, 811–12, 871.

Table 3.6
Relationship between population size and the number of trades and crafts businesses in the six case-study villages, 1861

Village	Population	Number of trades and crafts businesses						
		<4	<8	<12	<16	<20	<24	<28	<32
Stainforth	751								X
Fishlake	585							X	
Braithwell	422			X					
Rossington	400			X					
Warmsworth	385		X						
Sprotbrough	339		X						

Source: E.R. Kelly, *Post Office directory of the West Riding of Yorkshire, 1861* (London, 1861).

Table 3.7
Relationship between population size and the range of different trades and crafts in the six case-study villages, 1861

Village	Population	Range of different trades and crafts									
		1	2	3	4	5	6	7	8	9	10
Stainforth	751										X
Fishlake	585										X
Braithwell	422						X				
Rossington	400							X			
Warmsworth	385								X		
Sprotbrough	339					X					

Source: E.R. Kelly, *Post Office directory of the West Riding of Yorkshire, 1861* (London, 1861), pp. 871, 610, 811.

Communities in Contrast

Figure 3.5 Gravestone to George Nassau, Sprotbrough churchyard (author's own picture).

structures but comparable-sized populations, and accordingly had a similar number of trades and crafts. The total number of businesses in the larger multi-freeholder villages decreased between 1861 and 1877, although the range of different trades and crafts remained constant, while both the total number and the range remained more stable in the smaller estate villages. As population change did not correspond closely with these changes, it would suggest that competition eroded the foundations of micro-commerce, especially in rural communities where multiple businesses and people fulfilled the same or very similar roles.

Self-sufficiency and the extent to which rural communities could be self-contained cannot be determined by the quantity and range of trades and crafts businesses alone, and the presence of a trade or craft does not imply that everyone in that village used it. Factors such as the scale and scope of businesses, whether settlements were concentrated or scattered and the physical distance between rural and urban communities affected who used different trades and crafts businesses. Moreover, Mills considered a core group of trades and crafts vital to self-sufficiency and the notion of being self-contained, rather than the total number and range. These were a blacksmith, carpenter or wheelwright, a boot or shoemaker, a grocer or general shopkeeper, and licensed premises.[104] Each of the six villages had at least one shopkeeper, blacksmith and shoemaker in 1861. All but Sprotbrough had a wheelwright or carpenter and tailor, all but Rossington had a public house, and all but Braithwell had a butcher. Only Braithwell and Warmsworth had a mason, and only Fishlake and Stainforth had a bricklayer. None of the six villages had a baker.

The blacksmith was a linchpin in agricultural and rural society during the mid-nineteenth century, responsible for shoeing horses and making both agricultural tools and machinery and household goods.[105] On account of the crucial role he performed, the village blacksmith was generally held in high esteem within rural communities, and historians have even argued that they were the fourth constituent of rural society, alongside landowners, farmers and agricultural labourers.[106] The gravestone commemorating George Nassau, the village blacksmith at Sprotbrough, stands as a physical testimony to occupational identity and the pivotal role of the blacksmith (Figure 3.5). The iconography was overtly occupational, including a depiction of a blacksmith's tools and an occupational epitaph:

> *My Sledge and Hammer lies declined,*
> *My Bellows too have lost their wind;*
> *My Fire's extinct, my Forge decayed,*
> *My Vice now in the dust is laid;*
> *My Iron and my Coals are gone,*
> *My Nails are drove my work is done;*
> *My fire dried Corpse lies here at rest,*
> *My Soul is waiting to be blest.*[107]

Each of the six case-study villages had at least one blacksmith or wheelwright between 1837 and 1877, testimony to the predominantly agricultural nature of these communities and the importance of these crafts.[108] In the three multi-freeholder villages there were two or three blacksmiths until the 1870s, when this decreased to only one or two. Similarly, there were multiple carpenters or wheelwrights, and again the number had diminished by the 1870s. The continuity of family blacksmithing businesses was indicative of both a profitable business and demand for the craft.

---

104 Mills, *Rural community history*, p. 53; Crompton, 'Changes in rural service occupations', p. 193.

105 J.A. Chartres, 'The retail trades and agricultural service', in E.J.T. Collins (ed.), *The agrarian history of England and Wales*, Vol. VII, 1850–1914, Part 2 (Cambridge, 2000), p. 1161; Chartres and Turnbull, 'Country craftsmen', pp. 322–6.

106 Chartres and Turnbull, 'Country craftsmen', p. 323; Chartres, 'The retail trades', p. 1150.

107 For further information on epitaphs, gravestones and occupational identity see G.N. Wright, *Discovering epitaphs* (Aylesbury, 1972), p. 25; W. Andrews, *Curious epitaphs* (London, 1883), pp. 33, 43; K.D.M. Snell, 'Gravestones, belonging and local attachment in England 1700–2000', *Past and Present*, 179 (2003), p. 111.

108 White, *History, gazetteer and directory, 1837*, Vol. 2, pp. 165, 179–80, 188, 206–7, 200–201, 213; Kelly, *Post Office directory, 1861*, pp. 206, 276, 328–9, 610, 811–12, 871; Kelly, *Post Office directory, 1877*, pp. 217, 314, 385–7, 785–6, 1112, 1186.

Edmund Fitzgeorge at Warmsworth, members of the Johnson family in Rossington, Samuel Tomlinson and his son Samuel in Fishlake, George Mawson and his son John in Stainforth and different branches of the Thompson family at Braithwell maintained village blacksmith businesses between the 1830s and the 1870s.[109]

Skilled crafts, such as blacksmithing, had a long tradition of apprenticeships, which was still in evidence in some Doncaster villages during the mid-nineteenth century. Apprenticeships could be informal or formal in nature, and for both family members or unrelated persons. They could constitute either a source of cheap labour or a respected means of transferring knowledge and skills, and sometimes both.[110] Apprenticeships involving family members indicated the importance of transferring skills and knowledge, not just businesses and tools, to the next generation. At Rossington, Thomas Johnson was apprenticed as a blacksmith to his widowed mother, Maria Johnson, in 1851.[111] Similarly, at Fishlake, Samuel Tomlinson was apprenticed as a blacksmith to his father in 1851.[112] In contrast, apprentices not bound to family or by the poor law administration were generally more mobile, which meant that skills could be transferred between villages, towns and neighbouring counties. Of those young apprentice blacksmiths in the six Doncaster villages who were not related, the majority were born further afield, including Newark, Chesterfield and Huddersfield. Many of these apprentices later set up their own business in a nearby town. Charles Brooks, aged 17, was apprenticed to Edmund Fitzgeorge in Warmsworth in 1851. Thereafter he lived and worked as a blacksmith in Rotherham and Sheffield until at least 1911. Similarly, Mark Beevers, also 17, was apprenticed to George England in Fishlake in 1861 and later moved to Rotherham, where he worked as a blacksmith. Apprenticeships such as these provided village blacksmiths with a relatively cheap supply of labour and facilitated the transfer of knowledge and skills from both estate and multi-freeholder villages to towns.

The fortunes of village retail were closely interwoven with those of agriculture, as farmers, labourers and associated trades and crafts people provided retailers' custom. Whereas the services of a blacksmith were often a necessity, the use of shops and public houses was more likely to be a matter of choice. As such, shops, public houses and other retail trades provide further indications of the vitality of rural

---

109 White, *History, gazetteer and directory, 1837*, Vol. 2, pp. 165, 180, 188, 201; TNA, HO 107/2346, CEB Warmsworth 1851; TNA, HO 107/2346, CEB Braithwell 1851; TNA, HO 107/2348, CEB Rossington 1851; TNA, HO 107/2349, CEB Fishlake and Stainforth 1851; TNA, RG 9/3513, CEB Braithwell 1861; TNA, RG 9/3514, CEB Warmsworth 1861; TNA, RG 9/3522, CEB Rossington 1861; TNA, RG 9/3524, CEB Fishlake and Stainforth 1861; TNA, RG 10/4714, CEB Braithwell 1871; TNA, RG 10/4724, CEB Rossington 1871; TNA, RG 10/4714, CEB Braithwell 1871; TNA, RG 10/4726, CEB Fishlake and Stainforth 1871; Kelly, *Post Office directory, 1877*, pp. 217, 314, 386–7, 786.

110 K.D.M. Snell, *Annals of the labouring poor: social change and agrarian England 1660–1900* (Cambridge, 1985), pp. 228, 241–3, 256, 259; J. Lane, *Apprenticeship in England, 1600–1914* (London, 1996), pp. 1–8, 130–31.

111 TNA, HO 107/2348, CEB Rossington 1851.

112 TNA, HO 107/2349, CEB Fishlake 1851.

society.¹¹³ Retailers, especially shopkeepers, publicans and butchers, were far more prolific in the multi-freeholder villages of the Doncaster district, again corresponding with population size as well as with the concentration of landownership. However, this did not mean that estate villages were dependent on multi-freeholder villages: Doncaster was a retail hub, with the market and shops catering for the demands of rural communities.

It is hard to discern the nature of retail in the villages around Doncaster, as few business records survive for them. Trade directories and census enumerators' books frequently recorded 'shopkeepers', a designation either representing a move towards more general shopkeepers in the countryside or concealing a specialism. Many of the general shopkeepers in the six case-study villages were female, often unmarried or widowed, which was a feature of nineteenth-century rural retail.¹¹⁴ Mrs Susannah Trueman, a widow, was a farmer and grocer in Stainforth in 1861. Mrs Sarah Richardson, also a widow, was listed as a shopkeeper in 1877 and a grocer in 1881. As an unmarried young woman she had been a grocer and draper in Stainforth in 1851, together with her three unmarried sisters. Yet, during her marriage, her husband was recorded as grocer while no occupation was recorded for Sarah. Similarly, while the 1851 census recorded Hannah Collis as a shopkeeper in Warmsworth living with her husband, a blacksmith, a contemporary trade directory listed her husband as both blacksmith and shopkeeper. The 'separate spheres' ideology thus worked to influence the collection of occupational data in the nineteenth century, so that women who worked alongside their husbands were often hidden in the census as enumerators imposed their expectations that married women would remain within the domestic sphere while their husbands worked to provide for the family, whereas unmarried and widowed women were recorded as businesswomen in their own right.

Landownership was particularly important in creating a disparity in the number of public houses in the six villages. In total, there were more licensed premises and beer houses in multi-freeholder villages than estate villages, and these businesses were sustained from 1837 to 1877. The landowners at Rossington and Sprotbrough actually revoked the licences of their respective public houses during the mid-nineteenth century. Even at Warmsworth, where the retailing of beer continued throughout the nineteenth century, there was only one public house, in contrast to four public houses at Stainforth in 1861. At Stainforth, the majority of pubs were located close to the waterways.¹¹⁵ Public houses were also a focus for recreation and social gatherings in both estate and multi-freeholder villages, as discussed in chapter 6.

---

113 J. Stobart, 'Food retailers and rural communities: Cheshire butchers in the long eighteenth century', *Local Population Studies*, 79 (2007), p. 23; Chartres, 'County tradesmen', pp. 302–4, 312; Chartres, 'The retail trades', pp. 1152–3.
114 Chartres, 'County tradesmen', p. 308.
115 TNA, RG 9/3524, CEB Fishlake and Stainforth, 1861; Kelly, *Post Office directory, 1861*, pp. 328–9.

Industry

Industrial activities in Doncaster villages were primarily aligned to the needs of the rural community, or were extractive. Models of village typology suggest that limited industrial activity was characteristic of estate villages, owing to the constraints imposed by landowners, whereas industry was more prevalent in multi-freeholder villages. The relationship between landownership and industry was complex during the mid-nineteenth century. An important economic distinction existed between landowners who received an income from industry and those who did not, with a further division between those who merely received rents and royalties from industry and those who were active industrial entrepreneurs.[116] During the nineteenth century landowners increasingly had industrial and other non-agricultural sources of wealth, while industrialists and businessmen were investing in landed estates.[117] The industrial credentials of landowners do not fully explain the extent of industry within a rural community, however. Geological location also determined opportunities for extractive industries, which some landowners in the district were keen to exploit.

The wealth of the Copley family of Sprotbrough was generated predominantly from agricultural rents. Sir Joseph William Copley had minimal business interests, although he was a director of the South Yorkshire Railway Company and collected royalties on land that formed part of the Levitt Hagg Quarries at Warmsworth.[118] Copley appeared to epitomise the landowner of the Mills model, who had few industrial interests and restricted industry on his estate. However, the boundary of Sprotbrough parish adjoined the perimeter of Doncaster and its location was therefore conducive to the Don Foundry, a small-scale agricultural engineering firm (discussed in more detail below) that served both town and country.

In contrast, the Aldams, Battie-Wrightsons and Browns had significant industrial interests, although the majority of these were not located on their rural estates in the Doncaster district. William Aldam and William Battie-Wrightson had long legacies of combining landowning and business interests prior to the mid-nineteenth century. The Aldam family had been cloth merchants in Leeds from 1735, initially in partnership with Benson before becoming Aldam, Pease, Birchall and Co.[119] The partnership was terminated in 1839, and William Aldam senior retired to Warmsworth. However, William Aldam junior, who was gifted the Frickley estate in 1844, continued to pursue numerous business interests during the mid-nineteenth century. He was an active participant in both railway and canal navigation companies, including the Huddersfield and Manchester Railway, the Leeds and Liverpool Canal and the Aire and Calder Navigation Company, and regularly documented the business meetings he attended

---

116 Thompson, *English landed society*, p. 267; D. Spring, 'English landowners and nineteenth-century industrialism', in J.T. Ward and R.G. Wilson (eds), *Land and industry: the landed estate and the industrial revolution* (Newton Abbot, 1971), pp. 51–2.

117 Thompson, *English landed society*, pp. 242, 268.

118 Holland, *Sprotbrough in history*, p. 67.

119 Documents relating to these businesses are held at Doncaster Archives and are catalogued under DD/WA/B1.

Rural economies

in his diaries.[120] William Battie-Wrightson, of Warmsworth and Cusworth, similarly combined the ownership of agricultural land and industrial concerns, including collieries in the north-east of England and quarries in the parish of Warmsworth.[121]

The Brown family were woollen cloth manufacturers and merchants in Leeds, purchasing the Rossington estate only in 1838.[122] The transition from merchant to landowner through the profits of industry or trade was not uncommon, and the fortunes made in the Leeds woollen trade secured the place of at least two dozen families in Burke's Peerage.[123] Industrialists and businessmen had varied motives when investing in land and landed estates in the nineteenth century, including the intention to develop extractive industry. Indeed, the sale catalogue for the Rossington estate advertised the brickyard as having a 'bed of excellent clay, kiln and tile shed'.[124] Yet the exploitation of clay deposits was not a principal objective in the Browns' purchase of the estate, and the brickyard was maintained only to meet the estate's requirements. Many businessmen and industrialists, such as the Browns, in fact purchased landed estates to acquire social status and to access landed leisure.[125] The Browns adopted the role of paternalistic and leisured landowners, rebuilding cottages, farms and communal buildings in the village and staging fox hunts on the estate. Their passion for fox hunting was even immortalised in the carved fox heads that adorned the parish church they rebuilt in 1844.[126] It is unclear what impact, if any, this had on their cloth business. It has been argued that the purchase of landed estates by industrialists led to a decline in entrepreneurial spirit from the mid- to late nineteenth century, but, equally, it has been asserted that landownership alone did not damage business performance.[127] The Browns continued their business for a further 19 years after purchasing the Rossington estate, and it was election as member of parliament for Malton in 1857 that finally led James Brown to sever his links with manufacturing and business.

---

120 Documents relating to these businesses are held at Doncaster Archives and are catalogued under DD/WA/B2; William Aldam's diaries are held at Doncaster Archives and are catalogued under DD/WA/D1.
121 Documents relating to industry on Battie-Wrightson's estates are held at Doncaster Archives and are catalogued under DD/BW/E14 and DD/BW/E15.
122 E. Baines, *Directory of Yorkshire, 1822* (Leeds, 1822), p. 118; E. Baines and R. Newsome, *General and commercial directory of Leeds 1834* (Leeds, 1834), p. 415.
123 R.G. Wilson, *Gentlemen merchants: the merchant community in Leeds 1700–1830* (Manchester, 1971), pp. 111, 220.
124 DA, AB/7/3/63, Sale catalogue for the Rossington estate 1838, p. 4.
125 W.D. Rubinstein, 'New men of wealth and the purchase of land in nineteenth century Britain', *Past and Present*, 92 (1981), pp. 125–47; T. Nicholas, 'Businessmen and land ownership in the late nineteenth century', *Economic History Review*, 52/1 (1999), p. 28; F.M.L. Thompson, *Gentrification and the enterprise culture, Britain 1780–1980* (Oxford, 2001).
126 See chapter 5 for further details about the church and a photograph of the carved fox heads.
127 M.J. Wiener, *English culture and the decline of the industrial spirit, 1850–1980* (2nd edn, Cambridge, 2004), pp. 13–14, 97, 159; J.A. Smith, 'Landownership and social change in late nineteenth century Britain', *Economic History Review*, 53/4 (November, 2000), p. 775.

Nor was the transfer of capital necessarily unproductive.[128] Brown's entrepreneurial spirit remained active, albeit increasingly directed towards the newly acquired agricultural estate, specifically in relation to investment in the agricultural infrastructure at Rossington. Brown brought wealth and business acumen from industry to agriculture, and his investment epitomised a metamorphosis of the entrepreneurial spirit in the nineteenth century.

Extractive industries in the Doncaster district were closely aligned with the geological composition of the landscape. Their scale and scope thus varied considerably, with quarrying and brickmaking responding to local requirements and/or the growing demand for building materials from urban centres.[129] It was not uncommon for landed estates to have small brickyards and to employ a small number of people to make bricks from locally extracted clay to provide building materials sufficient for estate requirements. The aforementioned brickyard at Rossington was valued at £10 per annum in 1835, just before the estate was sold to the Brown family in 1838.[130] As mentioned, the Browns retained it as a small-scale venture that was used as and when required by the landowners for estate rebuilding. As such, the only mention of brick and tile makers resident and operative in the village coincided with the rebuilding of cottages and farms on the estate during the 1850s and 1860s.[131] Similarly, a clay pit and brick yard were maintained at Sprotbrough for estate use in the 1840s, which corresponded with Sir J.W. Copley rebuilding several estate cottages in the mid-nineteenth century.[132] In both instances, brick making fulfilled the requirements of the respective landed estates, but the limited scale and scope of the industry resulted in the employment of only a few people.

The scale and scope of extractive industries was no greater in the multi-freeholder villages in the district. At Fishlake a small clay pit is shown on the 1854 Ordnance Survey map, and Joseph Marshall was listed in the 1861 and 1877 directories as the brickmaker.[133] Like the estate brick makers mentioned above, Marshall provided bricks for local use as demand required, which again resulted in a low number of regular employees. Larger brickyards on the periphery of Doncaster, such as that at Balby, developed specifically to meet the demands of urbanisation in the Doncaster district.

---

128 Wilson, *Gentlemen merchants*, pp. 235–6.

129 J.A. Chartres, 'Rural industry and manufacturing', in E.J.T. Collins (ed.), *The agrarian history of England and Wales*, Vol. VII, 1850–1914, Part 2 (Cambridge, 2000), pp. 1139–43; G.E. Mingay, *Rural life in Victorian England* (London, 1976), p. 110.

130 Appendix to the first report of the commissioners appointed to inquire into municipal corporations: part III northern and north midland circuits (London, 1835), p. 1504; DA, AB/7/3/63, Sale catalogue for the Rossington estate, 1838.

131 White, *Gazetteer and general directory of Sheffield, 1852*; Kelly, *Post Office Directory, 1861*.

132 White, *History, gazetteer and directory, 1837*, Vol. 2, p. 207; Ordnance Survey, 1854, first edition county series, 6 inch map, Yorkshire (West Riding), surveyed 1850; G. Fardell, *Sprotbrough: or, a few passing notes for a morning's ramble* (Doncaster, 1850), pp. 8, 14, 55.

133 Kelly, *Post Office directory, 1861*, p. 276; Kelly, *Post Office directory, 1877*, p. 314; Ordnance Survey, Yorkshire (West Riding).

The only large-scale extractive industry in the district (prior to coal mining in the twentieth century) was the stone quarries at Warmsworth. Initially the extraction of stone here also corresponded with population growth and estate rebuilding from the eighteenth century onwards.[134] During the late eighteenth and through the nineteenth century quarrying activities expanded and Levitt Hagg, on the periphery of the estate, developed considerably. The Lower Magnesian Limestone was suitable for construction, while the lime could be applied to marginal agricultural land and used by builders and iron founders.[135] Consequently, stone and lime were transported out of the Doncaster district via the river, with small-scale boat building and specially constructed wagon ways facilitating the efficient movement of goods.[136] The geological location and spatial relationships within an industrialising county were of paramount importance in the growth and development of these quarries.

Many landowners wanted to 'extract the wealth beneath the soil', although by the mid-nineteenth century it was increasingly rare for them to directly manage mineral exploitation on their estates.[137] Management of the quarries at Warmsworth transferred from the landowners to lessees in 1766, corresponding with the inter-marriage of the Battie and Wrightson families.[138] As the scale of quarrying at Warmsworth increased, so did the number of landowners from which the quarries were leased. The Battie-Wrightsons continued to be the main landlords, but Mr Fox, William Aldam and Sir J.W. Copley also leased land for this purpose.

Lockwood, Kemp and Blagden (later Lockwood, Blagden and Crawshaw) leased the quarries and limekilns during the nineteenth century. Correspondence and agreements between the landowners and lessees dated from the 1840s address concerns over boundaries and how rents were calculated. Aldam and Battie-Wrightson maintained an active interest in the quarries and were vocal in such matters, applying their business acumen to negotiations. This was perhaps unsurprising, as Battie-Wrightson's income from the quarries exceeded that from his agricultural rents in Warmsworth.[139]

Key to the growth of the Levitt Hagg quarries and the value of the stone and lime were connections with external markets. A wide market existed for this limestone, and the commercial potential of these quarries was far greater than the requirements of the estate during the mid-nineteenth century. A notice in the *Leeds Intelligencer* in 1820 stated that a proposed warping sluice to be built on the south bank of the river

---

134 D. Holland, *Warmsworth in the eighteenth century: population change, agriculture and quarrying in a rural South Yorkshire community* (Doncaster, 1965), pp. 7–11.

135 Holland, *Changing landscapes*, p. 28; Kelly, *Post Office directory, 1861*, p. 871.

136 Holland, *Changing landscapes*, pp. 19–27.

137 Mills, *Lord and peasant*, p. 30; Spring, 'English landowners', p. 51; Thompson, *English landed society*, p. 264.

138 Thompson, *English landed society*, pp. 265–6.

139 DA, DD/BW/E11/77, Letter from Lockwood, Kemp and Blagden to W. Battie Wrightson, 27 November 1843; DA, DD/BW/E11/78, Agreements between Messrs. Lockwood, Kemp and Blagden and the Landowners (Aldam, Copley, Fox, Wrightson), 1846–47 (7 items); DA, DD/BW/E2/4, Rentals of Battie-Wrightson, 1827–1840; DD/BW/E2/7, Rentals of Battie-Wrightson, 1853–1856.

Ouse near Swinefleet was to be built of 'quality' stone and that Warmsworth stone was being considered.[140] In 1844 a feature in the *Sheffield Independent* on the proposed Doncaster Branch of the Lincoln, York and Leeds railway mentioned that Warmsworth stone had long been 'celebrated for its building purposes'.[141] Both the *Bristol Mercury* and the *London Standard* printed features in 1845 about the value of Warmsworth limestone for 'building purposes'.[142]

A similarly wide market existed for the lime from Warmsworth. The application of lime could reduce the acidity of soil and was thus beneficial to agriculture, and lime could also be used in construction work.[143] There was, however, some debate about the application of lime from Levitt Hagg to agricultural land. An advertisement for lime from the Warmsworth quarries published in the *Stamford Mercury* stated that it was 'the best quality for building and agricultural purposes'.[144] However, Charles William Hatfield, newspaper proprietor and editor, argued that while it was a 'superior quality' for building purposes it was not 'equal to that of Knottingley for agricultural purposes'.[145] In addition to the supply of lime directly from the quarry, merchants and agents acted as intermediaries between the quarry company and the purchasers. Significantly, the advertisements of the Sheffield-based agents took pride in the fact they were the sole agents for Warmsworth lime. This presumably enabled the agents to negotiate savings when purchasing the lime and to secure customers. Certainly, the advertisements placed by their agents increasingly announced reductions in the cost of lime as a result of special arrangements reached with the quarry company. For example, in 1851 and 1852 William Travis of Canal Street, Sheffield advertised a 'great reduction' in the price of Warmsworth building lime, from 13s 4d to 11s 8d per ton.[146] Easy carriage available from the Midland Railway Company meant that Mr G.O. Brown and later his widow (who continued to run the business) could offer a constant supply of Warmsworth lime at a reduced price.[147] By the 1860s and 1870s J.H. Sales was advertising fresh Warmsworth lime for between 9s and 10s per ton.[148]

---

140 *Leeds Intelligencer*, 23 October 1820, p. 1.
141 *Sheffield Independent*, 21 December 1844, p. 4.
142 *Bristol Mercury*, 27 September 1845, p. 1; *London Standard*, 9 October 1845, p. 7.
143 *Doncaster Chronicle*, 13 May 1842, p. 7; *Doncaster Chronicle*, 24 June 1842.
144 *Stamford Mercury*, 7 February 1873, p. 1.
145 Hatfield, *Hints to pedestrians*, p. 158.
146 *Sheffield Independent*, 12 March 1851, p. 1; *Sheffield Independent*, 22 March 1851, p, 1; *Sheffield Independent*, 29 March 1851 p. 1; *Sheffield Independent*, 12 April 1851, p. 1; *Sheffield Independent*, 19 April 1851, p. 1; *Sheffield Independent*, 10 April 1852, p. 4; *Sheffield Independent*, 14 Aug 1852, p. 1; *Sheffield Independent*, 28 August 1852, p. 1; *Sheffield Independent*, 11 Sept 1852, p. 1; *Sheffield Independent*, 25 Sept 1852, p. 1; *Sheffield Independent*, 4 December 1852, p. 1.
147 *Sheffield Independent*, 24 April 1852, p. 3; *Sheffield Independent*, 15 May 1852, p. 1; *Sheffield Independent*, 29 May 1852, p. 1; *Sheffield Independent*, 2 September 1854, p. 1; *Sheffield Independent*, 12 January 1856, p. 4; *Sheffield Independent*, 6 August 1854, p. 1.
148 *Sheffield Independent*, 16 April 1864, p. 2; *Sheffield Independent*, 15 October 1864, p. 2; *Sheffield Independent*, 10 April 1868, p. 1; *Sheffield Independent*, 9 June 1868, p. 2; *Sheffield Daily Telegraph*, 27 March 1869, p. 2.

Rural economies

The railways and use of commercial agents widened the market for lime from the quarry and, as with other quarries in the West Riding of Yorkshire, a close relationship developed between industry, urban society and the countryside.[149]

Owing to the extensive markets for, and trade in, stone and lime from the Levitt Hagg quarry at Warmsworth, this industry employed more people than any other single rural industry in the six villages. Moreover, the total number of Warmsworth residents recorded as employed at the quarries in the Census Enumerators Books increased between 1841 and 1871, reflecting growth in the sector nationally.[150] The majority of employees at Levitt Hagg were labourers and lime burners, with a handful of book-keepers. The total number may have been even greater because some labourers were employed in both quarries and agriculture, a distinction not always made on the census.[151] John Firth, a quarryman in 1841 and 1871, was also recorded as an agricultural labourer in 1851 and 1861, and may have undertaken employment on the land and in the quarries as and when required.[152]

Locational factors, spatial relationships and economic spheres of influence were important in the foundation and development of other industries in the Doncaster district. As mentioned above, the Don Foundry, located on the boundary between the parish of Sprotbrough and Doncaster on land owned by Sir J.W. Copley, catered for both town and country. Small-scale agricultural engineering businesses such as this represented the transitional phase between hand-made agricultural implements and the large-scale agricultural engineering industry.[153] John Walkinshaw junior, who had inherited his father's business, ran the foundry between at least 1847 and 1871.[154] In 1861 Walkinshaw was listed in the local directory as 'engineer, iron founder, and manufacturer of agricultural implements, weighing machines, crabs, blocks, jacks, pumps, hot water apparatus, kitchen ranges, pans, spouting, palisading and wire fencing'.[155] Such items were manufactured for town and country markets and for both industry and agriculture, and as such the foundry was well sited for stimulating trade.

Flint grinding for pottery occurred on the river Don at Lower Sprotbrough. The water mill there supplied the Don Pottery at nearby industrialised Swinton with the

---

149 M. Yasumoto, 'Industrialisation and demographic change in a Yorkshire parish', *Local Population Studies*, 27 (1981), pp. 10–25.

150 Chartres, 'Rural industry', p. 1139.

151 *Ibid.*, pp. 1139–43.

152 TNA, HO 107/1329, CEB Sprotbrough 1841; HO 107/2346, CEB Sprotbrough 1851; RG 9/3516, CEB Sprotbrough 1861; RG 10/4716, CEB Sprotbrough 1871.

153 D. Grace, 'The agricultural engineering industry', in E.J.T. Collins (ed.), *The agrarian history of England and Wales*, Vol. VII, 1850–1914, Part 2 (Cambridge, 2000), pp. 1000–1004; J.A. Chartres and R. Perren, 'Trade, commerce and industry: introduction', in E.J.T. Collins (ed.), *The agrarian history of England and Wales*, Vol. VII, 1850–1914, Part 2 (Cambridge, 2000), p. 948.

154 DA, P25/9/B1, Sprotbrough tithe apportionment and map, 1847; TNA, HO 107/2346, CEB Sprotbrough 1851; RG 9/3516, CEB Sprotbrough 1861; RG 10/4716, CEB Sprotbrough 1871.

155 Kelly, *Post Office directory, 1861*, p. 812.

ground flint used to temper their cream-ware pottery.[156] From 1801 to 1840 the Green family, who founded the Don Pottery, also occupied the mill at Sprotbrough. After the Green family were declared bankrupt in November 1840, including J. Green of Sprotbrough Mill and W. Green of Swinton, the mill and pottery were collectively acquired by Mr Barker, maintaining the inter-relationship between rural Sprotbrough and industrialised Swinton.[157] Even after 1860, when the owner of the pottery and the occupant of the mill were no longer the same, the relationship continued. For example, Benjamin Harris, commission merchant and flint grinder at Sprotbrough in 1877, supplied the Don Pottery with ground flint.[158] This relationship was sustained until the Don Pottery closed in 1893. The necessity of a geographical proximity to industry and a riverine location meant that this industry was reliant on the estate village of Sprotbrough throughout the mid-nineteenth century.

Location and spatial relationships also stimulated inter-connected networks of supply and demand, and of labour and skill, at Stainforth. Boat builders and sail makers were located on the banks of the Stainforth and Keadby Canal, which was an important artery for transporting goods, transferring knowledge and skills and connecting with other waterside communities. Two of the principal boat-building yards served both local and national markets. Benson's Yard, a family-run business, employed people in addition to family labour, including apprentices.[159] In 1851 they employed three men, two of whom were apprentices (John Garrett, 17, and John Foster, 14) who lived with the family.[160] Both apprentices were the sons of agricultural labourers, from Thorne and Stainforth respectively. By 1861 both had married and were working as a shipwright and a ship's carpenter respectively.[161] However, by 1871 both men had moved out of Stainforth, with Foster residing in Fishlake, where he worked as a ship's carpenter, and Garrett living in Hull, where he worked as a shipwright.[162] The boat builders also generated trade for sail makers, who made sails for new boats and replacements for older vessels. The total employment in boat building and associated trades, which included employees and apprentices who moved to Stainforth from elsewhere, increased between 1851 and 1871.[163] Many, such as William Shirtliff, were born in places such as Goole, which were renowned

---

156 DA, DD/BW/E7/50, Sketch plan of River Don, flint mill and canal cut at Sprotbrough, mid 19th century; Holland, *Sprotbrough in history*, p. 47.
157 White, *History, gazetteer and directory, 1837*, Vol. 2, p. 213; *Woolmer's Exeter and Plymouth Gazette*, 28 November 1840, p. 4.
158 Kelly, *Post Office directory, 1877*, p. 1112.
159 White, *History, gazetteer and directory, 1837*, Vol. 2, p. 188; TNA, HO 107/2349, CEB Stainforth 1851; Kelly, *Post Office directory, 1861*, p. 328; Kelly, *Post Office directory, 1877*, pp. 385–6.
160 TNA, HO 107/2349, CEB Stainforth 1851.
161 TNA, RG 9/3524, CEB Fishlake and Stainforth 1861.
162 TNA, RG 10/4726, CEB Fishlake 1871; RG 10/4782, CEB Hull 1871.
163 TNA, HO 107/2349, CEB Stainforth 1851; RG 9/3524, CEB Stainforth 1861; RG 10/4726, CEB Stainforth 1871; Kelly, *Post Office directory, 1877*, pp. 385–6.

for their canal trades and crafts.[164] Boat building and sail making in Stainforth were an integral part of much wider networks of production, marketing and knowledge transfer that were stimulated by the canal and the river.

The framework knitting workshop at Braithwell was a distinctive form of industry in Doncaster's rural hinterland, being focused on the endeavours of one family (the Clarksons). No mention was made of Braithwell or the Doncaster district in the 1845 Report into the Conditions of Framework Knitters. This is in contrast to parts of Leicestershire, Nottinghamshire and Derbyshire, where the framework knitting industry was more prevalent in terms of the numbers of both frames and employees. The report focused on the conditions of framework knitters and a series of grievances that had accumulated.[165] Complaints about wages, payment in kind and frame rents, however, largely did not apply to the small-scale family-run business at Braithwell. Members of the Clarkson family ran and worked at their framework knitting workshop, located in the village street, with the employment of minimal additional labour. It was a multi-generational business, with George Clarkson (67), his son William (41) and two grandsons, Mark (15) and Benjamin (13), working as framework knitters in 1851.[166] Female family members also worked on the frames. For example, in 1871, Ann (58) was recorded in the CEB as a hosiery manufacturer and her two daughters, Charlotte (23) and Jane (20), were framework knitters.[167] These employment patterns were typical of the hosiery industry in England, which continued to be predominantly rural and family-based in many places during the nineteenth century.[168] On occasion, however, non-family members were employed, such as Charles Hall in 1851 and William Mann in 1861.[169] Mann (51) was from Nottinghamshire, where he had previously resided and worked as a framework knitter, which suggests that the Clarksons valued his skill and experience.

Conclusion

Although positioned within an industrialised county, Doncaster remained a country market town and the rural economies in the district were predominantly agricultural throughout the mid-nineteenth century. Differentiation in rural economies was not clearly delineated by landownership. While, superficially, farm size and capital investment in the agricultural infrastructure were greater in the estate villages, and the extent of industry and micro-commerce were greater in multi-freeholder villages, this statistical comparison conceals variation and nuances. Differences in crops and

---

164 White, *History, gazetteer and directory, 1837*, Vol. 2, p. 188; Kelly, *Post Office directory, 1861*, p. 328; Kelly, *Post Office directory, 1877*, pp. 385–6; TNA, HO 107/2349, CEB Stainforth 1851; RG 9/3524, CEB Stainforth 1861.
165 PP 1845, XV, *Report of the commissioner appointed to inquire into the condition of the framework knitters*.
166 TNA, HO 107/2346, CEB Braithwell 1851.
167 TNA, RG 10/4714, CEB Braithwell 1871.
168 Chartres, 'Rural industry', pp. 1106–14; M. Palmer, *Framework knitting* (Aylesbury, 2002), p. 9.
169 TNA, HO 107/2346, CEB Braithwell 1851; RG 9/3513, CEB Braithwell 1861.

livestock were still largely determined by the geology of the district, as were extractive industries. Locational factors, such as proximity to urban areas or access to a river or canal, affected other aspects of local rural economies. A close alignment between some rural industries or micro-commerce and agriculture and the rural community meant that core trades and crafts such as blacksmithing were present in both estate and multi-freeholder communities. Crops were still processed locally, often for consumption in the community. Even where micro-commerce in multi-freeholder communities far exceeded that found in estate communities, this was primarily due to their larger populations.

The inter-relationships between rural communities, and between town and country, are important for understanding rural economies. Rather than a one-way dependency of estate villages on multi-freeholder communities, mutual dependency existed. This was stimulated by the availability of resources, skills and knowledge and by geography. Rural economies converged in the market town of Doncaster, which was an important trading hub. Doncaster Corporation was an active agent in this process and promoted a reciprocal relationship between town and country through the construction of market buildings. The knowledge networks facilitated by agricultural societies strengthened the relationships between rural communities and between town and country. These rural economies, and the distinct relationship between town and country, influenced the living and working conditions of agricultural workers in the Doncaster district, which are explored in the next chapter.

Chapter 4

Living and working conditions

Despite the popular notion of the countryside as a rural idyll, a space that was healthier to live and work in than were Victorian towns and cities, there was increasing awareness that rural areas contained their own challenges.[1] Social investigations of the 1830s and 1840s began to reveal the extent of rural poverty and prompted more detailed parliamentary enquiries examining the countryside. During these two decades, the *Morning Chronicle* drew attention to the condition of agricultural labourers in southern England, using testimonials from the labouring population, letters and observations.[2] The reports argued that the new poor law had 'unquestionably added to the privations of the agricultural labourers' and that landowners (among others) had a responsibility to attend to their needs.[3] In responding to these reports, the clergy and poor law guardians defended themselves and other rural elites from accusations that their actions, especially in administering the new poor law, were responsible for the condition of agricultural labourers. The 1867–8 parliamentary commission into the employment of children, young people and women in agriculture included northern counties and so had a broader geographical reach than earlier investigations, but drew its evidence largely from rural elites. As such, parliamentary commissions effectively set an agenda that understood the labouring poor within an upper- and middle-class interpretive framework.[4] In other words, the problems of the poor were reported by farmers, landowners and the clergy rather than by the labouring population itself, and the perceived causes of these problems often became interwoven with the economic or moral motivations of those giving evidence to the commission. Living and working conditions, which were to a large extent determined by landlords and employers, are defining characteristics in historians' models of village typology, as shaped by nineteenth-century reports. This chapter examines four

---

1 A. Howkins, 'Rurality and English identity', in D. Morley and K. Robbins (eds), *British cultural studies* (Oxford, 2001); E.K. Helsinger, *Rural scenes and national representation: Britain, 1815–1850* (Princeton, 1997); K. Sayer, *Country cottages: a cultural history* (Manchester, 2000); G.E. Mingay, 'The rural slum', in M. Gaskell (ed.), *Slums* (Leicester, 1990); M. Freeman (ed.), *The English rural poor* (London, 2005); K. Waddington, '"It might not be a nuisance in a country cottage": sanitary conditions and images of health in Victorian rural Wales', *Rural History*, 23/2 (2012), pp. 185–204.

2 *The Morning Chronicle*, 16 November 1838, p. 3; *The Morning Chronicle*, 27 November 1838, p. 3; *The Morning Chronicle*, 18 December 1839, p. 3; *The Morning Chronicle*, 5 April 1843, p. 6; *The Morning Chronicle*, 22 June 1844, p. 6; Freeman, *Social investigation*, p. 25

3 *The Morning Chronicle*, 16 November 1838, p. 3; *The Morning Chronicle*, 27 November 1838, p. 3; *The Morning Chronicle*, 1 November 1844, p. 3.

4 Freeman, *Social investigation*, p. 25; N. Verdon, *Rural women workers in nineteenth century England: gender, work and wages* (Woodbridge, 2002), p. 72.

key indicators of living and working conditions in the Doncaster district – wages and bonuses, employment patterns and hiring practices, attitudes to the employment of women in agriculture, and the quality and availability of housing and gardens – in order to examine the extent to which such conditions varied between estate and multi-freeholder communities.

In 1848 J.H. Charnock argued, in his *JRASE* prize essay, that perhaps nowhere in England were agricultural labourers 'better paid, better housed, and better cared for' than in the West Riding of Yorkshire.[5] Agricultural wages were generally higher in the industrial north, as they had to compete with those of industrial occupations.[6] According to Charnock, the wages of common labourers in the West Riding of Yorkshire were 14–16s a week, increasing to 18s per week for an occupation requiring more skill and judgement.[7] By contrast, the national average weekly wage for comparable work was between 11s and 12s.[8] Charnock also argued that Yorkshire labourers were more comfortable on account of the 'cheapness and excellency of fuel' there.[9] Nevertheless, within the county considerable variation existed, not simply between different parts of the region but also within localities. The situation also changed over time.

Evidence of living and working conditions in the Doncaster district can be drawn from wage reports, parliamentary enquiries and local commentators. The official reports and enquiries provide comparative evidence of living and working conditions, albeit imbued with the moral or social overtones of rural elites: as already described, it was usually members of the clergy or landowners who gave evidence to the commissioners. Those who wished to reform hiring practices, see a reduction in the employment of women in agriculture or improve cottage accommodation spent a disproportionate amount of time drawing attention to these issues in their evidence. The clergy were increasingly concerned with the ill health of the labouring population, as well as their perceived immorality, which was on occasion blamed for their general condition, and sought to use the commission as an opportunity to highlight the need for reform. In contrast, those who had something to gain from the status quo, such as farmers who relied on female labour, highlighted the benefits thereof. Nevertheless, such contributions still provide valuable insights, especially regarding contrasting attitudes, either in the absence of other data or when used in conjunction with other records, and can be used to evaluate existing models of village typology. After all, despite ostensibly being about the employment of women and children in agriculture, the 1867–8 commission was considered nothing short of a comprehensive survey of the labouring population in rural England.[10] The printed reports of the commissioners and T.E. Kebbel's *The Agricultural Labourer* (based largely on these reports)

---

5   Charnock, 'On the farming of the West Riding', p. 311.
6   Afton and Turner, 'Wages', p. 2013; E.H. Hunt, 'Industrialisation and regional wage inequality: wages in Britain, 1760–1914', *Economic History Review*, 46/4 (1986), p. 947.
7   Charnock, 'On the farming of the West Riding', p. 311.
8   Hunt, 'Industrialisation and regional wage inequality', p. 965.
9   Charnock, 'On the farming of the West Riding', p. 311.
10 Freeman, *Social investigation*, p. 38.

highlighted housing, modes of employment and hiring, wages, diet and education as affecting the condition of labourers and their position in society.[11]

Mills' 'open–closed' model of village typology suggested that the living and working conditions of agricultural workers can be clearly delineated according to the concentration of landownership. The conditions of the rural poor, while frequently attributed to the attitudes and actions of rural elites, are far more complex and nuanced than this suggests. Evidence from the Doncaster district demonstrates the difficulties of applying this model to a range of rural communities in close proximity to one another. Not only were there disparities in labourers' conditions in places with similar landowning structures, but concerns about living and working conditions were often shared by reformers in estate and multi-freeholder villages, thus transcending landownership. Moreover, living and working conditions were not synonymous with one another, especially as many agricultural workers did not live and work in the same place and the fluidity of the agrarian population and social hierarchies (defined by type of work, skill, wages and position in society) among agricultural workers meant that change and differentiation were characteristic.

Wages

Wage data for the Doncaster district is sparse. Few wage books survive and, in the absence of village-specific wage data for the six case-study communities, it is impossible to compare and contrast wages at the village level. Annual wage reports compiled by the House of Commons contain average weekly wages for the district, which can be compared to places elsewhere in the region and nationally. The average weekly wage of male agricultural labourers in the Doncaster district was consistently 2–3s more than the national average during the mid-nineteenth century, which was in line with Charnock's observations for the West Riding of Yorkshire made in 1848, and they steadily increased from 13s to 15s (Table 4.1). This was slightly lower than in other parts of the West Riding, on account of there being less industry in the Doncaster district. Of course, in reality wages were variable, with reported wage rates providing only a partial indication of such variation and concealing differentiation in the skill and regularity of employment.[12] Wages for core workers were more stable and consistent than those of casual workers, whose wages were subject to seasonality and market forces to a greater extent.[13] Weekly earnings by task (paid to workers employed to undertake specific tasks, often seasonal in nature, as part of a casual workforce) may have been 3–4s higher than the average weekly wage in the Doncaster district during the 1860s, but offered a less secure income. In the winter months there was very little task work, and jobs such as threshing, that previously would have formed task work, were noted as being almost entirely undertaken by machines, which

---

11 PP 1867–8, XVII, *Commission on the Employment of Children, Young Persons, and Women in Agriculture 1867*; T.E. Kebbel, *The agricultural labourer: a short summary of his position* (London, 1870).

12 Afton and Turner, 'Wages', p. 1993.

13 C. Yamamoto, 'Two labour markets in nineteenth century English agriculture: the Trentham Home Farm, Staffordshire', *Rural History*, 15/1 (2004), pp. 89, 104.

Table 4.1
Average weekly wages for agricultural workers, 1860–70

	National	Doncaster area			
	Average weekly wage (men)	Average weekly wage (men)	Average weekly earnings by task	Average weekly wage (women)	Average weekly wage (children)
Quarter ending Michaelmas 1860	10s 9d	13s 6d	15s		
Quarter ending Christmas 1860	10s 9d	13s	15s	5s	3s
Quarter ending Lady Day 1861	11s 1d	13s 6d		6s	4s
Quarter ending Midsummer 1861	11s 1d	13s 6d	16s 6d	6s	6s
1868	11s 8d	14s		6s	6s
1871	12s	15s			

Sources: national average weekly wage: B. Afton and M. Turner, 'Wages', in E.J.T. Collins (ed.), *The Agrarian History of England and Wales*, Vol. VII, 1850–1914, Part 2 (Cambridge, 2000), p. 2013; Doncaster area wages – Michaelmas 1860: PP 1861, L, *Return of the average rate of weekly earnings of agricultural labourers*, Part 1, 1860, p. 12; Christmas 1860: PP 1861, L, *Return of the average rate of weekly earnings of agricultural labourers*, Part 1, 1860, p. 12; Lady Day 1861: PP 1861, L, *Return of the average rate of weekly earnings of agricultural labourers*, Part 2, 1861, p. 9; Midsummer 1861: PP 1861, L, *Return of the average rate of weekly earnings of agricultural labourers*, Part 2, 1861, p. 9; 1868: PP 1868–9, L, *Return of the average rate of weekly earnings of agricultural labourers*, 1868, p. 15; 1871: PP 1871, LVI, *Return of the average rate of weekly earnings of agricultural labourers*, 1871, p. 27.

reduced the labour required. Weekly wages were also notably higher during harvest and haymaking and were often boosted by additional non-monetary allowances in response to the increased demand for agricultural labourers.[14] Supplements of food and drink served as an incentive to workers and literally fuelled the workforce to enhance productivity. In 1860 an experienced agricultural male labourer in the Doncaster district could be hired during harvest for up to four weeks at 18s per week, and would receive in addition a daily allowance of breakfast, dinner, supper and three pints of ale.[15] An allowance of ale, bread and cheese was also granted to those using the steam engine and threshing machine between 1860 and 1861. By 1868–9 a labourer could earn between 20s and 24s per week during harvest, although without supplementary allowances.[16]

The manner in which agricultural workers were hired also varied. Farm service and hiring fairs were prominent features of the Victorian labour market in the Doncaster district. Farm servants were usually hired annually for a wage agreed at the Doncaster

---

14 N. Verdon, *Working the land: a history of the farmworker in England from 1850 to the present day* (London, 2017), pp. 70–77.
15 PP 1861, L, *Return of the average rate of weekly earnings of agricultural labourers*, Part 1, 1860, p. 12.
16 PP 1868–9, L, *Return of the average rate of weekly earnings of agricultural labourers*, 1868, p. 15.

Statutes, whereas many agricultural labourers were hired by the week. The potential for higher wages, on account of the proximity to industrial and urban employment and the consequential increased competition for labour, bestowed agency on some agricultural workers in the Doncaster district, albeit engendering social hierarchies among workers. Farm servants were particularly adept at exerting their agency through their bargaining power. Their success was greatest during periods of agricultural prosperity, when demand for labour often exceeded the supply of farm servants. Bargaining favoured principally the most experienced and skilled farm servants, who were able to improve their wages and status accordingly. Between the 1850s and 1870s local newspapers regularly reported that 'first class servants' or 'good males with known ability' were 'readily engaged' and could demand the highest wages. These rose from 18s in 1858 to 34s in 1876, and were usually at least 10s more than those paid to young, unexperienced farm servants. Farm servants who possessed a skill shared with industry or required by towns, such as those skilled in working with horses, were particularly in demand and could command higher wages.[17]

As wage demands escalated, resistance from farmers intensified. While the campaign to reform hiring practices focused on the demoralising process of hiring servants in public and the immorality (drink and disorder) associated with the fairs, an economic undercurrent bubbled under the surface. Local clergy had begun to discourage farmers and farm servants from attending the Doncaster Statutes from the 1840s on moral grounds, with the Revd C.E. Thomas (Warmsworth) and the Revd Dr Vaughan (Doncaster) actively securing places for young people beforehand and attempting to establish a proto-system of registry offices.[18] Almost 20 years later, in 1861, ten registry offices were established in Doncaster and its environs, in which hiring agreements took place in private. These were a cross-district alternative to the very public hiring fair, and were perceived to be part of the campaign to tackle the immorality associated with hiring fairs, but the fact that they were supported by farmers who refused to pay more for their agricultural workers suggests economic motivations under an umbrella of morality. By removing hiring negotiations from public view, some local farmers hoped it would reduce the bargaining position of farm servants. The servants, however, were seemingly suspicious of reform and, despite media reports suggesting some initial success, the Statutes continued to thrive. For servants, abolishing the hiring fairs was tantamount to eradicating their day of leisure (discussed further in chapter 6) and diminishing their limited agency.[19] By refusing to use the registry offices and commenting they would not be 'driven inside', farm servants not only exerted their agency but also exhibited an awareness of possessing that agency.

Wage rates also indicate social hierarchies among the hired workforce. Although the average wages for agricultural work were much higher in the Doncaster district

---

17 Holland, 'Farm service', pp. 183–202; S. Caunce, *Amongst farm horses: the horselads of East Yorkshire* (Stroud, 1991), pp. 5, 11–15; Holland and Robinson, 'The fluidity of the "farming ladder"', pp. 106–28; Verdon, *Working the land*, pp. 23–53.

18 PP 1867–8, XVII, *First report of the Commission on the Employment of Children, Young Persons, and Women in Agriculture 1867*, pp. 99–100.

19 Holland, 'Farm service', pp. 199–200.

than in many other places, young and unskilled labourers frequently received lower than these average wages and were often without work, as differentiation in wages and hiring was dependent on skill and experience. In 1853 it was reported that those newly entering service were numerous and that supply exceeded demand.[20] By the 1870s the difference between the number of farm servants hired and not hired had widened further, with 'young and inexperienced boys being hard to dispose of'. Despite demanding more, the majority of farm servants did not receive higher wages because they were not skilled and their labour was not in demand.

Wages and hiring also fluctuated as a result of broader economic conditions. During the 1840s and early 1850s the local press reported that hiring notably diminished when agriculture was depressed, with all farm servants having to accept lower wages. In 1842 the *Doncaster Gazette* reported that local farmers were 'not only reducing the number of labourers annually employed by them in the winter season, but also reducing the rate of wages paid to those who are returned [hired]'.[21] By December 1850 the *Doncaster Chronicle* proclaimed that pauperism in the Doncaster district had increased rapidly and was expected to continue to grow. Countless labourers were reported to be out of work for long periods of time or only able to secure part-time work, with many farm servants returning weekly to the marketplace up to a month after the statutes in the hope of finding employment.[22] Similarly, in February 1851 it was reported that for many agricultural labourers it was a time of great misery and privation, with large numbers out of work.[23]

In summary, while average wages were higher in the Doncaster district than nationally, not all labourers received them or indeed were in employment. Such disparities were a district-wide phenomenon associated with the inherent skill-based social hierarchies of the labouring population, the relative agency of different agricultural labourers and the demand from farmers for their labour. The bargaining power of skilled and experienced farm servants at the hiring fairs in Doncaster suggests that opportunities to exert their agency were to a large extent focused on the town where they were hired, rather than on the rural communities in which they lived and worked.

The employment of women in agriculture

Concerns about the employment of women, young people and children in agriculture during the mid-nineteenth century were shared in estate and multi-freeholder villages. Women's field labour was the subject of parliamentary investigations in 1843 and 1867–8. The second enquiry scrutinised all aspects of women's agricultural labour, including the tasks undertaken, the duration of their working day, how the women were employed and the impact on their health, morality and family life. Evidence was often collected from rural elites and the subsequent

---

20 *Doncaster Gazette*, 18 November 1853, p. 5.
21 *Doncaster Gazette*, 25 November 1842, p. 4.
22 *Doncaster Chronicle*, 13 December 1850, p. 5.
23 *Doncaster Chronicle*, 21 February 1851, p. 5.

reports were imbued with the middle-class ideology of 'separate spheres', which deemed fieldwork unfeminine. Yet, in reality, many women were compelled to work to supplement the family income, and in some cases they exhibited resistance to this moral opposition to their labour.[24]

The extent to which the Victorian ideology of separate spheres permeated the commission of 1867–8 is evident in the juxtaposition of waged work with the domestic. This ideology firmly positioned women within the domestic sphere, a space destined to suffer should women work elsewhere. The Revd S. Surtees perpetuated this notion when he gave evidence to the commission about female labour at Sprotbrough. He proudly noted that most young girls from the parish went into domestic service. Of the women who did work in the fields, he commented they were 'mostly widows, and some few of the labourers' wives', adding, 'You might mark them out by the general untidiness of the home, and the discomfort of the cottages.'[25] Similarly, at Warmsworth, the Revd C.E. Thomas reported that 'Where women go out regularly to field work it has the effect of making them dirty and slovenly in their homes, careless of the comforts of their husbands and families, and coarse in their manners, their children go about neglected in appearance, and their husbands for want of home comforts are drunken.'[26] The association of fieldwork with deficiencies in the home and family show that these opinions were irrefutably underpinned by moral ideologies.

A spectrum of 'acceptability' was applied to the tasks performed and methods of employment. Dairy work, traditionally associated with femininity, domesticity and cleanliness, was considered particularly suitable and appropriate work for women, whereas gang work (a form of sub-contracting between a farmer and gangmaster that saw the employment of groups of women and children in the open fields, was notorious for harsh working practices and the coercion of the gangmaster, and was often associated with immorality) was unequivocally not.[27] Local clergy, when giving evidence to the parliamentary commissions, differentiated between the types of labour undertaken by women in their parishes. The Revd Thomas of Warmsworth noted that occasional employment during harvest or stone-picking 'makes them industrious, tends to healthiness, and rubs off that finery and pride which is apt to grow among our cottagers'.[28] Conversely, he considered turnip cutting and pulling during winter to be 'a cruel employment for women'. He went so far as to argue that females should not work outside at all during the winter months, as 'many go out poorly clad and worse shod and so

---

24   K. Sayer, 'Field-faring women: the resistance of women who worked in the fields of nineteenth-century England', *Women's History Review*, 2/1 (1993).

25   PP 1867–8, XVII, *First report of the Commission on the Employment of Children, Young Persons, and Women in Agriculture 1867*, p. 398 – letter from the Rev. Scott Surtees of Sprotbrough to Hon. E. Portman (15 May 1868).

26   PP 1867–8, XVII, *First report of the Commission on the Employment of Children, Young Persons, and Women in Agriculture 1867*, p. 402.

27   Verdon, *Rural women workers*; Verdon, *Working the land*, pp. 67, 97.

28   PP 1867–8, XVII, *First report of the Commission on the Employment of Children, Young Persons, and Women in Agriculture 1867*, p. 402.

get into bad health'.[29] The Revd Surtees noted that certain jobs, including 'potato-setting and ingathering', were carried out by Irish women and girls who lived in the centre of Doncaster.[30] As such, he physically and morally distanced his parish from such work, suggesting that the women engaged in certain tasks in the fields of Sprotbrough did not reside there.

John Bladworth, an owner-occupier of Stainforth, viewed the employment of women in agriculture more favourably, stating that he would have preferred to have more women and children in the fields and certainly would not place any restriction on female employment, as he believed it to be in the interests of both women workers and farmers. As an employer, he was particularly transparent as to his motivations, commenting that 'The labour of women and children is the most economical the farmer can employ, in work which requires suppleness of finger, or activity rather than strength, they will do as much as a man.'[31] With regard to Stainforth, he noted that it was principally widows who did fieldwork, it being very difficult to get married women to work when the men were fully employed. As such, he implied that these were women who had little or no other means of subsistence, 'who would be deprived of a great aid to their means if prevented from working'.[32] Moreover, he argued that the work injured neither their health nor their morals. 'They are never called upon to do work unfitted to their strength and the fresh air is conducive to their health.'[33] On the subject of the gang system, he commented that, while there were no gangs in Stainforth, he had observed them in neighbouring villages. In his opinion the gangmaster was obligatory 'as their tongues are more likely to be in motion than their hands', yet 'His presence will neither cause them to overtax their strength nor be detrimental to their morals.'[34] It is perhaps unsurprising that a farmer, dependent on the labour of these women, adopted such a perspective.

The wages of female agricultural workers were much lower than those of their male counterparts. Charnock noted that women and older children were able to obtain employment on farms in the West Riding of Yorkshire with wages of about 1s per day.[35] Female agricultural wages in the Doncaster district were comparable with this. The average weekly wage for women in Doncaster between 1860 and 1870 was between 5s and 6s, which was considerably lower than the 13–15s paid to men. John Bladworth at Stainforth noted that wages for women and boys were ordinarily 1s per day, rising to 1s 3d in potato time. Work regularly undertaken by women in the district was similar in estate and multi-freeholder villages, albeit varying on account of land type and the demands of different farms. It included bird tenting, handpicking twitch or couch grass, dibbling beans, weeding, singling and cutting and pulling turnips and gathering potatoes, and accordingly provided employment at different points during the year.

---

29 Ibid.
30 Ibid., p. 398.
31 Ibid., p. 401.
32 Ibid.
33 Ibid.
34 Ibid.
35 Charnock, 'On the farming of the West Riding', p. 311.

In summary, contrasting perceptions of female labour were indicative of the different perspectives of those giving evidence to the commissioners, rather than the experience of female labourers. Evidence was underpinned by either a moral or economic rationale, often shared by those in estate and multi-freeholder villages according to their occupation or status, and thus reflected the agency of clergy and farmers, alongside landowners, in rural society. Of course, these prevailing attitudes could affect employment patterns and the number of women employed on the land, but female agricultural labourers appear to have worked in all of the six case-study villages during the mid-nineteenth century – albeit not always women resident in those communities, which was emphasised a number of times in the parliamentary reports.

Cottage accommodation and gardens

The quality of cottage accommodation was similarly examined during the nineteenth century. The reality was often far removed from the idyllic imagery of country cottages that was prevalent in Victorian England.[36] Living conditions could be as bad, if not worse, in the countryside as in urban areas – and it was often only the scale and concentration of the problems that differed.[37] The *Seventh report of the medical officer of the privy council*, commissioned in 1864, was the first national survey into rural labourers' dwellings, and revealed the extent of poor housing in the countryside. It was followed shortly afterwards by the 1867–8 Royal Commission on the employment of children and women in agriculture. Common themes running through the reports included the shortage of cottages, the poor quality of the buildings and overcrowding.[38] These parliamentary enquiries were part of a wider discourse evident from the 1830s that recognised the impact of standards of living and the availability of cottage accommodation and gardens on the health and wellbeing of inhabitants in rural communities. In 1845 the *JRASE* published an article by John Grey entitled 'On the building of cottages for farm-labourers' in which he argued that the construction of dwellings for agricultural labourers deserved at least as much attention as that devoted to farm buildings. One of the objectives of the Royal Agricultural Society of England was to promote the comfort and welfare of labourers and to encourage the improved management of their cottages and gardens. Grey's article explained the inter-relationship between living conditions and the health, comfort, wellbeing and moral character of the inhabitants, and argued that landlords were accountable.[39] Numerous other authors outlined essential requirements for healthy living, although many were coupled with the aesthetics favoured in estate villages. Examples include Henry Robert's cottage designs

---

36 Sayer, *Country cottages*, pp. 1–6; Freeman, *Social investigation and rural england*, p. 36.
37 G.E. Cherry and J. Sheail, 'Town and country: an overview – housing' in E.J.T. Collins (ed.), *The agrarian history of England and Wales*, Vol. VII, 1850–1914, Part 2 (Cambridge, 2000), p. 1551.
38 Sayer, *Country cottages*, p. 5.
39 J. Grey, 'On the building of cottages for farm-labourers', *Journal of the Royal Agricultural Society of England*, 5 (1845), pp. 237–8.

produced for the Society for Improving the Condition of the Labouring Classes, Sir Henry Acland's *Health in the village*, and J.C. Loudon's *Encyclopaedia of cottage, farm and villa architecture*.[40]

The 1867–8 parliamentary commission argued that Yorkshire cottages were 'vastly superior to the average dwellings in the southern counties', just as Charnock had observed two decades earlier.[41] Mr Portman, an assistant commissioner for the 1867–8 report, commented that 'there is much comfort in them [labourers' cottages]', and that gardens were 'almost universally attached to them'.[42] Nonetheless, standards were not uniform across Yorkshire or the Doncaster district, with both exceptionally good-quality housing and extremely poor cottages. The commissioners and those giving evidence often drew a distinction between estate and multi-freeholder villages, as do recent models of village typology. Mills argued that estate villages had superior accommodation but a shortage of cottages[43] as, with parish poor rates levied on individual houses until 1865, landowners had an incentive not to build new cottages, and even to demolish existing ones.[44] Conversely, multi-freeholder villages were assumed to have a greater supply of cottages, often constructed by speculative builders, that were in a poorer condition.[45] While this was true of some houses in the estate and multi-freeholder villages in the Doncaster district, contrasts in the quality of housing could often be seen in the same village.

Evidence for the Doncaster district certainly demonstrates that some good-quality cottage accommodation existed in the estate villages. At Rossington, James Brown junior erected a group of model estate cottages at the heart of the village shortly after he inherited the estate in 1845 (Figure 4.1). These mock-timber brick cottages combined aesthetic considerations with the latest recommendations regarding labourers' cottages. Each had three bedrooms, some of which had fireplaces, thus addressing contemporary concerns about overcrowding and comfort, and they were described as 'attractive and well built'.[46] The *Seventh report of the medical officer*, published in 1865, revealed that only 4.7 per cent of labourers' dwellings had more than two bedrooms, making the model cottages at Rossington exceptional.[47] A more subjective account of estate cottages came from the Revd J.G. Fardell, who described Sprotbrough as a 'pretty village' with flower-covered cottages that had been rebuilt

---

40 G. Darley, *Villages of vision* (London, 1975), pp. 94–5; J.C. Loudon, *An encyclopedia of cottage, farm and villa architecture* (London, 1846); H. Roberts, *The Dwellings of the Labouring Classes, Their Arrangement and Construction* (London, 1851); H.W. Acland, *Health in the village* (London, 1884).
41 PP 1867–8, XVII, *First report of the Commission on the Employment of Children, Young Persons, and Women in Agriculture 1867*, p. xxv.
42 *Ibid.*
43 D.R. Mills, *Lord and peasant*, p. 117.
44 G.E. Cherry and J. Sheail, 'Rural housing', in E.J.T. Collins (ed.), *The agrarian history of England and Wales*, Vol. VII, 1850–1914, Part 2 (Cambridge, 2000), p. 1553.
45 Mills, *Lord and peasant*, p. 117.
46 DA, DY/DAW/9/29, Sale catalogue for the Rossington estate, 1938.
47 PP 1865, XXVI, *Seventh report of the medical officer of the Privy Council*, Appendix.

Living and working conditions

Figure 4.1 Cottages at Rossington (author's own picture).

during the 1840s 'in a style both pleasing and ornamental'.[48] The new cottages in Sprotbrough, he wrote, 'are replete with the comforts and necessaries of that station of life' and built in a style 'both pleasing and ornamental', 'so that the peasantry now enjoy homes not to be rivalled by the poor of any parish around'.[49] This lack of any attempt to quantify the comforts and necessaries he mentioned typified the rural elite's attitude to the housing of the labouring population, but although his perspective was somewhat romanticised he did allude to the differences in living conditions that existed within rural communities in the district.

The shortage of cottage accommodation and the distance often travelled to work in estate villages in the Doncaster district was highlighted by the landowners and clergy who gave evidence to the parliamentary commissioners. The *Fourth report from the Select Committee on Settlement and Poor Removal* argued in 1847 that the scarcity of cottages in estate villages was an 'evil' of the open–closed parish system. The process whereby landowners restricted building in an attempt to lower poor law expenditure, in turn increasing overcrowding in neighbouring multi-freeholder villages, was pivotal to the accusations of a moral scandal discussed in chapter 1.[50] Latterly it also underpinned Mill's inter-dependency theory, whereby the actions of landowners in estate villages exacerbated problems in multi-freeholder communities.[51] Even

---

48   Fardell, *Sprotbrough*, pp. 8, 14, 55.
49   *Ibid.*, p. 55.
50   PP 1847, XI, *Fourth report from the Select Committee on Settlement and Poor Removal*, p. 15.
51   Mills, *Lord and peasant*, pp. 119–20.

James Brown, who had built the model estate cottages at Rossington, had to admit that, although the quality of housing was reasonably good, the number of cottages was not sufficient for the requirements of the land.[52] Similarly, Thomas Wood argued that 'more cottages are wanted' at Sprotbrough, while the Revd Surtees noted that

> The main grievance of the agricultural labourer in this part of the world is that he has to walk often so far to his work, as many villages have not sufficient cottage accommodation in proportion to their acreage, and if he has to walk three miles to his work, still he has to be on the spot at 6am with the others.[53]

The Revd C.E. Thomas highlighted deficiencies in the supply of cottages at Warmsworth. He noted that the parish had no more than one cottage to every 100 acres, whereas the recommendation was for three cottages for every 200 acres. As such, agricultural workers had to live elsewhere, often some distance from their place of work, leading Thomas to argue 'I do not think that any person of any age ought to go four miles backwards and forwards to work daily; it must in the end tell upon the workmen as well as upon the employer very disadvantageously.'[54] The *Seventh report of the medical officer* (1865) also drew attention to this, observing that 'Warmsworth, Loversall, Alverley, and other places hereabout do not afford the accommodation required for the number of men necessary to the land, and so people are drawn from the open villages of Balby and Conisbro.'[55] It added 'A walk in the fresh air may be pleasant to the engine smith but it is no luxury to the ploughman, and most of all it must be remembered that peasant women travel from home to work under the compulsion of poverty.'[56] Providing some explanation for this, William Aldam remarked with regard to Frickley and Warmsworth that 'The rent in purely agricultural villages is so comparatively small to the cost of building [cottages] that there is no inducement to build them.'[57]

Nor were living conditions consistent in estate villages. For instance, although Brown constructed some superior cottages at Rossington, many houses were older, unimproved and lacked a sufficient number of bedrooms, while the domestic accommodation was often over a cowshed or piggery, or adjoined a workshop.[58] The Revd C.E. Thomas argued that, while some improvements had been made at Warmsworth, many cottages were still inadequate, with poor drainage and ventilation and only one or two bedrooms, compelling parents and children to share rooms

---

52 PP 1867–8, XVII, *First report of the Commission on the Employment of Children, Young Persons, and Women in Agriculture*, 1867, p. 395.
53 *Ibid.*, pp. 396–8.
54 *Ibid.*, p. 402.
55 PP 1864, XXVIII, *The Medical Officer of the Privy Council: Seventh Report 1863*, p. 300.
56 *Ibid.*, p. 301.
57 PP 1867–8, XVII, *First report of the Commission on the Employment of Children, Young Persons, and Women in Agriculture 1867*, p. 395.
58 DA, AB/7/3/63, Sale catalogue for the Rossington estate, 1838; DA, DY/DAW/9/29, Sale catalogue for the Rossington estate, 1938.

and use kitchens as additional sleeping quarters.[59] In his opinion, good cottage accommodation was essential for the health, comfort and morality of labourers; he commented that he had known healthy children waste away on account of being in overcrowded accommodation. Thomas argued that, where work was plentiful and labour well paid, good and comfortable cottages could be constructed, with every necessity, at a cost that would repay the landed proprietor, taking into consideration how much he and his tenants were losing by labourers coming from a distance of even two miles to their work. He also noted that if the accommodation was comfortable then labourers would pay rent of £5 or £6 a year, instead of the £3 to £4 they paid for inferior housing.[60] Absentee landownership was associated with poor accommodation in estate villages in the *Fourth report from the Select Committee on Settlement and Poor Removal* in 1847.[61] While this may have played a role at Warmsworth, the agency of the incumbent, the Revd Thomas, in championing the condition of the labouring population was paramount in drawing attention to deficiencies in their living conditions, where elsewhere they often remained hidden.

In the multi-freeholder villages accommodation was more plentiful, as envisaged in the Mills model. John Bladworth, providing evidence about the cottages in Stainforth for the 1867–8 commission, remarked that 'the accommodation in the cottages is good and there are sufficient numbers of them … . The rooms are 10 to 12 feet square, the ventilation is good, and on average there would be two low and two bedrooms, with pantry and out-buildings.'[62] At Braithwell the number of cottages was again considered to be adequate, although they were apparently too small.[63] Similarly, at Barnby Dun (a multi-freeholder village located between Doncaster and Stainforth), the cottages were described as 'sufficiently numerous but rather small and not in good condition'.[64] This evidence would suggest that there was less variation in housing in the multi-freeholder villages than in the estate villages. The adequate supply but small size of cottage accommodation was a recurrent theme, the main variation being whether or not cottages were in a respectable condition.

Cottage gardens were considered advantageous during the mid-nineteenth century, both in respect of village aesthetics and as a means of supplementing the diet of labourers. Mr Portman, assistant commissioner, commented that a labourer could 'spend a half hour in the morning, or in the evening on his return from work, in his garden, where he can, without inconvenience, have the assistance of his wife or children'.[65] Those giving evidence to the 1867–8 commission from the Doncaster district specifically commented on the provision of gardens and agreed that they

---

59 PP 1867–8, XVII, *First report of the Commission on the Employment of Children, Young Persons, and Women in Agriculture 1867*, p. 402.
60 Ibid.
61 PP 1847, XI, *Fourth report from the Select Committee on Settlement and Poor Removal*, p. xxv.
62 PP 1867–8, XVII, *First report of the Commission on the Employment of Children, Young Persons, and Women in Agriculture 1867*, p. 402.
63 Ibid., p. 395.
64 Ibid., p. 396.
65 Ibid., p. 105.

were a great advantage to the labourer. Gardens were attached to most cottages in Rossington, Sprotbrough, Cadeby, Cusworth, Warmsworth and Stainforth, while about 20 cottages at Braithwell were singled out as being without gardens.[66]

Warmsworth provides evidence of how paternalism, social control and the agency of the labouring population could converge through the provision and use of cottage gardens. William Aldam, giving evidence to the Commission on the Employment of Children, Young Persons and Women in Agriculture, remarked, 'I have always considered gardens an advantage, they enable a labourer to utilise much of his spare time, conduce to steady habits, and add to his comfort.'[67] Aldam's comments were underpinned by a desire to see labourers engaged in worthwhile activity during their spare time that was linked to his need to control the behaviour of tenants, and by a paternalistic streak that addressed the welfare of his tenants. The majority of his tenants at Warmsworth had gardens attached to their cottages.[68] Moreover, the Aldam family established the Warmsworth Cottagers' Horticultural Show, which offered prizes for the best-kept garden and house front as well as for the best specimens of fruit, vegetables and flowers. The *Doncaster Chronicle* reported that the show made tenants more industrious, encouraging them to take pride in their homes, improving social order and benefiting rural society.[69] The Revd C.E. Thomas commented that the shows and prizes were conducive to making tenants 'take a pride in the neatness and respectability, and comfort of their homes as well as making them more industrious, sober, and contented'.[70] Morality and social control certainly appeared to be paramount in these appraisals.

Nevertheless, it is crucial not to undermine the importance of these gardens to the labourers themselves. The produce grown in these gardens supplemented a labourer's food supplies and therefore helped their income go further, while prizes provided families with practical items for use in the home and garden, as well as signifying an opportunity for social mixing. The lists of people awarded prizes or commendation for their produce suggest that a range of people actively participated in the shows, including agricultural labourers, quarry workers, shopkeepers and crafts people.[71] For agricultural workers, the provision of a garden, whether motivated by paternalism or social control, could be an opportunity to improve their living conditions.

Ultimately, the living and working conditions of agricultural workers were shaped by a combination of factors. High wages, secure employment, desirable occupational

---

66 *Ibid.*
67 *Ibid.*, p. 396.
68 DA, DD/WA/E6/1, Rental book, 1860, pp. 62–3.
69 *Doncaster Chronicle*, 11 July 1845, p. 5; *Doncaster Chronicle*, 22 July 1859, p. 5; *Doncaster Gazette*, 17 June 1842, p. 5.
70 PP 1867–8, XVII, *First report of the Commission on the Employment of Children, Young Persons, and Women in Agriculture 1867*, p. 403.
71 *Doncaster Gazette*, 17 June 1842, p. 5; *Doncaster Gazette*, 2 August 1844, p. 4; *Doncaster Chronicle*, 11 July 1845, p. 5; *Doncaster Chronicle*, 7 June 1850, p. 5; *Doncaster Chronicle*, 25 June 1852, p. 5; *Doncaster Chronicle*, 8 September 1854, p. 5; *Doncaster Chronicle*, 22 August 1856, p. 5; *Doncaster Chronicle*, 22 July 1859, p. 5; *Doncaster Chronicle*, 21 June 1861, p. 5; *Doncaster Chronicle*, 17 July

skills, good-quality cottage accommodation and the provision of a garden collectively contributed to a high standard of living. The Revd Surtees of Sprotbrough even argued that 'it is the rule not the exception for a labourer to leave at his death 50l to 100l', noting that some farm servants and labourers bequeathed sums far in excess of this. He attributed this to the high wages in the district and 'the almost universal possession by the labourer of a garden or allotment', contending that 'I see no reason to doubt that a man commencing life as farm servant and exercising ordinary prudence can, by the assistance of a savings bank, lay up a fair provision for his old age.'[72] While this was a somewhat idealised view of the circumstances of many agricultural workers it provides an important reminder that occupational groupings were fluid and contained social hierarchies in which skilled and experienced workers could take advantage of higher wages and the provision of a small plot of land to improve their relative position in rural society.

Conclusion

Living and working conditions in the Doncaster district were generally superior to those in southern England. Across the West Riding of Yorkshire proximity to industry increased agricultural wages, as both sectors competed for labour. While opportunities for good wages and cottage accommodation existed across the district, there were variations that meant that living and working conditions were not identical between or within rural communities, and nor were they determined solely by landownership. Nor were living and working conditions necessarily coterminous, as agricultural workers could work in a different village from the one in which they lived. Indeed, many had long distances to travel to work, which itself was a concern. Agricultural workers often moved during their lifetime, meaning that experiences of work and housing were not stable. Moreover, concerns about cottage accommodation and working practices in the district transcended landownership and village type. Local clergy were prominent in these debates.

The presence of a market town affected wages and work in the countryside: agricultural workers who worked with horses shared a skill set with those who worked in the town, especially the railways, breweries and carriers, and their labour was therefore in demand in both town and country, which meant that they could demand higher wages. Hiring practices for farm servants were largely centred on the market town, which again provided opportunities for experienced and skilled farm servants to

---

1863, p. 5; TNA, HO 107/2346, CEB Sprotbrough 1851; HO 107/2346, CEB Warmsworth 1851; HO 107/2348, CEB Rossington 1851; HO 107/2346, CEB Braithwell 1851; HO 107/2349, CEB Fishlake and Stainforth 1851; RG 9/3516, CEB Sprotbrough 1861; RG 9/3514, CEB Warmsworth 1861; RG 9/3522, CEB Rossington 1861; RG 9/3513, CEB Braithwell 1861; RG 9/3524, CEB Fishlake and Stainforth 1861; RG 10/4716, CEB Sprotbrough 1871; RG 10/4715, CEB Warmsworth 1871; RG 10/4724, CEB Rossington 1871; RG 10/4714, CEB Braithwell 1871; RG 10/4726, CEB Fishlake and Stainforth 1871.

72 PP 1867–8, XVII, *First report of the Commission on the Employment of Children, Young Persons, and Women in Agriculture 1867*, pp. xxv–xxvi, 398.

command better renumeration. This bargaining power democratised hiring practices and bestowed agency on some agricultural workers, and yet it also fed into social hierarchies within the labouring population, with many agricultural workers earning low wages if indeed they could secure employment in the Doncaster district. The agency of agricultural workers and attempts to control the labouring population are discussed further in the next two chapters, which explore religion, education and recreation in the Doncaster district.

Chapter 5

Religion and education

Religion and education were inextricably linked facets of rural society during the mid-nineteenth century, especially as most rural schools were run by the Anglican church in this period. They were manifestations of Victorian morality, paternalism and social control, with landowners, clergy and school teachers acting as influential co-agents, and as such have underpinned historical interpretations of rural communities. This chapter examines religious and educational provision and participation in the Doncaster district and attempts to determine whether the churches, chapels and schools forged a distinctive social identity in rural communities, and the role of rural inhabitants in this process. Comparisons are made between estate and multi-freeholder villages, and the extent to which landownership provided impetus and agency for differentiation is also explored. Similarities between village types are also identified in order to establish how both wider social trends and the geography of the Doncaster district helped to shape religion and education in these rural communities, thus transcending patterns of landownership. The first part of the chapter uses evidence from the fabric and location of places of worship, alongside the 1851 religious census, to provide a survey of religious institutions and practices in the six case-study villages. The second part of the chapter examines the provision of education in these communities and the relationship between school attendance and child labour in agriculture, using evidence from a series of nineteenth-century parliamentary commissions and reports.

Religion

The church or chapel was intrinsic to the fabric of a rural community. Tangible evidence of the role and, often, the dominance of religion is provided by the location and appearance of places of worship. The church building usually occupied a central position in a village, and, owing to the close relationship between landowners and the Church, was often in close proximity to the landed residence in estate villages. The architecture and layout of both church and chapel embodied social hierarchies, from symbolic carvings and private chapels to pew rents. New buildings, or the rebuilding of existing churches or chapels, could be representative of the challenges and opportunities faced by particular communities or by the Anglican Church during the nineteenth century. The Anglican Church built or rebuilt churches in response to a perceived decline in church attendance, but this soon led to concerns that 'whilst churches come of religion, religion does not come of churches': simply providing more places of worship would not necessarily result in greater attendance at them.[1] Landowners would similarly support

---

1   B.F.L. Clarke, *Church builders of the nineteenth century – a study of the gothic revival in England* (2nd edn, Newton Abbot, 1969), p. 21.

the rebuilding or expansion of the parish church with a view to either impressing or controlling parishioners, but they were not always successful.

Quantitative data drawn from the 1851 census of religious worship provides an indication of provision of, and attendance at, a place of worship. The census was carried out in response to concerns about the state of religion and whether religious provision had kept pace with population growth and redistribution. It captured attendance at morning, afternoon and evening services in Anglican, nonconformist, Catholic and Jewish places of worship on Sunday 30 March 1851 and gathered information about the construction date of buildings, the seating space available for worship, whether there were pew rents or fees, the average attendance and any endowments.[2] It is important to remember that this census was a snapshot in time and failed to capture many facets of Victorian religious practice (for example, attending multiple services or places of worship, attending church or chapel only on special occasions, reasons for attendance or non-attendance, religious belief without attendance at a place of worship, and the ways in which religion permeated other aspects of life). Nonetheless, as J. Wolffe argues, 'despite its obvious flaws and limitations, [it] provides vital evidence regarding early-Victorian religious activity and observance', which has implications for understanding the development of rural communities.[3] The 1851 religious census, together with the 1865 visitation returns and village-specific evidence, permits comparative analysis of religion in rural communities. Furthermore, both sources provide an indication of what members of the Anglican clergy believed to be the causes of declining attendance at village churches.

According to the 1851 religious census, 54.97 per cent of the total population of Yorkshire attended a place of worship. This figure was slightly lower than the national average for England and Wales (58.1 per cent), but still higher than that for some other northern and industrial counties. The West Riding of Yorkshire, however, as a result of industrialisation, rapid population growth and outmoded religious provision, had the lowest attendance at places of worship within the whole county. Attendance at Anglican churches was lower than at nonconformist places of worship across Yorkshire. Notable differences also existed between town and country, with provision and attendance greater in rural communities than in towns.[4]

Yet patterns of religion also varied considerably between rural communities. Dennis Mills attributed this largely to landownership, contrasting strong Anglicanism in estate villages with the prevalence of nonconformity in multi-freeholder villages. For landowners, the parish church was a symbol of their power, wealth and status, and could be a vehicle for social control and community cohesion.[5] The church could also contribute to the cultural self-containment of a village by providing a focal point for the community and permeating different aspects of society, although in reality (as David

---

2   Snell and Ell, *Rival Jerusalems*, p. 31.
3   J. Wolffe (ed.), *Yorkshire returns of the 1851 census of religious worship, vol. 3: West Riding* (York, 2005).
4   Snell and Ell, *Rival Jerusalems*, pp. 60–65.
5   Mills, *Lord and Peasant*, p. 117; D.G. Hey, 'The pattern of non-conformity in South Yorkshire 1660–1851', *Northern History*, 8 (1973), pp. 116–17.

Table 5.1

Provision of and attendance at Anglican churches in the six case-study villages, 1851

Place of worship	Population size	Provision (services and sittings)	Index of sittings	Attendance (per service)			Index of attendance (per service)			Index of occupancy (per service)		
				Morning	Afternoon	Evening	Morning	Afternoon	Evening	Morning	Afternoon	Evening
St Mary's parish church, Sprotbrough	528	2 services; 300 sittings (free: 130, other: 170)	56.8% (parish) 82.9% (township)	142	61		26.9%	11.5%		47.3%	20.3%	N/K
St Michael's parish church, Rossington	402	2 services; 250 sittings (free: 50, other: 200)	62.2%	N/K	N/K	N/K	N/K	N/K	N/K	N/K	N/K	N/K
St Peter's parish church, Warmsworth	389	2 services; 150 sittings (free: 50, other: 100)	55.5%	80	70		20.5%	17.9%		53.3%	46.6%	
St James' parish church, Braithwell	493	2 services; 234 sittings (free: 74, other: 160)	47.5%	48		54	9.7%		10.9%	20.3%		20.5%
Chapel of ease, Stainforth	881	1 service; 200 sittings (free: 200)	22.7%	32			3.6%			16%		
St Cuthberts' parish church, Fishlake	642	2 services; 420 sittings (free: 420)	65.4%	100	60		15.5%	9.3%		23.8%	14.2%	

Source: 1851 Religious Census

Table 5.2
Provision of and attendance at non-conformist chapels in the six case-study villages, 1851

Place of worship	Provision (services and sittings)	Index of sittings	Attendance (per service)			Index of attendance (per service)			Index of occupancy (per service)		
			Morning	Afternoon	Evening	Morning	Afternoon	Evening	Morning	Afternoon	Evening
Wesleyan Meeting House, Rossington	N/K	N/K			30			7.5%	N/K	N/K	N/K
Primitive Methodist Chapel, Warmsworth	1 service Sittings N/K	N/K			15			3.8%	N/K	N/K	N/K
Primitive Methodist Chapel, Levitt Hagg	1 service 20 sittings (free: 20)	N/K		12						60%	
Dwelling House (Wesleyan), Warmsworth	1 service 36 sittings (free: 36)	N/K			33			8.5%			91.6%
Wesleyan Methodist Chapel, Braithwell	2 services 200 sittings	24.3%		77	24		15.6%	4.8%		38.5%	12%
Wesleyan Methodist Chapel, Stainforth	3 services 280 sittings (free: 120 other: 160)	56.8%	57	125	144	6.5%	14.2%	16.4%	20.3%	44.6%	51.4%
Primitive Methodist Chapel, Stainforth	3 services 142 sittings (free: 60, other: 82)	16.1%	60	50	100	6.8%	5.7%	11.3%	42.2%	35.2%	70.4%
Unitarian Chapel, Stainforth	1 service 70 sittings (free: 40, other: 30)	7.9%		24			2.7%			34.3%	
Wesleyan Chapel, Fishlake	1 service 80 sittings (free: 40, other: 40)	12.5%		40			6.2%			50%	
Zion (Methodist New Connexion) Chapel, Fishlake	3 services 230 sittings (free: 80, other: 150)	35.8%	30	85	60	4.7%	13.2%	9.3%	13%	36.9%	26.1%
Primitive Methodist Chapel, Fishlake	2 services 100 sittings (free: 50, other: 50)	15.6%		62	40		9.7%	6.2%		62%	40%

Source: 1851 Religious Census

Religion and education

Brown highlighted) this is extremely difficult to measure. Tables 5.1 and 5.2 provide an overview of provision of and attendance at Anglican and nonconformist places of worship in the six case-study villages in 1851. A clear differentiation in religious provision and participation is discernible between the estate and multi-freeholder villages, with Anglicanism strongest in the former and nonconformity prevailing in the latter. Methodism was the dominant form of nonconformity and the main alternative to Anglicanism in these rural communities, as was the case elsewhere in the country.[6] This summary, however, conceals nuances in religious activity and variation in villages with similar landowning structures. Attendance at more than one place of worship or at multiple services on the same day was common, although very difficult to discern from the 1851 religious census. Horace Mann, who was responsible for organising and reporting on the 1851 religious census, devised a calculation to take multiple and dual attendance into consideration, but this is not considered reliable.[7] Even in estate villages where Anglicanism was strong and actively supported by a resident landowner, an undercurrent of nonconformity was often present. Moreover, the challenges faced by the Anglican Church were comparable in estate and multi-freeholder villages, with non-attendance at an Anglican church frequently attributed to nonconformity, social hierarchies, occupational structures, distance from a place of worship and proximity to the market town of Doncaster.

Of the six case-study villages, Sprotbrough is perhaps most closely aligned with the models as far as the relationship between concentrated landownership and Anglican religion is concerned. The only purpose-built place of worship in the village was the parish church, St Mary's, which also served Cusworth and Cadeby. It was located at the physical and social heart of Sprotbrough village, adjacent to the original manor house and on the boundary of Sprotbrough Hall's grounds, from which it was accessible via a private entrance. The church architecture, chapels and family memorials were representative of the power, authority and wealth of the resident landowning family. Built by the Fitzwilliam family in the twelfth century, it was maintained by their descendants, the Copleys, from the sixteenth century to 1925. While the Copleys were the sole landowners of Sprotbrough township, within the parish the Battie-Wrightsons also owned land, at Cusworth. Despite having their own personal chapel in Cusworth Hall and the parish church at Warmsworth, they also made their presence known at St Mary's, occupying the north aisle (adorned with their family memorials) during services. The chapel in the south aisle was the private chapel of the Copley family.

Sir Joseph Copley was noted for his proactive stance toward the church. The Revd Surtees, incumbent of Sprotbrough, commented that the landowners directed their 'whole weight into the scale for right and good, and with their servants attend most regularly Divine Service'.[8] This resident landowner's good working relationship with the clergy was reflected in the 1851 census, with attendance at the morning

---

6 Hey, 'The pattern of non-conformity', pp. 116–17; Wolffe, *Yorkshire returns*, p. 5.
7 Snell and Ell, *Rival Jerusalems*.
8 R. Larsen and E. Royle (eds), *Archbishop Thomson's visitation returns for the diocese of York, 1865* (York, 2006).

service considerably greater than at any other place of worship in the six villages: 26.9 per cent of the population, who occupied 47.3 per cent of the seating in the church. In total, a higher proportion of the population may have attended at least one service at this church, but it is impossible to know with any certainty how many of those who attended the afternoon service has also been at the morning service. Although it is likely that some attendees were present at both services, it is probable that a high proportion of the population was going to services at this church. In 1856 the Copleys extended their reach, and that of the Anglican Church, by constructing a chapel of ease dedicated to St John at Cadeby. Expressions of their power, wealth and status were once again paramount. Sir George Gilbert Scott, who was then in the process of reconstructing Doncaster parish church, was commissioned to design a neo-Gothic church in the village. The architecture of Cadeby church was similar to that of Skelton church, near York, also designed by Scott, and was described as 'one of the most beautiful little churches in the county'.[9] The total cost, all met by Sir J.W. Copley, was reported to have exceeded £5,000.[10] The designs even incorporated a heating apparatus, which 'warms and purifies the air in the church', a notable addition that both reflected the agency of the landowner and responded to concerns that the inhospitable nature of churches was a cause of low attendance.[11]

The building of the new church at Cadeby was at least in part motivated by the landowners' desire to exert social control over the periphery of their estate. On the one hand, this was a proactive means of bringing spiritual instruction to the rural population at a time when the distance that people had to travel to attend church was recognised as affecting church attendance. Copley was reported to be anxious 'to provide the rural population of the district with every spiritual necessity',[12] and the incumbent believed that the new church increased church attendance in the parish, although distance from the parish church had not previously been mentioned as a factor impeding church attendance.[13] Moreover, the 1851 religious census had revealed the presence of nonconformity in Cadeby. On the other hand, Copley also wanted to assert himself over neighbouring landowners, and the new church was a tangible symbol of his presence in a village owned partially by the Fountayne Wilson family of High Melton.

Owing to absenteeism or landowner apathy, Anglicanism was not always as strong in estate villages. Resident and proactive landowners created the impetus for church-going by encouraging or expecting attendance among their tenants and servants. Their presence within the village also meant that they could observe who was and was not attending, and tenants and servants would be aware of this. At both Rossington and Warmsworth, long periods without a resident landowner corresponded with at least some neglect of the churches within these communities. Although Doncaster

---

9 *Sheffield Daily Telegraph*, 26 September 1856, p. 3.
10 *Yorkshire Gazette*, 27 September 1856, p. 3; *Sheffield Daily Telegraph*, 26 September 1856, p. 3.
11 *Doncaster Chronicle*, 26 September 1856, p. 8.
12 *Yorkshire Gazette*, 27 September 1856, p. 3.
13 *Doncaster Chronicle*, 10 March 1856, p. 5; *Doncaster Chronicle*, 26 September 1856, p. 8; Larsen and Royle, *Archbishop Thomson's visitation returns*.

Corporation possessed the living, Rossington lacked the impetus of a resident landowner until 1838. Interest in St Peter's church at Warmsworth began to wane from the mid-eighteenth century, when the Battie-Wrightson family moved to reside solely at Cusworth Hall. The hall incorporated a private chapel and was located within the parish of Sprotbrough, which meant that the physical connection the family had with Warmsworth church was severed and there was no resident landowner within that parish to actively encourage church attendance. Nevertheless, the medieval church was rebuilt in red brick between 1803 and 1809, when William Battie-Wrightson provided £600 and the parishioners a further £100 by subscription, suggesting the family's continued moral connection with Warmsworth.

Renewed residency partially rehabilitated the respective parish churches in these rural communities. R.H. Wrightson (the son of William Battie-Wrightson) moved to Warmsworth in the 1830s and enlarged the church in 1849, motivated by an acknowledgement that the church had 'long been inadequate to the requirements of the congregation'.[14] Warmsworth church had also been subject to a sacrilegious attack in 1839, which perhaps provided additional impetus for R.H. Wrightson to take an active interest in the building. The *Doncaster Chronicle* reported that 'scoundrels' entered the church and 'stole a large bible, a large prayer book, three window curtains, [and] a quantity of green baize from the pews'.[15] Little explanation is given as to why this robbery took place, but it may have been due to the secluded location of the church, which was approximately half a mile from the village. The enlarged church of 1849 remained on the same site as its predecessor, suggesting that – apart from any physical constraints restricting new building work in the village – distance from the place of worship was not in fact perceived as a major impediment to attendance and continuity of the historical consecrated site was important. A bell tower incorporated within the boundary wall of Warmsworth Hall was used to call people to services at Warmsworth church, providing a physical link between the village and the church. This connection between the two sites was immortalised by Edward Miller, who wrote:

> A gentleman from the neighbourhood of Doncaster happening to go to London, went one morning to see St Paul's Cathedral. The verger who conducted him ... enlarged greatly upon the length, breadth, height, and other particulars of that noble structure. Why, says the gentleman, it really deserves the praise you have been bestowing upon it, but yet, I must tell you that we have a church in Yorkshire which, though it may not be equal in breadth or height to yours, is a full twenty yards longer from one end to another. Twenty yards longer exclaimed the astonished verger, and pray where is this extraordinary church? At Warmsworth, 3 miles from Doncaster replied the man.[16]

Although the church was by no means as long as St Paul's Cathedral and the remark was made in jest, the evidence suggests that, in spite of its physical distance

---

14   *Doncaster Chronicle*, 7 September 1849, p. 4.
15   *Doncaster Chronicle*, 23 February 1839, p. 3.
16   Miller, *The history and antiquities of Doncaster*, p. 221.

Communities in Contrast

Figure 5.1 St Michael's Church, Rossington (author's own picture).

from the village, Warmsworth church was an important part of this rural community. The enlargement of the church cost £200, of which £40 was given by the Society for Enlarging Churches. The 1851 census shows that approximately a fifth of the population were in attendance at both the morning and afternoon services, and that the church was just over half full in the morning and just under half full in the afternoon. In 1865 the recently appointed incumbent, the Revd C.E. Thomas, believed that attendance at the church equated to a good proportion of the population, and that this was in part due to his agency, that of the landowners and the rebuilding of the church. This level of attendance was sustained through continued efforts to make the church more hospitable. For example, in 1869 money was raised for 'the warming of Warmsworth Church'.[17]

Rossington also experienced renewal in this period. Following the purchase of the Rossington estate in 1838 the Browns rebuilt the parish church in 1844 (Figure 5.1).[18] With the exception of the tower and some Norman decoration over the doorway and chancel arch, the church was entirely rebuilt in sandstone and enlarged by the addition of north and south transepts. The church was the product of Brown's industrial wealth and his desire to become a member of the country gentry. Symbolic embellishments, including carved fox heads around the eaves representing the family's passion for fox hunting (Figure 5.2), were the hallmarks of a landowner's church. Aside from the enlargement, which provided greater capacity, the Brown family gave money for ongoing improvements to the church, thus provided impetus

---

17 *Doncaster Chronicle*, 16 April 1869, p. 6.
18 Kelly, *Post Office directory, 1861*, p. 610.

Religion and education

Figure 5.2 Carved fox heads, St Michael's Church, Rossington (author's own picture).

for additional attendance.[19] By 1865 the Revd Bower suggested that attendance had increased accordingly.

Despite the momentum provided by resident landownership and the close relationship fostered between landowners and the clergy, the Anglican Church still faced challenges in estate villages. The 1851 religious census revealed that over 50 per cent of 'sittings' (the seating spaces available for worship) were appropriated, meaning that they were reserved for the use of particular individuals and often subject to pew rents.[20] In the three estate villages a high proportion of 'sittings' in the Anglican churches, ranging from 46 per cent at Sprotbrough to 77 per cent at Warmsworth and 80 per cent at Rossington, were subject to fees.[21] This meant many of the labouring population in these villages were largely excluded from attending. Joseph Arch, a Primitive Methodist preacher and leader of the National Agricultural Labourers' Union (founded by Arch in 1872), identified the social hierarchies of the established church as alienating labourers and pushing them towards nonconformist congregations.[22] Nonconformity was often cited as the main impediment to the Anglican Church, especially in terms of attendance, even in rural communities where nonconformity was weak, suggesting that in some instances at least it was a scapegoat for deficiencies within the Anglican Church. Methodism nevertheless

---

19 Instances were reported in the local newspaper, including *Doncaster Chronicle*, 17 May 1850, p. 5 when James Brown contributed £20 to further improve the interior of the church.
20 Snell and Ell, *Rival Jerusalems*, pp. 321–37.
21 Wolffe, *Yorkshire returns*.
22 J.G. O'Leary (ed.), *The autobiography of Joseph Arch* (London, 1966), p. 92; P. Horn, *Joseph Arch 1826–1919: the farm workers' leader* (Kineton, 1971), pp. 71–3.

did gain ground in agricultural and quarrying settlements across South Yorkshire and, while it was more prevalent in multi-freeholder communities, undercurrents of nonconformity and dissent were discernible in estate villages.[23]

Even in Sprotbrough, where the Anglican Church was undoubtedly strong and received the ongoing support of resident landowners, nonconformity was evident in the early nineteenth century. Premises in lower Sprotbrough were licensed for Methodist meetings, including a cottage in 1817 and the mill in 1830.[24] The physical detachment of this hamlet from the main village may have facilitated the presence of nonconformity, and there is no evidence for nonconformist meetings in the heart of the village. By 1851 a private dwelling house at Cadeby in Sprotbrough parish, occupied by Thomas Heardley, was licensed for Wesleyan Methodist meetings. John Jefferson, a large tenant farmer on the estate, signed the return. In spite of Dennis Mills' assertion that tenant farmers were deferential to their landowners, Jefferson's role indicates the independence and agency exhibited by some.[25] Of the 60 nonconformist sittings the house offered on Sunday evenings, all were free, which meant that in principle they were available to anyone. In real terms this did not pose a great threat to the Anglican parish church in Sprotbrough, as it represented provision for only 11.7 per cent of the parish population and as few as 34 people (6.4 per cent of the parish population) attending the evening service in 1851. However, the proportion of people attending the Wesleyan Methodist meetings increases to 30.1 per cent when only the residents of Cadeby are taken into consideration. This suggests that these meetings both responded to the demands of local people and reflected the hostility they felt towards existing social hierarchies in the Anglican Church, and that they were able to flourish owing to their physical distance from the main village. It is possible that the founding of this meeting was at least a partial motivation in the building of the aforementioned new Anglican church at Cadeby in the mid-1850s.

At Rossington, nonconformity developed prior to 1838, when Doncaster Corporation were absentee landlords, and was seemingly tolerated by the Brown family thereafter. A dwelling house in the village continued to be licensed for Wesleyan use in 1851. Socio-economic factors appear to have influenced the development of nonconformity at Rossington. The steward who signed the Wesleyan return was Thomas Holmes, a shoemaker, who also occupied the dwelling house where meetings took place; here, as in many other places, there were strong links between trades and crafts people and principal leaders in Methodism.[26] Similarly, the two resident Primitive Methodist preachers were railway plate layers, reflecting the dominance of labourers in Primitive Methodism. Nonconformity was particularly associated with the labouring population, Mann identifying the 'labouring myriads' as those most frequently absent from the Anglican church.[27] As at Cadeby, however, the number of people attending this Sunday evening service in 1851 was low (30).

---

23 Hey, 'The pattern of non-conformity', pp. 111–12.
24 W. Pierson, *Methodism in Sprotbrough* (Sprotbrough, 1980).
25 Wolffe, *Yorkshire returns*.
26 Mingay, *Land and society*, p. 85.
27 Larsen and Royle, *Archbishop Thomson's visitation returns*, p. 64; J.R. Moore, *Religion in Victorian Britain: sources* (Manchester, 1988).

Warmsworth had a long history of nonconformity. Thomas Aldam, one of the main landowners in the village during the seventeenth century, had been an active Quaker who preached publicly and wrote associated publications. The village was home to a Quaker Meeting House, which welcomed George Fox in the seventeenth century and hosted regular religious meetings.[28] Although these village meetings had been disbanded by the mid-nineteenth century and William Aldam aligned himself with the Anglican Church, a foundation had been laid on which nonconformity continued to flourish. The economic and occupational composition of Levitt Hagg, a satellite settlement of Warmsworth, facilitated this process and added to the religious complexity of this estate village. The inter-relationship between industry and nonconformity, whether in urban or rural communities, has long been recognised by historians,[29] and the quarrying settlement at Levitt Hagg engendered a culture of nonconformity, independence and autonomy. Primitive Methodist and Wesleyan meetings were held in the estate village of Warmsworth and there were Primitive Methodist and Wesleyan chapels at Levitt Hagg. The landowners and the Anglican church tried to counter the effects of nonconformity by enlarging the parish church in Warmsworth and building a missionary chapel at Levitt Hagg. In 1865 the Revd Thomas reported that Warmsworth village had no dissenting chapel, and yet nonconformity was still considered an impediment by the Anglican church, with about 25 known dissenters in the parish.

Despite the anxieties of the established Church, however, the challenge posed by nonconformity was often not that great. In some rural communities in the Doncaster district evidence suggests that people attended both the Anglican Church and nonconformist chapels. At Adwick-le-Street the incumbent explained that 'the Wesleyans have closed their chapel during hours of Divine worship and all the Dissenters without exception attend Church' on account of the 'plain and often extemporaneous preaching'.[30] Similarly, at Brodsworth, it was noted that 'frequenters at the Chapel are very few, and their leaders are Communicants in Church'.[31]

Many labourers, in fact, did not attend any place of worship. Even at Sprotbrough, where attendance at the parish church was reasonably high, the incumbent, the Revd S. Surtees, argued that 'many of the agricultural labourers and their families never attend a place of worship'.[32] He added: 'a large proportion, as far as attendance at a place of worship is concerned, are practically living without God in the world'. The Anglican clergy of the Doncaster district may not have considered that 'a fair proportion of the labouring population' attended their churches, but they did recognise that agricultural work and Sunday worship were sometimes incompatible.[33]

---

28 Miller, *The history and antiquities of Doncaster*, pp. 220–21.
29 A. Everitt, *The patterns of rural dissent: the nineteenth century* (Leicester, 1972); A.D. Gilbert, *Religion and society in industrial England: church, chapel and social change, 1740–1914* (London, 1976); Snell and Ell, *Rival Jerusalems*.
30 Larsen and Royle, *Archbishop Thomson's visitation returns*, p. 9.
31 Ibid., p. 74.
32 Ibid.
33 Ibid.

The work of feeding or attending to livestock meant that some labourers had to work on a Sunday, whether in estate or multi-freeholder villages.

Another issue was the close proximity of many of these rural communities to Doncaster, which allowed external distractions and spheres of influence to affect patterns of religious behaviour in villages. The Revd C.E. Thomas, incumbent of Warmsworth, identified both the Doncaster races and the statute fairs at Doncaster as having a negative impact on church attendance.[34] This was a view shared by the incumbents of town-centre churches. The Revd Vaughan, of St George's Church, Doncaster, argued that the late market on Saturday and the races affected attendance at Sunday services. Regarding the market, he wrote: 'I should suppose that the late Saturday Market is an evil in many ways in its effects upon the observance of the Sunday.'[35] Similarly, the incumbent of Christ Church in Doncaster, referring to the drinking and gambling that took place there, stated that 'The annual races in September have the most demoralising effect.'[36]

Nonconformity was undoubtedly more prevalent in terms of provision and participation in the multi-freeholder communities around Doncaster. This correlation between non-concentrated landownership and the spread of nonconformity was recognised and understood during the nineteenth century. The *Imperial Gazetteer* (published in the 1870s using information from the 1851 religious census) noted that most dissenting chapels were located in parishes with divided or multiple ownership.[37] Nonconformity, according to both contemporaries and historians, filled a vacuum and reached out ideologically to the very people the Anglican Church alienated. By 1851, almost 80 per cent of parishes had at least one nonconformist meeting place, and between 33 and 50 per cent of religious attendees were nonconformist.[38]

At Fishlake, the number of people attending nonconformist chapels during the nineteenth century was almost twice the number going to the Anglican Church. By the mid-nineteenth century the parish church was described as being near to a state of collapse and in need of urgent repair. Not only was landownership fragmented at Fishlake, but the living was also vacant for some time. Fresh impetus for the Anglican Church came from a new and proactive incumbent, the Revd Ornsby (1850–1886), who initiated a programme of restoration. Although he secured finances from the dean and chapter of Durham for some of this restoration work he was adamant that money from the parish rates should supplement this. He was anxious to actively engage the parishioners in this process by having them literally buy into the Anglican Church. He believed that this would foster a more engaged congregation who would embrace collective ownership, but in fact it displeased many parishioners. The proportion of people attending Fishlake Church continued to be lower than Ornsby hoped for, with dissent and the size of the parish cited as the main impediments in 1865.[39]

---

34 Ibid.
35 Ibid., pp. 119–20.
36 Ibid., p. 122.
37 Snell and Ell, *Rival Jerusalems*, pp. 370–71.
38 Ibid., pp. 71–3, 122; A.D. Gilbert, 'The land and the church', in G.E. Mingay (ed.), *The Victorian countryside*, Vol. 1 (London, 1981); Everitt, *The patterns of rural dissent*, p. 5.
39 Larsen and Royle, *Archbishop Thomson's visitation returns*, p. 157.

Like Warmsworth, Fishlake had a long legacy of dissent. In 1676, 136 dissenters resided in Fishlake – the largest number in any parish in South Yorkshire with the exception of Sheffield.[40] By the nineteenth century it had three chapels: Methodist New Connexion – Zion, Primitive Methodist and Wesleyan.[41] Leading figures in these chapels were often those with money and influence in the community: men with their own business interests who were in a financial and social position to promote the chapel they supported. For instance, the steward and signatory for the Zion chapel in Fishlake was Charles Thorpe, a grocer; and the Primitive Methodist preacher, Mr Dearman, was the local cordwainer and coal dealer. As at Rossington, the link between nonconformity and trades and crafts occupations is highlighted.[42] The ability of nonconformity to transcend social barriers is illustrated again in Fishlake by Briggs, an agricultural labourer, who, like the railway plate layers in Rossington, was recorded as a Methodist preacher.[43]

With no historical Anglican presence, nonconformity and dissent were especially fervent at Stainforth. The parish church was some distance away, at Hatfield, and it was not until 1820 that a small red-brick chapel of ease was erected and licensed at Stainforth. The new chapel was unable to accommodate everyone in Stainforth, and the number of people attending services remained low.[44] Attendance was far greater at the three nonconformist chapels: the Unitarian (1817), the Wesleyan Methodist (1822, considerably enlarged in 1844) and the Primitive Methodist (1835, rebuilt in 1870).[45] While only 32 were recorded as attending the Anglican chapel of ease in 1851, 144 were present at the Wesleyan Methodist evening service, in addition to 125 in the afternoon and 57 in the morning. At the Primitive Methodist chapel, attendees were 60 at the morning service, 50 at the afternoon one and 100 in the evening. Only the Unitarian Chapel had fewer people attending its afternoon service (24). Navigation and nonconformity went hand in hand at Stainforth, with the river and canal fostering demographic and cultural diversity, which in turn stimulated dissent. The largest attendance in Stainforth was at the Wesleyan Methodist Chapel. The *Doncaster Chronicle* reported that, to commemorate the reopening of this chapel after enlargement in 1844, a social tea was held in addition to the sermons. Over 200 persons sat down together, both people from the community and other Wesleyan Methodists from Doncaster.[46] A similarly large gathering occurred for the reopening of the Primitive Methodist Chapel at Stainforth in 1870. Around 300 people from across the Doncaster district were present, from Stainforth, the surrounding villages of Sykehouse, Fishlake and Hatfield Woodhouse, and from further afield: Doncaster,

---

40 Hey, 'The pattern of non-conformity', p. 211.
41 Wolffe, *Yorkshire returns*, pp. 159–60; Larsen and Royle, *Archbishop Thomson's visitation returns*, p. 157.
42 Mingay, *Land and society*, p. 85.
43 TNA, RG 9/3524, CEB Fishlake and Stainforth, 1861. Labourers were generally more prominent in Primitive Methodism than in Methodism.
44 Wolffe, *Yorkshire returns*, p. 159.
45 *Doncaster Chronicle*, 4 October 1844, p. 5; *Doncaster Chronicle*, 8 July 1870, p. 5; Wolffe, *Yorkshire returns*, p. 159.
46 *Doncaster Chronicle*, 4 October 1844, p. 5.

Thorne, Balby, Mexborough, Conisborough and Epworth – demonstrating the spheres of influence and interconnections at play. Open-air services were accompanied by a variety of rural sports, and a large marquee, with tea and a bazaar, was run by ladies from the parish.[47] Such events brought communities together, as well as indicating their independent identities.

Even at Braithwell, a multi-freeholder village with just one small Wesleyan Methodist chapel (erected in 1800), dissent was perceived as a problem by the Anglican Church.[48] The Anglican incumbent considered nonconformity to be the greatest impediment to the Anglican ministry, and talked of the 'antagonistic influence of Methodism'. His response was pastoral visiting and sympathy, which he felt occasionally brought people to church.[49] In fact, non-attendance was the real problem at Braithwell, with twice as many people absent from any place of worship than attending nonconformist services.

Contrasting experiences of religion were undoubtedly a feature of rural communities in the Doncaster district. The Anglican Church had greater presence and attendance in the estate villages, whereas nonconformity was more prevalent in multi-freeholder villages. However, this categorisation of estate and multi-freeholder villages conceals the variation in and complexities of religious provision and attendance. Differentiation was evident between estate villages with and without resident landowners, for example. The economic composition of a rural community, too, had a pronounced impact on its religious diversity. A greater proliferation of nonconformity within a village was associated with a more diverse occupational structure. Nonconformity and dissent were frequently cited as impacting negatively upon Anglican attendance, but the perception was often stronger than the reality, especially in estate villages. Non-attendance at either church or chapel was common among the labouring population in both multi-freeholder and estate villages; whether labourers were working, dissatisfied with authority, lived a long way from a place of worship or were distracted by the nearby market town remains a matter for speculation.

Education

Until the 1870 Education Act, which made it compulsory to provide elementary education to children aged between 5 and 13 in England and Wales, and the subsequent 1880 Education Act, which made school attendance compulsory between the ages of 5 and 10, provision of and attendance at schools were sporadic. The 1833 Factory Act had stated that children under nine should not work and that employers must have an age certificate for their child workers, while those children who did work should receive two hours' schooling each day. This was not always implemented, however, and did not apply to children working in agriculture.

Many Victorian village schools originated from collaborations between the Anglican Church and landowners. The National Society for Promoting the Education

---

47 *Doncaster Chronicle*, 8 July 1870, p. 5.
48 It was erected of stone in 1800, and included a gallery.
49 Larsen and Royle, *Archbishop Thomson's visitation returns*, p. 64.

Religion and education

of the Poor in the Principles of the Established Church throughout England and Wales was founded in 1811, and established National Schools.[50] Earlier endowed schools also often became National Schools during the nineteenth century. By 1851, 80 per cent of elementary day schools were connected with the Anglican Church.[51] Concurrently, the British and Foreign Society, established in 1814, offered educational provision that represented nonconformist interests. This chapter now examines the provision of, and participation in, education in rural communities of the Doncaster district.

The closely intertwined relationship between landownership and the Church was also evident in educational provision in the Doncaster region. The earliest village schools in the locale, such as those at Rossington, Fishlake and Braithwell, were endowed. Such schools were so called because they were endowed with income, land or property by a wealthy benefactor – often a landowner or the clergy – which paid for or contributed to the running costs. Endowed and grammar schools were the subject of the Schools Inquiry Commission in 1868, which aimed to determine the extent to which these schools fulfilled the purpose for which they had been founded and served the evolving needs of the rural communities in which they were located.[52] The commissioners observed that Rossington and Fishlake were among a handful of endowed schools in the northern counties that 'furnish the only means of education in a parish or village'.[53]

Nevertheless, a strong link existed between these two schools and the Anglican Church and clergy, and by the 1860s they had adopted many of the characteristics of a National School. The free school at Rossington was founded in the mid-seventeenth century by a wealthy clergyman, the Revd William Plaxton, and was endowed with farmland. By the nineteenth century Doncaster Corporation also provided support for and maintained the school until the Brown family purchased the estate in 1838, after which the Browns provided additional financial support. The free school was located in Littleworth Lane, a short distance from the centre of the village, and although plans to relocate it to a more central location with scope to expand were discussed from the late eighteenth century it was not until the mid-nineteenth century that this occurred. In 1857 Brown erected a new village schoolroom, with an accompanying house for the school teachers, adjacent to the church.[54] The brick-built school, with mock timber framing (Figure 5.3), was aesthetically integrated with the estate rebuilding taking place at that time, and was described as 'a picturesque and substantial schoolroom' in the 1867–8 Royal Commission on Education.[55] The school still operated under

---

50 T.W. Bamford, *The evolution of rural education 1850–1964* (Hull, 1965), pp. 10–13; Larsen and Royle, *Archbishop Thomson's visitation returns*, xliii.
51 Larsen and Royle, *Archbishop Thomson's visitation returns*, p. xliii.
52 PP 1868, *Schools Inquiry Commission*, Vol. IX, General Reports of Assistant Commissioners, Northern Counties, pp. v–ix. This Commission led to the Endowed Schools Act of 1869, which restructured endowed grammar schools.
53 *Ibid.*, p. 216.
54 Kelly, *Post Office directory, 1877*, p. 785.
55 PP 1869, *School Inquiry Commission*, Vol. XVIII, Yorkshire, p. 226.

Communities in Contrast

Figure 5.3 Rossington school (author's own picture).

its endowment at this point, but its relocation was symbolic of an educational transformation, and by 1877 it was described as a church school.

The endowed grammar school at Fishlake was founded in 1640 by the Revd Richard Randes (who was born in Fishlake but by then was incumbent of the parish of Hartfield, in Sussex), who gave £300 for this purpose. This was invested in land, the return from which provided funds to build the school, maintain it and pay the schoolmaster. By 1868 the Royal Commission noted that Fishlake school had 'long ceased to be a grammar school', with Latin no longer taught, and had virtually become a National School.[56] This was facilitated by the Revd Ornsby, who was proactive in promoting education in Fishlake during his incumbency (1850–86) and supported the construction of an additional brick classroom in 1874, which expanded educational provision in the parish. The local press reported that Ornsby 'takes great interest in the school', while the Royal Commission observed that he 'evinces a great interest in the improvement of the school'.[57]

At Braithwell John Bosvile, a local landowner, founded the free school in 1693, again supported by a number of endowments of land. An inscription over the door and the family coat of arms over the fireplace offered a reminder of the school's dependence on his patronage. Members of the Bosvile family still owned land in

---

[56] PP 1868, *Schools Inquiry Commission*, Vol. IX, General Reports by Assistant Commissioners, Northern Counties, p. 86.

[57] Ibid.; *Doncaster Chronicle*, 5 April 1867, p. 5.

Braithwell in the nineteenth century, and other members of the family continued to donate money to the school during the early nineteenth century. The school building was expanded in 1826 as a result of the combined efforts of the Bosvile family, other local landowners, the schoolmaster and local residents. It was enlarged again in 1871 in response to the 1870 Education Act, when it became a National School, with the construction of a new schoolroom and the conversion of the old one to the schoolmaster's house.[58] At a public meeting to mark the opening of the new school the incumbent, the Revd C. Hodgson, impressed upon landowners and occupiers alike that they were expected by the government not only to provide the school building but also to 'support and sustain sufficient, efficient and suitable teaching', and that they would be compelled to do so if they did not.[59] He also appealed to parents to send their children to school and for employees to not employ children under 12 without a certificate of school attendance confirming that they could read, write and do simple sums, as they too would eventually be compelled by legislation.

Sprotbrough, Warmsworth and Stainforth acquired purpose-built schools only during the mid-nineteenth century. These relied not only on the National Society but also on landowners and local benefactors. William Aldam erected a school at Warmsworth in 1831, at a cost of £500, which he continued to support thereafter.[60] The *Doncaster Chronicle* noted that his daughter Miss Aldam took 'a warm interest in its prosperity and success, and frequently applies, very assiduously, many an hour to the culture of the children'.[61] The Aldams' domination of educational provision in the village occurred in spite of the Battie-Wrightson family owning the largest proportion of land at Warmsworth and being active in promoting education and the National Society throughout the Doncaster district. At Warmsworth, children made penny payments each week and the school was well attended, with many scholars being drawn from neighbouring communities.[62]

Other local landowners also responded positively to the impetus to expand educational provision in the countryside. The Copleys supported the construction of schools in both Sprotbrough and Cadeby and the payment of salaries to teaching staff. The initial impetus for this appears to have been a response to wider societal concerns about deficiencies in educational provision in the Doncaster district. A meeting of the Doncaster Board of Education in 1839 reported the difficulty of getting scholars into Sunday School on account of a lack of purpose-built school accommodation, noting that it was desirous to build a schoolroom at Sprotbrough and provide a master and mistress to manage the school.[63] The schoolroom at Sprotbrough opened in 1840. Nevertheless,

---

58 N. Hawker and L.A. Pugh, *A goodly heritage: a history of the parish of Braithwell and Micklebring through the millennium* (Doncaster, 2000); *Doncaster Chronicle*, 14 July 1871, p. 8; Kelly, *Post Office directory, 1877*, p. 217.
59 *Doncaster Chronicle*, 14 July 1871, p. 8.
60 *Doncaster Chronicle*, 14 November 1839, p. 6; Hatfield, *Hints to pedestrians*, p. 157.
61 *Doncaster Chronicle*, 14 November 1839, p. 6.
62 PP 1835, *Education enquiry: abstract of answers and returns*, Vol. 1, p. 1201; *Doncaster Chronicle*, 16 November 1839, p. 6.
63 *Doncaster Chronicle*, 16 November 1839, p. 6.

concerns about educational provision throughout the Doncaster district continued to surface. In 1843 a meeting of the Doncaster National Society argued that the 'present accommodation is far from adequate to the efficient discharge of the increased duties of the schools' and emphasised the need for 'benevolence and generosity'.[64] Copley, however, continued to maintain an interest in education in the district and to support the school at Sprotbrough, and in response to the 1870 Education Act, anxious to maintain his influence on local education, Copley not only expanded the school at Sprotbrough but also constructed a new school at Cadeby in 1872.

In the multi-freeholder village of Stainforth local benefactors supplemented an endowment that supported a school. In the 1830s Mr Traver's charity continued to provide £15 per year for 14 children to be instructed. In addition, a donation of £2 8s per year from the Hon. J. Simpson paid for six more, while further children were taught at the expense of their parents.[65] The vicar of Thorne, the Revd G. Jennings, expressed his satisfaction at the condition of this school when he inspected it in 1867.[66]

The close alliance between village education and the Church was also evident in the employment of the teaching staff. Under the National System, teachers were required to be established members of the Anglican Church and familiar with the National Society's system of tuition. An advert for a schoolmaster and mistress for the newly erected school at Wadworth near Doncaster in 1841 stated a preference for a married couple who were members of the established church,[67] as did one for the post of schoolmaster at Fishlake in 1854.[68] Fishlake was an endowed school, bound by the trustees to elect a graduate of either Oxford or Cambridge University. However, the trustees were determined to dispense with this rule from 1854 and it was considered obsolete by 1868.[69]

The nature of the education offered varied, with differences in what was taught relating predominantly to the foundation of school and the changing needs of the community, rather than the type of village and concentration of landownership. The foundation of Fishlake school had stipulated that children be taught the rudiments of Latin, but the 1867–8 Commission noted that the 1827 commissioners had already reported a shift in the nature of education offered at Fishlake. The master had initially instructed a small number of boys in Latin, but from the mid-nineteenth century Henry Brooks provided a non-classical education, teaching reading, writing and accounts.[70]

The school had also begun to admit girls, but no adjustments had been made to the curriculum to accommodate female scholars. The Schools Inquiry Commission

---

64 *Doncaster Chronicle*, 13 January 1843, p. 5.
65 PP 1835, *Education enquiry: abstract of answers and returns*, Vol. 1, p. 1169.
66 *Doncaster Chronicle*, 5 April 1867, p. 5.
67 *Doncaster Chronicle*, 27 February 1841, p. 1.
68 *Doncaster Chronicle*, 5 May 1854, p. 1.
69 PP 1868, *Schools Inquiry Commission*, Vol. IX, General Reports of Assistant Commissioners, Northern Counties, p. 135; PP 1869, *Schools Inquiry Commission*, Vol. XVIII, Yorkshire, Special Reports of Assistant Commissioners, p. 340.
70 PP 1869, *Schools Inquiry Commission*, Vol. XVIII, Yorkshire, Special Reports of Assistant Commissioners, pp. 86–7.

Religion and education

noted the need for sewing and other domestic crafts to be taught for girls.[71] On examining the children, the commissioners found that 'they had been carefully instructed in the humbler rudiments; and that the general attainments, though not high, or characterized by much intelligence, were of a useful and respectable kind'.[72]

The clergy of Sprotbrough, Warmsworth and Fishlake emphasised a link between education, social order and social mobility. The 'cleanly state' of the school buildings and grounds at Warmsworth was considered to be 'sufficiently indicative of the order and propriety with which the school is conducted'.[73] According to the Revd Fardell, parents of children attending Sprotbrough School spoke of how their children had become 'cleanly, teachable, orderly and obedient', and he felt that the lessons learnt at school were disseminated through society.[74] The ability to influence the wider rural community through the village school was desirable in the eyes of rural elites, who were keen to uphold social order and encourage a deferential society. The clergy also suggested that there was no resistance to their endeavours, arguing that parents were favourably inclined to send their children to school. Indeed, the Revd Surtees, incumbent of Sprotbrough in the 1860s, stated that, 'With regard to the education of boys, there is no disinclination of parents, quite the reverse, to have their children taught, nor do the farmers set themselves against it.'[75]

Prize-giving ceremonies were used to cultivate a sense of pride in achievement and to impress upon young people the importance of making good use of their knowledge and skills. In some villages, such as Warmsworth, this was taken a step further by the clergy, who urged people to take advantage of the other facilities for learning, in the form of the Sunday and evening schools.[76] The public expression of achievements, through annual examinations to which parents and others were invited, was reported in the local newspapers and was evidently important in these communities.[77] The clergy and school teachers took a lead in organising and promoting these events in both estate and multi-freeholder villages. At Fishlake in 1857, for example, it was noted that the children performed well, especially in key subjects such as scripture and arithmetic, and that many parents were present at the examinations. The Revd Ornsby of Fishlake said that, through the giving of prizes, it was hoped that children would value 'their industry in youth' and he used these occasions as opportunities to encourage them to 'continue in perseverance and good behaviour through the whole course of their lives'.[78] This suggests that the ideals of social order and good social conduct were as important to multi-freeholder communities as to estate villages, and were championed by the clergy.

---

71 Ibid., p. 86.
72 Ibid.
73 Hatfield, *Hints for pedestrians*, p. 157.
74 Fardell, *Sprotbrough*.
75 PP 1867–8, XVII, *First report of the Commission on the Employment of Children, Young Persons, and Women in Agriculture 1867*, p. 399 – letter from the Rev. Scott Surtees of Sprotbrough to Hon. E Portman (15 May 1868).
76 *Doncaster Chronicle*, 3 February 1871, p. 5.
77 *Doncaster Chronicle*, 27 February 1857, p. 5.
78 Ibid.

There is limited evidence regarding attendance at schools in the six case-study villages, and whether or not the rural elites were successful in their efforts to get children to attend school. Children were not always accurately returned in the CEBs as 'scholars' and even if they were attending a school it may have been outside the parish; attendance may also have been irregular.[79] Nevertheless, evidence for scholars in the census indicates the occupational background of at least some of those who sent their children to school. At Warmsworth and Rossington the majority of parents with children designated as scholars were agricultural labourers, whereas at Sprotbrough they were farmers.[80] The occupations of scholars' parents in Stainforth was more diverse, with boat hauliers, mariners and sailors listed alongside the most usual farmers and agricultural labourers. The 1869 Schools Inquiry Commission also provides information about school attendance. At Fishlake the children of farmers, artisans and labourers from within a two-mile radius attended the village school.[81] At Braithwell, a large proportion of those attending the village school were the children of labourers, who were taught alongside the children of farmers and trades and crafts people.[82] In some instances, evidence demonstrates that children were educated outside the village where their family lived. For instance, the son of a miller from Sprotbrough attended Doncaster Grammar School. He was highlighted in the Royal Commission on Education (Yorkshire) for poor levels of attainment, unfortunately falling within the lowest ten students in the school.[83]

The survival of admission registers and log books is sporadic for schools in the Doncaster district during the mid-nineteenth century, and yet, combined with evidence from newspapers and the commissioners' reports, it is possible to gauge comparative educational provision and attendance in the villages around Doncaster. A number of schoolmasters in the district highlighted the difficulty of enforcing attendance. Of 60 scholars on the books at Fishlake, 44 were present on the day of the commissioners' visit (29 boys and 15 girls). The schoolmaster testified that he had 'great difficulty in enforcing the attendance of free scholars, whose parents seem to set a lower value on their instruction than the parents of paying children'.[84]

The role of child labour in agriculture impeded school attendance, especially at certain times of the year. The incumbent of Braithwell, for example, stated that in a 'small agricultural parish composed principally of poor people, the children at

---

79 E. Higgs, *A clearer sense of the census* (London, 1996), p. 102.
80 TNA, HO 107/2346, CEB Sprotbrough 1851; HO 107/2346, CEB Warmsworth 1851; HO 107/2348, CEB Rossington 1851; RG 9/3514, CEB Warmsworth 1861; RG 9/3516, CEB Sprotbrough 1861; RG 9/3522, CEB Rossington 1861; RG 10/4715, CEB Warmsworth 1871; RG 10/4716, CEB Sprotbrough 1871; RG 10/4724, CEB Rossington 1871.
81 PP 1869, *Schools Inquiry Commission*, Vol. XVIII, Yorkshire, Special Reports of Assistant Commissioners, p. 87.
82 DA, P71/8/1, *Admission register of Town School at Braithwell*, 1867–1877.
83 PP 1869, *Schools Inquiry Commission*, Vol. XVIII, Yorkshire, Special Reports of Assistant Commissioners, p. 75.
84 *Ibid.*, pp. 86–7.

Religion and education

an early age are sent out to the towns or farm service'.[85] While 47 children regularly attended the school in the winter, only 35 did in the summer, and the school log book specifically recorded high levels of absence as a result of children doing agricultural work at certain times of the year. For example, in May 1872 it was noted that 'several boys away from school this week on account of their parents sending them to work in the fields'.[86] Similarly, at Fishlake, the incumbent stated that attendance at the village school was far greater when children were not required for agricultural labour.[87] In both instances they were unable to retain students at Sunday school after they left day school because of employment patterns.[88] The establishment of evening schools in rural communities was thus a response to the socio-economic impediments to daytime education. The one at Warmsworth was considered a success, with some male scholars attending an evening school three days a week in winters until the age of 20 and some female students engaged in sewing and reading classes during the summer before they entered domestic service.[89]

Debates during the nineteenth century about the education of children in rural communities paid close attention to their employment in agriculture. It was argued that introducing either recommended or obligatory attendance and/or certification would impact negatively on farmers and farming, as it would limit the availability of children (a relatively cheap source of labour) to work on the land. Without limitations on the age at which children should undertake paid farm work, however, attendance at school was hard to enforce. The 1867–8 Commission regarding the employment of women and children in agriculture included a discussion of proposed schemes to educate agricultural children. Mr Portman, assistant commissioner reporting on Yorkshire, argued

> The most feasible plan for obtaining continuous education appears to be to fix an age below which no child shall go to work for hire, with or without compulsory attendance at school, to require a certain amount of school attendance from that age to 13 or 14 years of age, and perhaps, in addition, the production of a certificate of such school attendance before hiring. Very few objections will be found to this plan, with the exception of the certificate, but I think that when a good system of registering, which might be combined with a register for farm servants, is once established, the supposed difficulties and inconveniences will soon vanish.[90]

Support for similar schemes came from the Doncaster district. James Brown, a landowner at Rossington, argued that children should not be permitted to work

---

85 Larsen and Royle, *Archbishop Thomson's visitation returns*, p. 64.
86 DA, P71/8/2, *Log book of National School, Braithwell*, 1871–1910.
87 Larsen and Royle, *Archbishop Thomson's visitation returns*, p. 157.
88 Larsen and Royle, *Archbishop Thomson's visitation returns*.
89 *Ibid.*; Wolffe, *Yorkshire returns*.
90 PP 1867–8, XVII, *First report of the Commission on the Employment of Children, Young Persons, and Women in Agriculture 1867*, p. liii.

regularly on the land until they were 12 years old and had a certificate of school attendance. Taking into account the agricultural calendar, he added that 'All children should attend school pretty regularly from the beginning of November till the latter part of March till they are 13 years old. In April, May and June they can be usefully employed in field labour; in July they may again attend school until harvest.'[91] The incumbent of Warmsworth, the Revd Thomas, similarly recommended that attendance at school be enforced during the winter months and also advocated limiting the age at which children worked on the land, stating

> I would not allow boys to go to work at all before 8 years of age, and not regularly before 13. No child under 13 should work more than eight hours a day. I would recommend that an endeavour be made to enforce attendance at school during the six winter months, i.e. from October to March.[92]

William Aldam, of Frickley and Warmsworth, also supported a specified duration for school attendance. He argued that

> The principal of education embodied in the Factory Acts might be conveniently carried out in agriculture by requiring each child, as the condition of his being allowed to be employed, to have a certificate of the requisite school attendance in the previous year, such certificate being necessary up to 13 years of age, so as to secure school attendance up to 12 years.

With specific reference to Warmsworth, Aldam observed that, while a good school existed, 'Parents are not always careful to send their children to school, and I think the stimulus of a certificate would be useful.'[93]

Mr Portman's report regarding Yorkshire did recognise, however, that the loss of child labour on small farms could be serious, as 'they are too poor to hire labour, and the assistance rendered by a child of 8 or 9 years of age is of great value'.[94] Within the Doncaster district there was some resistance to aspects of the proposed changes – particularly the half or alternate day system (introduced for child labour in factories whereby children would work for half a day and attend school for half a day or work one day and go to school the next), on account of its being incompatible with the requirements of agriculture. William Law, a farmer from Braithwell, argued such a system 'could not be worked'.[95] C.T. Ward, a farmer from Cadeby, similarly stated that

> Children of average age of 10 years are employed in agriculture, and I do not consider such employment injurious, either to health or morals. As a rule it is not necessary to place any restriction. Half days or alternate days at school and

---

91 *Ibid.*, p. 395.
92 *Ibid.*, p. 402.
93 *Ibid.*, p. 395.
94 *Ibid.*, p. liii.
95 *Ibid.*

work are impossible. Six months' school attendance during the year might be required, but it would not be desirable to require the production at hiring of a certificate of such attendance.[96]

Thomas Wood (Sprotbrough) and James Brown (Rossington) also argued that half or alternate days would not work and were not desirable.[97] John Bladworth (Stainforth) stated that 'the farmer must have them altogether or not at all; the winter months might be devoted to education'.[98]

School attendance was also affected by parents' economic circumstances and attitudes. The same John Bladworth asserted that 'school attendance is affected in some cases by the pecuniary resources of the parent, and a man with a large family cannot spare the elder ones for school as he requires their services for the support of the family', and that, while free education might be provided in Fishlake parish, 'the population is the most ignorant in the district'.[99] To illustrate the resistance to education on the part of some farming and labouring families, he described how he had offered to send his shepherd's child to school for free. The shepherd had declined, as his son earned 5s a week in light work, and argued that bread was better than learning. Even when challenged with the fact he might soon be compelled to send his children to school until they had reached a certain age, the shepherd expressed his hope that it would not be for a couple of years, as he had a large family to support. Bladworth went on:

> The working classes, generally speaking, do not properly appreciate education, and the man with large family cannot afford, even if he felt inclined, to send his children to school. And unless some provision was made to meet the latter case, and a compulsory attendance at school for a given time [imposed] on all classes of the poor, any prohibitory labour enactment with a view to education would be inoperative, and fail to secure the object aimed at.[100]

The provision of and participation in education varied in the rural communities of the Doncaster district. While landowners provided and supported schools in these villages, these actions were often in response to external stimuli such as the 1870 Education Act and the commissions into educational provision that preceded it. Moreover, many of the early schools in both estate and multi-freeholder communities were endowed by wealthy benefactors. Rural elites, predominantly landowners and the clergy, promoted village schools, and yet concerns over low attendance were found in both estate and multi-freeholder communities. The rural economy, principally in terms of the employment of children in agriculture, undermined attempts to compel young people to attend school. Even following educational legislation in 1870, rural communities had to balance the demands of agriculture with the legal requirement to educate their children.

---

96 *Ibid.*, p. 397.
97 *Ibid.*, p. 396.
98 *Ibid.*, p. 401.
99 *Ibid.*
100 *Ibid.*

Conclusion

Religion and education in the rural communities of the Doncaster district were closely intertwined, and yet patterns of provision and attendance of each varied. Superficially, the provision of and participation in religion could be delineated in accordance with village type. This conceals important variations between and within communities, however, and, significantly, common challenges and concerns that were shared in estate and multi-freeholder communities alike. The contrast in education between village types was less distinct, as the availability of schooling depended more on endowments and the National Society than on concentrated landownership. Religion and education were an integral part of rural communities in the mid-nineteenth century, and religious and educational institutions had a powerful impact on how and why rural communities developed. Both were closely interlinked with historical determinants and rural elites in the community, and with external stimuli. Alongside landowners, the church, chapel or school, and the clergy and school teachers, were also integral to the provision of recreation in some rural communities, and it is to this subject that we now turn.

Chapter 6

Rural recreation

Life in the Victorian countryside was not merely about work, religion or education. Recreational and cultural activities were integral aspects of rural society, and as such should be central to understanding how and why rural communities developed. This chapter explores the extent to which the experience of rural recreation and culture in the Doncaster district was different in estate and multi-freeholder villages, and whether this was determined exclusively by landownership. It focuses on who provided, facilitated and participated in rural recreation; what activities were undertaken; and where these took place. The relationship between recreation and other aspects of country life, including work, religion and education, is also considered. It is argued that agency extended beyond landowners, and the role of other rural elites (the clergy, school teachers and farmers) and of labourers is examined, emphasising their status as 'active participants'.

Landowners have, as with other aspects of rural life, been placed at the heart of recreational and cultural provision in the Victorian countryside. Historians such as Hugh Cunningham and Alun Howkins have argued that landowners attempted to revive paternalism and recreate a sense of community through leisure and culture, but in the process sought to repress popular culture and impose more rational forms of entertainment.[1] Rational recreation was a middle-class ideal that sought to control and improve the leisure activities of the labouring population.[2] The emphasis was on self-improvement and abstinence, although not necessarily at the expense of entertainment. In rural communities, rational recreation could take the form of educational lectures, organised sports, choral music, horticultural shows or village feasts. Recreation could also be a tool for exerting social control more generally.[3] Landowners were certainly in a position, both socially and financially, to organise grand social events, to coerce tenants into attending them and to attract media publicity to showcase their paternalistic efforts, ensuring that these events were recorded for posterity. However, not all landowners were actively engaged in this process, and they were certainly not the only agents. They often acted in conjunction with the clergy, schoolmasters/mistresses or farmers, demonstrating the importance of leadership and collaboration above patterns of landownership. The clergy's role in recreation not only transcended that of landownership but also consolidated their moral and social duties in both estate and multi-freeholder villages.

---

1. H. Cunningham, *Leisure in the industrial revolution, c.1780–c.1880* (London, 1980), p. 122; A. Howkins, 'Social, cultural and domestic life', in E.J.T. Collins (ed.), *The agrarian history of England and Wales*, Vol. VII, 1850–1914, Part II (Cambridge, 2000), pp. 1402–4, 1407–8.
2. P. Bailey, '"Rational recreation": the social control of leisure and popular culture in Victorian England, 1830–1885', PhD thesis (University of British Columbia, 1974); P. Bailey, *Leisure and class in Victorian England: rational recreation and the contest for control, 1830–1885* (London, 1978).
3. Mills, *Lord and peasant*, pp. 125–8.

The location and nature of recreational opportunities are also important in explaining patterns of recreational provision and participation. The use of existing cultural sites, especially the church, chapel or school, that were closely aligned with authority was an effective way in which landowners and clergy could reinforce deference and social and moral control. Appropriating these sites for recreational purposes, rather than using purpose-built village halls, to some extent influenced the scope and tone of recreation, but could also strengthen community cohesion by expanding the cultural remit of these familiar institutions.

Recreational provision in the rural communities of the Doncaster district, both estate and multi-freeholder, was to a large extent self-improving in nature. It was an integral part of the agenda of order and harmony espoused by landowners and the clergy. Such activities ranged from lectures and church choirs to entertainments for children, but all were underpinned by an underlying tone of morality and self-improvement. A series of lectures held at Fishlake school in the 1860s had the explicit objective of providing working people with 'the means of acquiring sound, useful and entertaining information ... with a view of cultivating a taste for mental recreation, of heightening their enjoyment and of elevating their social condition'.[4] The lectures were also a means of fundraising, with collections going to the speaker's nominated cause and to the school for examination prizes.

Choirs were established in estate and multi-freeholder villages in the Doncaster district, including in Sprotbrough and Warmsworth under the patronage of the landowners, but also at Stainforth and Fishlake.[5] In addition to providing the desired 'harmonious music in the church', choirs in estate villages were symptomatic of landowners' desire to weave the thread of harmony through the fabric of the rural community. Choir members tended to be self-selecting, but audiences were drawn from a wider cross section of the rural community. This was particularly the case where concerts were staged to raise money for a cause such as the victims of the Sheffield Flood in 1864, or when secular music was performed alongside the sacred.[6] To accommodate enlarged audiences and enable them to see and hear the performances fully, Sir Joseph William Copley funded a gallery in the schoolroom at Sprotbrough.[7] Village choirs also facilitated the interaction of inhabitants from different rural communities or the town. The Doncaster Choral Union Festival, established in 1863, for example, welcomed choirs from Warmsworth, Stainforth and Fishlake.[8]

Activities arranged by the clergy for local children were more entertaining in nature, and the available evidence suggests that the participants enjoyed them. The Revd J.G. Fardell organised the annual National School feast at Sprotbrough in 1844, at which

---

4 *Doncaster Chronicle*, 21 February 1868, p. 5; *Doncaster Chronicle*, 11 June 1869, p. 5; *Doncaster Chronicle*, 17 December 1869, p. 5.
5 *Doncaster Chronicle*, 9 January 1863, p. 5; *Doncaster Chronicle*, 5 February 1863, p. 5; *Doncaster Chronicle*, 5 February 1868, p. 5; *Doncaster Chronicle*, 9 April 1869, p. 5; *Doncaster Chronicle*, 20 January 1870, p. 5.
6 *Doncaster Chronicle*, 29 April 1864, p. 5; *Doncaster Chronicle*, 9 April 1869, p. 5.
7 *Doncaster Chronicle*, 6 May 1864, p. 5.
8 *Doncaster Gazette*, 5 June 1873, p. 5; *Sheffield Telegraph*, 6 June 1873, p. 4.

the children were entertained and provided with tea, cake and fruit.[9] The children of Warmsworth were invited to the Revd C.E. Thomas' home in December 1867, where they gathered around the Christmas tree and were given a prize, sweetmeats and other treats.[10] Similarly, at Fishlake in 1856 the Revd Ornsby invited village children to enjoy food and games and welcomed children from Thorne workhouse to partake in games, tea and cake.[11] Local newspaper reports suggest that the children enjoyed these events: 'The happy faces of the children testified the pleasure they felt, and their hearty cheers while leaving the grounds told of their gratitude for this great annual treat.'[12]

Nevertheless, such events were still underpinned by concerns about morality, authority and control, whether in estate or multi-freeholder villages. The use of processions was symbolic of the authority of both landowners and clergy, and provided a physical reinforcement of this. The processions placed great emphasis on order, leadership and hierarchy, and were carefully planned to start and finish at key institutions of authority. Children in both Sprotbrough and Fishlake paraded on foot through the village from the school to the rectory as part of entertainments provided. At Sprotbrough, it was reported of the children that 'Their neat attire and becoming deportment could not fail to elicit the delight and gratification of the inhabitants.'[13] Such occasions also featured toasts to the landowner and/or incumbent of the village, and at Sprotbrough the Revd J.G. Fardell delivered a speech impressing upon them the importance of attending school.[14] Under the guise of recreation and leisure, landowners and the clergy were able to assert their agency and instil social order in the inhabitants. This was partially responsible for creating passive recipients who conformed to patterns of deference. It did not, however, preclude people from enjoying themselves or becoming active participants in some of the prescribed, 'rational' activities organised by rural elites. Nor were all recreational opportunities of an explicitly improving nature.

The public house, often at the heart of village society, was a more contested space, being both the subject of moral reform and the home of organised recreational activities. Landowners had an equivocal relationship with pubs on their estates, and in the Doncaster district fewer were located in estate villages than in their multi-freeholder counterparts. Alcohol was frequently blamed for social evils in the Victorian era, with moral opposition to alcohol consumption and the rise of the temperance movement coupled with concerns about social order and productivity.[15] Drunkenness was associated with the labouring classes and was blamed for crime, disease and illness, especially within urban areas.[16] Landowners in the Doncaster district retained tight control over pubs and were responsive to problems and tensions. For example, a series of drunken incidents at Sprotbrough, culminating in a man drowning in 1857,

---

9   *Doncaster Chronicle*, 7 August 1844, p. 4.
10 *Doncaster Chronicle*, 5 February 1868, p. 5.
11 *Doncaster Chronicle*, 30 May 1856, p. 5.
12 *Doncaster Chronicle*, 11 February 1870, p. 5.
13 *Doncaster Gazette*, 15 August 1845, p. 5.
14 *Doncaster Gazette*, 9 August 1844, p. 4.
15 B. Harrison, *Drink and the Victorians: the temperance question in England 1815–1872* (London, 1971).
16 *Sheffield Independent*, 5 January 1850, p. 2.

Communities in Contrast

Figure 6.1 Sprotbrough pub (author's own picture).

resulted in the pub's licence being revoked shortly after.[17] Limitations were placed upon licensed premises, with an application for extended opening by the landlord of the Moon Inn, Carcroft, denied on the grounds that 'extensions had never been granted for small villages. Ten o'clock was long enough for the inns to be open … '.[18]

Nevertheless, public houses performed an important social role. The Sprotbrough annual subscription ball was held at the village pub (Figure 6.1), and both the event and the physical infrastructure of the pub bore the hallmarks of concentrated landownership. The speeches and toasts to the family coat of arms adorning the building demonstrate how the Copley family were at the heart of this event – and, equally, they dominated its subsequent media coverage. The ball, a lavish affair, with music, decorations and food, was held in the large function room in the pub, which was described as 'brilliantly illuminated, and tastefully decorated with evergreens and flowers'.[19] A local band provided music to accompany the dancing. The ball brought together tenants and employees from the estate, while members of the social elite from across the district paid a subscription fee to attend. This event, and others like it, fostered social interaction within a controlled environment, albeit one that essentially reinforced the hierarchical structure of the countryside and its deferential relationships.

Far more pubs and beer houses were located in the multi-freeholder communities of the Doncaster district, forming the basis of an informal network of rural recreation. While there is little evidence to suggest that this led to excessive drink-related incidents, the temperance movement had a presence in some of these villages

---

17 *Sheffield Daily Telegraph*, 27 July 1857, p. 3; Holland, *Sprotbrough*, p. 61.
18 *Sheffield Independent*, 15 July 1895, p. 8.
19 *Doncaster Gazette*, 7 January 1853, p. 5.

and attempted to impose alternative recreational activities. At Fishlake an annual temperance festival was held in the village Temperance Hall, although the low attendance led contemporary accounts to question the popularity of the event.[20]

Recreational activities or social occasions that occupied communal or open spaces, such as fields or the whole village, provided opportunities to create a sense of belonging within rural communities, and in some instances allowed labourers to exert more agency. Cricket played an important role in Victorian society, instilling a sense of 'Englishness' and perpetuating the social hierarchies of the nineteenth-century countryside. The landed gentry were confident of the inherent social value of cricket, and the sport was promoted as an acceptable and respectable form of recreation accordingly.[21] Between the 1850s and 1870s most villages in the vicinity of Doncaster had a cricket team supported by landowners and/ or the clergy.[22] In spite of elite patronage, the membership of these village cricket teams suggests that participation was socially and occupationally diverse. Teams in both estate and multi-freeholder villages were notably occupationally diverse, including farmers, agricultural labourers, tradesmen, craftsmen and domestic servants. A low turnover of team members was common, as was the presence of multiple members of the same family or household in teams.[23] The distance teams travelled to play one another and the types of village (estate or multi-freeholder) they played varied considerably. Both Rossington and Sprotbrough played within an insular geographical network, focused predominantly on other estate villages and sometimes limited to the parish, with teams representing the hall and village playing one another.[24] In contrast, the teams at Warmsworth, Braithwell and Fishlake played a wide range of different rural communities, both estate and multi-freeholder villages, across the district.[25]

---

20   *Doncaster Chronicle*, 12 April 1867, p. 5.
21   D. Allen, 'England's golden age: imperial cricket and late Victorian society', *Sport in Society: Cultures, Commerce, Media, Politics*, 15/2, (2012), pp. 210, 218.
22   P.L. Scowcroft, *Cricket in Doncaster and district: an outline history* (Doncaster, 1985), pp. 5–7.
23   *Doncaster Gazette*, 17 August 1849, p. 8; *Doncaster Chronicle*, 17 August 1855, p. 8; *Doncaster Chronicle*, 15 August 1856, p. 8; *Doncaster Chronicle*, 24 May 1861, p. 8; *Doncaster Chronicle*, 28 June 1861, p. 5; *Doncaster Chronicle*, 12 June 1863, p. 8; *Doncaster Chronicle*, 26 June 1863, p. 7; *Doncaster Chronicle*, 3 July 1863, p. 8; *Doncaster Chronicle*, 10 July 1863, p. 8; *Doncaster Chronicle*, 14 August 1863, p. 8; *Doncaster Chronicle*, 6 November 1863, p. 8; *Doncaster Chronicle*, 22 July 1864, p. 8; *Doncaster Chronicle*, 5 August 1864, p. 8; *Doncaster Chronicle*, 12 August 1864, p. 8; *Doncaster Gazette*, 11 July 1873, p. 8; TNA, HO 107/2346, CEB Sprotbrough 1851; HO 107/2346, CEB Warmsworth 1851; HO 107/2348, CEB Rossington 1851; HO 107/2346, CEB Braithwell 1851; HO 107/2349, CEB Fishlake and Stainforth 1851; RG 9/3516, CEB Sprotbrough 1861; RG 9/3514, CEB Warmsworth 1861; RG 9/3522, CEB Rossington 1861; RG 9/3513, CEB Braithwell 1861; RG 9/3524, CEB Fishlake and Stainforth 1861; RG 10/4716, CEB Sprotbrough 1871; RG 10/4715, CEB Warmsworth 1871; RG 10/4724, CEB Rossington 1871; RG 10/4714, CEB Braithwell 1871; RG 10/4726, CEB Fishlake and Stainforth 1871.
24   *Doncaster Chronicle*, 12 June 1863, p. 8; *Doncaster Chronicle*, 26 June 1863, p. 7; *Doncaster Chronicle*, 1 June 1854, p. 5; *Doncaster Chronicle*, 10 August 1866, p. 8; *Doncaster Chronicle*, 28 August 1866, p. 8.
25   *Doncaster Chronicle*, 2 September 1859, p. 6; *Doncaster Chronicle*, 3 July 1863, p. 8; *Doncaster Chronicle*, 7 August 1863, p. 8; *Doncaster Chronicle*, 5 August 1864, p. 8; *Doncaster Chronicle*, 12 August 1864, p. 8; *Doncaster Chronicle*, 30 June 1865, p. 8; *Doncaster Chronicle*, 18 August 1865, p. 8; *Doncaster Chronicle*, 5 July 1867, p. 8.

Communities in Contrast

The notion of creating or rediscovering a sense of community was evident in how villagers came together for national events. Rural communities across the Doncaster district shared in the celebrations of the Prince of Wales' marriage in 1863. Similar communal celebrations had taken place to mark other national events, including the marriage of Queen Victoria to Prince Albert in 1840. The impetus for and organisation of the celebrations in 1863 came from the rural elites – landowners, clergy and farmers. At Sprotbrough, the Copleys provided every cottage in the village with 'a substantial dinner, beer and tea', welcomed 200 inhabitants to the Hall, held a tea party for the children in the schoolroom and entertained their servants to a ball in the evening.[26] Although the Brown family oversaw the celebrations at Rossington, W.B. Tate and other principal farmers of the parish were responsible for putting them into action and providing each cottage with a 'good piece of beef and a pound of tea'.[27] In the absence of a principal landowner, the Revd Ornsby presided over celebrations at Fishlake. Despite being organised by rural elites, such events embodied a sense of community cohesion founded on active participation. The *Doncaster Chronicle* reported that, at Sprotbrough, 'everyone seemed to be up and doing' from an early hour, decorating the village with colourful flags.[28] Of Rossington, it was said that 'most people imagined an earthquake could scarcely move' the village and its inhabitants, and yet the celebrations had set both in motion 'without the aid of so very destructive a propeller'.[29] At Fishlake every inhabitant was invited to a subscription tea in the schoolroom, where 'adults, rich and poor, without distinction, sat down to eat'.[30] Sports, including pig racing and sack jumping, were also a prominent feature of the celebrations.

Village horticultural shows, although a form of rational recreation and another vehicle used by rural elites to promote social control, provided opportunities for tenants and labourers to become more active participants. While amateur gardening was an elite recreation during the nineteenth century, with landowners and principal farmers from the Doncaster district members of the Doncaster Horticultural Society, the social and economic benefits of gardening for the labouring population were also recognised.[31] The possession of a garden was highly valued, as discussed in chapter 4, and shows and prize-givings stimulated pride and diligence. The Warmsworth Cottagers' Horticultural Show, established by the Aldam family, aimed to make the Aldams' tenants more industrious and encouraged them to take pride in their community. The *Doncaster Chronicle* heralded the show as being exemplary, citing the improved order among tenants as being tangible in their homes and gardens.[32] Prizes of a practical nature, such as pans or blankets, were awarded for the best specimens of fruit, vegetables and

---

26 *Doncaster Chronicle*, 13 March 1863, p. 5.
27 Ibid.
28 Ibid.
29 Ibid., pp. 5, 8.
30 Ibid., p. 4.
31 S. Constantine, 'Amateur gardening and popular recreation in the nineteenth and twentieth centuries', *Journal of Social History*, 14/3 (1981), pp. 390–93.
32 *Doncaster Chronicle*, 22 July 1859, p. 5.

flowers.³³ The *Doncaster Gazette* wrote that 'of all societies established for the benefit of a rural population, there is none which can be more advantageous' than the Warmsworth Cottagers' Horticultural Society, while the *Doncaster Chronicle* reported that the shows it hosted were 'worthy of transcript in every village in the neighbourhood'.³⁴ Newspaper reports also observed that 'The benefits of such a society are already exhibiting themselves in the habits of industry and improved order established amongst the cottagers; and the considerate promoters of this society have the satisfaction of seeing their praise-worthy efforts crowned with success.'³⁵

Nevertheless, many participants enjoyed the process and the Warmsworth Show cultivated a genuine interest in gardening among the tenants and labourers. The very nature of the show necessitated individuals working independently towards a common goal. Each year, the profusion, variety and quality of specimens exhibited were acknowledged as testimony to the agency of the cottagers, who had taken 'ownership' of the show.³⁶ Moreover, participants came from a diverse range of occupational groups, including shopkeepers, crafts people, agricultural labourers and quarry workers. Whole family groups were involved, including women and children.³⁷ This inclusive nature extended the horticultural show from the schoolroom, where specimens were exhibited twice a year, to the gardens of each and every participant throughout the year.

The notion of the entire village as a cultural and recreational site was epitomised by the annual village 'feast'. These communal celebrations were usually organised in association with the church or school, but their physical 'openness', encompassing different spatial foci (including not only the church and school but also the village hall and open fields), fostered active participation and community identity, and in some instances facilitated the democratisation of rural recreation. The *Doncaster Chronicle* reported in 1855 that village inhabitants who would normally not mix with one another were 'friends not strangers' after the feast.³⁸ While this was perhaps an overly optimistic interpretation of rural relations, the feast irrefutably provided opportunities for positive

---

33 *Doncaster Chronicle*, 11 July 1845, p. 5; *Doncaster Chronicle*, 17 July 1863, p. 5.
34 *Doncaster Gazette*, 17 June 1842, p. 5; *Doncaster Chronicle*, 22 July 1859, p. 5.
35 *Doncaster Chronicle*, 11 July 1845, p. 5.
36 *Doncaster Chronicle*, 25 June 1852, p. 5; *Doncaster Chronicle*, 22 July 1859, p. 5; *Doncaster Chronicle*, 17 July 1863, p. 5.
37 *Doncaster Gazette*, 17 June 1842, p. 5; *Doncaster Gazette*, 2 August 1844, p. 4; *Doncaster Chronicle*, 11 July 1845, p. 5; *Doncaster Chronicle*, 7 June 1850, p. 5; *Doncaster Chronicle*, 25 June 1852, p. 5; *Doncaster Chronicle*, 8 September 1854, p. 5; *Doncaster Chronicle*, 22 August 1856, p. 5; *Doncaster Chronicle*, 22 July 1859, p. 5; *Doncaster Chronicle*, 21 June 1861, p. 5; *Doncaster Chronicle*, 17 July 1863, p. 5; TNA, HO 107/2346, CEB Sprotbrough 1851; HO 107/2346, CEB Warmsworth 1851; HO 107/2348, CEB Rossington 1851; HO 107/2346, CEB Braithwell 1851; HO 107/2349, CEB Fishlake and Stainforth 1851; RG 9/3516, CEB Sprotbrough 1861; RG 9/3514, CEB Warmsworth 1861; RG 9/3522, CEB Rossington 1861; RG 9/3513, CEB Braithwell 1861; RG 9/3524, CEB Fishlake and Stainforth 1861; RG 10/4716, CEB Sprotbrough 1871; RG 10/4715, CEB Warmsworth 1871; RG 10/4724, CEB Rossington 1871; RG 10/4714, CEB Braithwell 1871; RG 10/4726, CEB Fishlake and Stainforth 1871.
38 *Doncaster Chronicle*, 24 August 1855, p. 5.

social interaction. Residents had a vested interest in the village feast, not least because many were funded by subscription. It was therefore their day of pleasure and, as such, they endeavoured to make it successful and congenial. Moreover, in estate villages, estate employees often took responsibility for collecting subscriptions for the feast and for organising the programme. For instance, Messrs Sharp, Chandler and Ramsden (coachman, gardener and agricultural labourer respectively) organised the subscriptions and planned the Warmsworth Feast in 1870.[39]

The extent and diversity of entertainment, and thus the participation and agency of labourers, varied. For example, at Sprotbrough the village feast was restricted to a church service, choral performances, cricket and refreshments,[40] whereas entertainment featured much more strongly at the feasts in Warmsworth and Fishlake. Cricket, dancing, donkey racing, flat and hurdle racing, sack jumping and women's races characterised the entertainment at Warmsworth,[41] where, according to the *Doncaster Chronicle*, large numbers assembled to enjoy the entertainments; it was specifically noted that the annual festival 'was kept up with great spirit by the villagers', inferring agency on their part.[42] Similarly, the feast at Fishlake was dominated by athletic sports, side shows, merry-go-rounds, rifle galleries and a photo caravan, which attracted large numbers of people.[43] This difference between the types of entertainment offered was only partially attributable to patterns of landownership. The attitudes of the rural elites and the agency of the labouring population also came into play.

On occasion the village feast could become a contested space. Controversy erupted in 1869 over the donkey races at the Warmsworth Feast. Residents objected to 'practiced and well trained riders' from outside the village being permitted to compete without contributing to the subscription fund. On the surface, this may suggest that insular attitudes pervaded rural society, but it also reveals evidence of agency. The funding of the event by subscription instilled a sense of perceived ownership, and subscribers were thus gatekeepers of the event. It also suggests, perhaps, an uneasy relationship between some rural communities, especially as the influx of 'outsiders' was from nearby Balby, a newly industrialising community that was home to many of Doncaster's railway workers.

Doncaster

Beyond the village, rural inhabitants could access recreational and cultural opportunities in the neighbouring market town, with social occasions often partnering economic functions. Doncaster provided an extensive range of recreational opportunities and cultural venues, including the racecourse, fairs and circuses, pubs, theatres and railway excursions, which drew visitors from far and wide. The close proximity of the market town to the villages

---

39 *Doncaster Gazette*, 8 July 1870, p. 8; TNA, RG 9/3514, folio 44, CEB Warmsworth 1861, p. 6; RG 10/4715, folio 42, CEB Warmsworth 1871, p. 3; RG 10/4715, folio 44, CEB Warmsworth 1871, p. 8.
40 *Doncaster Chronicle*, 24 August 1855, p. 5.
41 *Doncaster Chronicle*, 16 July 1869, p. 5; *Doncaster Chronicle*, 15 July 1870, p. 5.
42 *Doncaster Chronicle*, 15 July 1870, p. 5.
43 *Doncaster Chronicle*, 22 September 1871, p. 8.

examined here allowed rural inhabitants access to a multitude of experiences beyond the cultural and recreational remit of the community in which they resided.

The Doncaster Statutes were a notable social occasion, independent from their economic function. As the *Doncaster Chronicle* reported,

> a great many of the country population came into the town; avowedly for the purpose of securing a master or mistress; but secretly, we believe, with the intention of enjoying a day's recreation amongst their relations, friends, and sweethearts, dairy maids and agricultural labourers, – who find this an excellent opportunity for a rustic reunion.[44]

The entertainments at the Statutes were varied and increasingly focused on the mechanical attractions typical of the Victorian age. In 1843 entertainments included stalls selling gingerbread and lollipops, shooting stalls, a sparring booth, a funfair, leopards and tigers, and 'the showyard, which as if touched by the hand of a magician, or subjected to the influence of Aladdin's wonderful lamp, had risen in all its showy splendour'.[45] After reports that both the quantity and quality of shows had diminished in 1861, a far greater array of entertainments was boasted in 1863, although they were of varying quality. These included 'penny circuses, shooting galleries, pummelling saloons, cheap jacks, photographic galleries, fine art exhibitions, "spirometers", "muscular indicators", "coggy boats", "cock horses", and two circuses with animals, acrobats and clowns'.[46] By 1870, the pleasure fair was considered the main inducement for the farm servants to attend the Statutes and was described as 'a more extensive affair than ever, there being more shows, roundabouts, velocipedes, shooting galleries, &c, than a great number of years past'.[47] The Statutes were thus entrenched in tradition as a day of leisure, and the campaign to reform hiring practices unsurprisingly met fierce opposition from those who felt that their day of privilege was threatened.[48]

The countryside as a destination for leisure

The relationships between town and country, and between rural communities, are further evidenced through the use of the countryside for leisure pursuits. Doncaster's rural hinterland attracted both urban and rural dwellers, whether for the natural beauty of the Don Valley or the spa resort of Askern. The local countryside catered to the Victorian fascination with the natural world and provided a rural retreat within an increasingly industrialised county. The appetite for a rural idyll was expressed in

---

44 *Doncaster Chronicle*, 17 November 1843, p. 8.
45 *Doncaster Chronicle*, 17 November 1843, p. 8.
46 *Doncaster Chronicle*, 20 November 1863, p. 5. Cheap jacks were street traders usually selling inferior goods and often travelling to fairs and markets.
47 *Sheffield Daily Telegraph*, 16 November 1870, p. 3. Velocipedes, in this context, were bicycle roundabouts that relied on people cycling to power the ride.
48 *Doncaster Chronicle*, 15 November 1861, p. 5.

the Revd J.G. Fardell's *Sprotbrough; or a few passing notes for a Morning's Ramble*, published in 1850 – a publication typical of the topographical and antiquarian works written by the clergy during the nineteenth century. It began lyrically, by quoting Wordsworth, and asserted that 'there is no country in the whole world where green fields and quiet out of the way places are more eagerly sought than in Old England'.[49] Drawing attention to the natural beauty in the parish, and advocating walks through the pretty village of Sprotbrough, Fardell wrote:

> The river is seen winding its course through the valley; on the one side are green fields and hills, advancing here and retiring there; and on the other side high cliffs and rocks, crowned everywhere with the richest foliage; cottages of the peasantry and an old mill occupy the foreground, and a delightful murmur from the water flowing over the breakwater.[50]

Fardell's commentary was also imbued with the social hierarchies of the Victorian countryside and the relative position of labourers within them: 'There is nothing more delightful than for a poor man to have the pleasure granted him of walking over some rich man's estate.' In positioning the labouring population as poor men who, he felt, benefited from the benevolence of the landowner in allowing access to his estate, Fardell highlighted both the social hierarchies and inequalities of the Victorian countryside and the extent to which rural elites valued the rural environment as a source of relaxation and pleasure. Moreover, it further illustrates how rural elites sought to impose respectable and improving leisure on the labouring population.

In his book Fardell also noted that, in the summer months, the Don valley was 'much frequented by those who enjoy a ramble in the country' and that it was here that 'parties meet and walk through the varied scenery'.[51] Even Sir Walter Scott is said to have visited this area, and to have written a part of *Ivanhoe* in the public house at Sprotbrough.[52] The river Don was thus a focal point for rural recreation, an anonymous letter-writer arguing that for 'the lover of natural beauty and antiquarian research there are few more interesting districts of country than that which is traversed by the winding river Don from Doncaster towards Sheffield'. The letter, written to the *Yorkshire Post* and reprinted in other regional papers, noted that

> On an acclivity of the beautiful vale of the Don [...] about three miles from Doncaster, is situate the pleasant village of Sprotbrough. Viewed from beneath a bright July sun, it presents a perfect blaze of beauty – long-reaching limes and clumps of great chestnut, beech, and elm trees, greet the eye, whilst the feathery lime and evergreen bushy shrub seem but a fairy step to most exquisite floriculture, which bespangles and odourises the cottage of the poor as well as the mansion of the rich. In this model, almost regal-looking village, on the

---

49 Fardell, *Sprotbrough*, p. 1.
50 Ibid., p. 4.
51 Fardell, *Sprotbrough*.
52 *Barnsley Chronicle*, 18 September 1869, p. 2.

limestone, with its ornamental bridge, stretch across the valley and river in its bed, famous for the fertility of its soil, and abounding with rustic walks and drives through wood and ravine, is situated [...] Sprotbrough Hall.[53]

Similarly, an advertisement in the *Doncaster Gazette* in May 1843 invited readers to sail in the Aquabus that traversed the river between Doncaster and Swinton through 'The beautiful vale of the Don, with its fair outstretched arms ... – a scene redolent of picturesque grandeur ... '.[54] It observed that passengers or pleasure parties disembarked at Sprotbrough, where the village pub welcomed visitors passing through the parish, whether on the river or riverside paths. The report noted that the pub was to be rebuilt to be 'more commodious, more convenient, more ornamental, for the reception of the stranger-visitor ... ',[55] and concluded by stating that:

> Thus, for the purposes of business or for pleasure, the facilities and advantages presented by the Aquabus are manifold ... expeditious, convenient, and cheap; ... . The country through which this iron boat passes is, indeed, as highly interesting, as it is varied in its character. Even-surfaced meadow and sloping corn field, hall and tower, park and pasture, village and hamlet, rock and river, wood and water, weir, lock, and mill, villa, farmstead, and cottage, quarry and lime-kilns, cliff and mountain.[56]

The Magnesian Limestone belt along the river Don was an attractive destination for walkers and picnic parties. Of particular note were the picturesque cliffs, Edlington and Wadworth Woods, Conisborough Castle, Sprotbrough Hall and Cusworth Park and Hall.[57] Levitt Hagg was a noted destination for picnic parties, and the local press included adverts for picnic baskets.[58] Again, occasional tensions surfaced, as evidenced by a letter published in the *Doncaster Gazette*, which told a cautionary tale of a party of four men and four women who had disembarked from their boats at Levitt Hagg for a picnic and had a narrow escape from a man who threw a stone weighing 28lb towards them.[59]

On the other side of Doncaster, Askern Spa boasted a number of springs promoted for their medicinal properties. Local and regional newspapers featured advertisements for the baths in Askern, and lists of people visiting them appear in the society news. William Ward, occupier of the Swan Hotel and Manor Baths, announced that the baths were located immediately over the original spring, which was 'unequalled by any other

---

53 *Barnsley Chronicle*, 18 September 1869, p. 2. The letter, 'A Ramble in South Yorkshire', was written to the *Yorkshire Post* and republished in the *Barnsley Chronicle*.
54 *Doncaster Gazette*, supplement, May 1843.
55 *Ibid.*
56 *Ibid.*
57 Kelly, *Post Office directory, 1877*, p. 1186.
58 *Doncaster Gazette*, 26 August 1870, p. 1; *Doncaster Gazette*, 2 September 1870, p. 2.
59 *Doncaster Gazette*, 23 September 1870, p. 5.

Spring in the Vicinity' for its medicinal properties.[60] Mr Dyson and Mr Thompson of Braithwell, Mr Marsdin of Stainforth and Mrs Wainwright and family of Rossington, all farming families, were noted in the *Doncaster Chronicle* as visiting Manor Baths in either 1843 or 1844.[61] Similarly, Mr and Mrs Chester Sailes of Fishlake and Mr Bradford of Rossington, again farmers, were noted as visiting Saul's Terrace Steam Baths in 1841.[62] People from across the Doncaster district, as well as from further afield, went to Askern for the baths and spring water – including farmers and tradespeople from rural communities who had the time, money and inclination to do so.

Conclusion

Rural communities could be vibrant cultural and recreational centres, operating within and outside existing institutions. In the Doncaster district, physical and ideological cultural centres were interchangeable, with inhabitants occupying the village church, chapel, school and other public and private spaces to fulfil multiple objectives, including recreation. The way in which events and functions occupied multiple sites, including public and private buildings and open spaces, meant that the village itself was a site of recreation. This was a foundation on which residents could construct networks of active participation and begin to democratise rural recreation, despite the involvement of landowners and other figures of authority in orchestrating many of the activities and events. It also provided opportunities for shared and distinct rural identities to be forged.

Landowners and the clergy controlled many of these sites and placed great emphasis on activities of an improving nature. Yet that did not equate to the restrictive, unimaginative provision of leisure in all villages in the district. Nor did it prevent the tenant or labourer from becoming an active participant in their leisure and culture within the village and taking some ownership of it, or being exposed to leisure and entertainment in the nearby market town. Beyond the village, rural inhabitants in the district could access recreational and cultural opportunities in Doncaster, with social occasions often partnering economic functions. Moreover, the Victorian countryside was increasingly a recreational destination for those living in towns or other rural communities. The Magnesian Limestone belt and riverside walks to the west of Doncaster, and the spas to the east, were popular venues for town and country dwellers alike. Relationships between town and country, and between rural communities, especially in an industrialising county, are undoubtedly important for understanding patterns of rural recreation.

---

60 *Hull Advertiser and Exchange Gazette*, 17 May 1850, p. 1.
61 *Doncaster Chronicle*, 9 June 1843, p. 5; *Doncaster Chronicle*, 14 July 1843, p. 5; *Doncaster Chronicle*, 26 July 1844, p. 5.
62 *Doncaster Chronicle*, 12 June 1841, p. 4; *Doncaster Chronicle*, 17 July 1841, p. 4.

Chapter 7

Conclusion

The extent of variation between nineteenth-century rural communities in the Doncaster district is striking. Some of these contrasts are still evident in the landscape today, while others have been subsumed by later development. Evidence of the nature of these communities is preserved in archival collections, the comparative analysis of which has been at the heart of this study. Although models of village typology, with their potential to characterise and delineate rural communities, retain value, they cannot adequately explain the nuanced development and differentiation of the rural communities described in this book. Through its thematic chapters, new theoretical and geographical perspectives have been offered that reinterpret village differentiation.

The evidence from the Doncaster district does not entirely refute existing models of village differentiation. In so far as a broad range of classificatory attributes and traits can be assigned to rural communities on the basis of the concentration of landownership, the Mills model has utility.[1] Superficially at least, Doncaster villages did exhibit some of these hallmark characteristics. Farms were larger in estate villages, with little industry and few trades and crafts; some cottage accommodation was very good quality yet generally in short supply; and the Anglican Church was a dominant presence. In contrast, multi-freeholder villages were characterised by smaller farms, rural industries and micro-commerce, poor but plentiful housing, non-conformity and independence. Differences between the estate and multi-freeholder villages of the Doncaster district are undeniable, but the categorisation is far from definitive given other differences that cannot be explained by these factors.

Such broad-brush classification disregards the variation and nuances within and between rural communities. Many villages in the Doncaster district do not in fact neatly comply with the expectations of theoretical models, despite initial impressions. This is discernible in terms of differences between villages with similar landowning structures, similarities between estate and multi-freeholder communities, and variation within particular communities. For instance, within villages there were wide variations in farm size, living and working conditions, and religious practices and modes of recreation. Moreover, industry and micro-commerce such as corn milling and blacksmithing were important elements of the rural economy, often complementing the agricultural sector, and as such they could be indicators of the vitality of rural society in both estate and multi-freeholder villages. Thus, while the Mills model is a useful starting point for understanding village differentiation, the classificatory argument embodied in it cannot account for the nuanced variation found in rural communities in the Doncaster district.

---

1   Mills, *Lord and peasant*; Mills, 'Canwick (Lincolnshire) and Melbourn (Cambridgeshire)'.

Thinking of the differences between villages as a continuum goes some way to alleviating the constraints embodied by the open–closed model by moving beyond a dichotomy of rural communities – an acknowledged weakness.[2] Although advocated by Mills, Howkins and Short, it is perhaps unsurprising that the continuum has not itself been adequately modelled. Differences between communities are often subtle rather than glaring, while the position of a village in relation to a variety of criteria may vary both across the criteria and over time, making positioning any community on a single spectrum challenging. Contrasts between communities, however, certainly cannot be explained by landownership alone. Land did bestow agency on its owners, and landownership directly influenced some aspects of rural society, but its effects were neither unlimited nor consistent. Analysis of why rural communities developed in different ways certainly requires an examination of different landownership patterns and types of landowner, however. Important differences include not only residency (as emphasised in Sarah Banks' work) and levels of wealth but also attitudes and inclinations. Not all landowners behaved in the same way, with expectations and practice often very different. For example, according to the Mills model, landowners restricted industrial development in estate villages, and yet large quarries were developed on the periphery of Warmsworth because of the availability of and demand for limestone and lime, with both William Battie-Wrightson and Sir Joseph Copley actively involved. Similarly, while agricultural writers such as James Caird advocated employing professional land agents, local landowners adopted different strategies. Sir Joseph Copley, a resident and long-standing landowner, employed a tenant farmer as land agent at Sprotbrough, while James Brown, an industrialist who purchased the Rossington estate, and his descendants, who were resident landowners in Rossington, directly engaged in agricultural management on the estate, investing heavily in the development of model farms.

Landownership should also be positioned within the context of other types of agency within rural communities. Landowners were part of a wider rural elite within which the clergy were also prominent. In many instances, the willingness to take on leadership roles, rather than the fact of landownership, was the factor instrumental in bringing about change. For example, the Revd Ornsby, incumbent of Fishlake, was more influential than the small freeholders of the parish in terms of leading change in the community. Landowners were in fact often reacting to external pressures, such as legislation they perceived might undermine their control. Moreover, external agents such as Doncaster Corporation (who were also landowners at Rossington until 1838) and the local press influenced rural communities across the Doncaster district and affected the relationship between town and country. This is particularly evident through the expansion and development of Doncaster market, undertaken by Doncaster Corporation and reported on extensively by both the *Doncaster Chronicle* and *Doncaster Gazette*; the creation and promotion of knowledge networks via agricultural societies, shows and reports supported and discussed by the Corporation

---

2   Mills, *Lord and peasant*, p. 93; Mills, 'Canwick (Lincolnshire) and Melbourn (Cambridgeshire)', p. 5; Howkins, *Reshaping rural England*, pp. 25–6; Short, 'The evolution of contrasting communities', p. 37.

and the local press; and the hiring of farm servants and the campaign to reform the Doncaster hiring fairs. It can also be seen through the movement of people for work, worship and recreation. Finally, the agency of the labouring population should not be underestimated. Many agricultural workers of the Doncaster district were active participants in the development of the rural communities in which they lived and worked.

The concepts of agency and social hierarchies have underpinned the analysis of why rural communities developed throughout this book. The idea of agency tries to capture the balance of power within communities, alongside the willingness to act. Those who had the potential for powerful agency, such as landowners, did not always act accordingly. Others took up that agency in their place. People with less wealth and status also found ways to leverage agency in the communities in which they lived and worked. Opportunities for agency were often situational and fluid, with agents acting and reacting in response to people, places and events. Beyond human agency, historical, geographical and geological determinants shaped rural communities, influencing, for example, the different types of crops and livestock produced, the location of extractive and food-processing industries, and the interests and agenda of agricultural societies as reflected by their meetings and shows.

Ultimately, a model can never truly represent the complexities of rural communities and thus is not the most effective way to explain the differences between villages. Models tend to reduce rural communities to quantifiable variables and, as Barry Reay argued, few places correspond with these. This study of the rural communities of the Doncaster district provides evidence of the extent to which characteristics can vary between villages with and without similar landowning structures, and demonstrates that these can be explained by factors other than the concentration of landownership. Although a continuum, as discussed by Mills, Short and Howkins, moves beyond the strict dichotomy of the original Mills model, it still cannot effectively represent every scenario. Similarly, although differences in landownership were important, as highlighted by Sarah Banks and David Spencer, those differences went beyond the residency of landowners. Moreover, other agents, such as the clergy, Doncaster Corporation and even labourers, affected rural communities in the Doncaster district. The difficulties with models go deeper than their failure to capture the nuanced variation, subtle disparities and shared experiences that a detailed case study of rural communities can demonstrate. A model cannot engage effectively with the people who lived and worked in these rural communities – and yet such interactions are at the heart of many studies of rural history. Nor can it adequately represent complex relationships, external determinants and spheres of influence.

This case study of a northern market town, Doncaster, and its rural hinterland has revealed that rural communities cannot be understood without examining the relationship between villages and between town and country. A mutual interdependency existed between many Doncaster villages and a reciprocal relationship was fostered between town and country. Acknowledging reciprocity between communities seems a more accurate depiction of inter-village relationships than the dependency model proposed by Mills, who claimed that a negative interdependency operated between villages, with 'close' villages dependent on 'open' villages for labour, which exacerbated problems of overcrowding and poverty in the latter. In contrast, evidence from the Doncaster district demonstrates mutual interdependency, including factors such as the forging of knowledge networks via farmers' clubs and agricultural societies, the location of resources and food-processing industries, and the provision of and attendance at places of worship. The inter-relationship between Doncaster and its rural hinterland was especially important in terms of agricultural knowledge networks, market facilities, forums for political debate, the extension or limitation of the agency of different social groups, opportunities for labourers to renegotiate their agency and influence their living and working conditions, and as a place of recreation. Town and country converged in the market place, where the differences between estate villagers and freeholders were of little importance. District-wide concerns about living and working conditions, especially the quality and availability of cottage accommodation and the employment of women in agriculture, gained momentum through the complex spatial dynamics in operation. Not only were these issues of concern to the local clergy and some local landowners, but they were also the focus of national parliamentary enquiries that subjected both estate and multi-freeholder villages to scrutiny. Contrasts in living and working conditions also revealed much about the divergent perspectives of those giving evidence as well as about geography and village typology. Moreover, they were the focus of debates that took place in the market town or were reported in local and regional newspapers with district-wide circulation. The interplay between town and country was a two-way process, as demonstrated by the urban dependency on the products of agriculture and the town dweller's appetite for the beauty of the Victorian countryside. Urban visitors were particularly drawn to the Magnesian Limestone belt and the estate villages beside the river Don, thus opening these rural communities up to wider social interactions. Rural communities were also shaped by external stimuli from farther afield in the form of Victorian legislation and parliamentary investigation.

Doncaster and its rural hinterland were located in an industrialising northern county. How and why rural communities developed within the vicinity of this market town was specific to this particular situation. Nevertheless, the approach advocated here to understanding village differentiation has broader application. The village and landowner are part of a complex web in which agency and social hierarchies – leadership not landownership – and the spatial dynamics between places are instrumental. The process of drawing contrasts between communities is both a means of exploring differences between villages and an approach to understanding how and why they developed.

Bibliography

Primary sources, manuscript
Doncaster Archives

AB/2/2/4, Rossington committee meeting minutes in the Corporation Committee Orders and Papers, 1808–1840

AB/2/6/21/3, Council and committee records of Doncaster Corporation, 1836–1843

AB/2/6/21/4–7, Council and committee records of Doncaster Corporation, finance committee including markets, 1843–1888

AB/7/3/5, Survey of Rossington, 1826

AB/7/3/42, Survey of the manor of Rossington, early 18th century

AB/7/3/43, Field book and survey of the manor of Rossington, *c.*1768

AB/7/3/63, Sale catalogue for the Rossington estate, 1838

DD/BW/A/26–31, Private account books [Battie-Wrightson family], 1842–1871

DD/BW/A/33–37, Copy estate cash books [for Battie-Wrightson family], 1788–1868

DD/BW/B/149–153, Account books for cereals ground at the Sprotbrough Mill, 1853, 1858, 1860 x2, 1862

DD/BW/E2/4–12, Rentals of Battie-Wrightson, 1827–1868

DD/BW/E3/14–15, Cash book of Thomas Wood [Warmsworth], February 1839–December 1872

DD/BW/E4/10–11, Letters, calculations, memoranda and miscellanea regarding tithes, 1826–48

DD/BW/E7/50, Sketch plan of River Don, flint mill and canal cut at Sprotbrough, mid 19th century

DD/BW/E11/18–19, Field book of the Lordship of Warmsworth, from 1860

DD/BW/E11/41–42, Warmsworth tithe apportionment and map, 1838–1841

DD/BW/E11/71, Brief memorandum regarding boundary stakes between the land of John Wrightson and Mr Aldam [Warmsworth], 1760s

DD/BW/E11/77, Letter from Lockwood, Kemp and Blagden to W. Battie Wrightson, 27 November 1843

DD/BW/E11/78, Agreements between Messrs Lockwood, Kemp and Blagden and the landowners (Aldam, Copley, Fox, Wrightson) [Warmsworth], 1846/47 (7 items)

DD/BW/E11/88, Memorandum book about farms and lands allocated to tenants in Warmsworth, 1830–1859

DD/BW/E11/89, Miscellaneous memoranda by W.B. Wrightson about tenancies and field areas, mid 19th century [Warmsworth], 1830–1859

DD/BW/E11/109, Tenancy agreement between Battie-Wrightson and John Wood [Warmsworth], 24 January 1837

DD/BW/E11/126, Miscellaneous papers, including Doncaster Agricultural Society leaflets

DD/BW/E14/16, Rentals for County Durham estates [Battie-Wrightson], 1831–1849

DD/BW/E14/87–88, Miscellaneous letters on estate business for Durham and North Yorkshire [Battie-Wrightson], 1828–1878

DD/BW/E14/91, Application book for farm tenancies [Battie-Wrightson estates in North Yorkshire and County Durham], 1874–1879

DD/BW/E15/97–112, Mickley rental and accounts of agents nos 33–106, May 1837–November 1876

DD/BW/F4/1, Pocket diary [Battie-Wrightson referring to Warmsworth], 1875
DD/WA/B1, Records of Benson family and Aldam, Pease, Birchall and Co., 1732–1840
DD/WA/B2, Business records of William Aldam, 1847–1890
DD/WA/D1/1–28, Diaries of William Aldam, 1848–1877
DD/WA/E5/4, Notebook of William Aldam, 1860s
DD/WA/E6/1, Rental book, 1860
DD/WA/E7/5, Farm memoranda and cattle book [Warmsworth], 1864–1883
DD/WA/P/1, Leeds parliamentary election handbills and other publicity, 1841
DD/WA/P/5, Petition to W. Aldam (Leeds) opposing the Corn Laws, 1843
DD/WA/P/10, Letters [William Aldam], 1841
DD/WA/P/12, Letters regarding the Corn Laws [William Aldam], 1843
DD/WA/P/16, Draft speech on the Corn Laws and free trade [William Aldam], 1841
DD/WA/P/19, Speech delivered in Leeds [William Aldam], 1841
DD/WA/P/24–29, Speeches delivered by Aldam, 1843
DD/WA/P/36–55, Parliamentary papers including speeches and House of Commons business [William Aldam], 1841–1843
DY/DAR/1, Ledger for the Darley brewery, 1863–1891
DY/DAR/3, Complimentary booklet produced by W.M. Darley, 1938
DY/DAW/7/4, Thorne, Hatfield and Fishlake enclosure award, 1825
DY/DAW/9/29, Sale catalogue for the Rossington estate, 1938
DY/Wall/1–2, Hatfield tithe apportionment and map, 1843 (includes Fishlake and Stainforth)
DZMD/569, 1847, Order of procession for the laying of the first stone for New Market, 24 May 1847
P25/9/B1, Sprotbrough tithe apportionment and map, 1847
P58/9/B1–2, Rossington tithe apportionment and map, 1838
P71/6/B2/1, Apprenticeship indenture of George Burton (pauper child) [Braithwell], 1834
P71/8/1, Admission register of Town School, Braithwell, 1867–1893
P71/8/2, Log book of National School, Braithwell, 1871–1910
P71/9/B1–2, Braithwell tithe apportionment and map, 1839–1840

Durham University Library Special Collections

G18/2/193, Miscellaneous box of papers relating to Miss Copley, rules of the Sprotbrough Farmers' Club, 1848

Royal Agricultural College Archives, Cirencester

RAC/16/004/2, Class lists and prize lists, 1859–1870
RAC/16/27/1, Student register, 1863–1883

The National Archives

HO 107/1329, CEB [Census Enumerators' Book] Sprotbrough 1851
HO 107/2132, CEB Nottingham 1851
HO 107/2346, CEB Braithwell 1851
HO 107/2346, CEB Sprotbrough 1851
HO 107/2346, CEB Warmsworth 1851
HO 107/2348, CEB Rossington 1851

Bibliography

HO 107/2349, CEB Fishlake and Stainforth 1851
MAF 68/81, The agricultural returns (livestock) for the West Riding of Yorkshire, 1866
MAF 68/82, The agricultural returns (crops) for the West Riding of Yorkshire, 1866
RG 9/3513, CEB Braithwell 1861
RG 9/3514, CEB Warmsworth 1861
RG 9/3516, CEB Sprotbrough 1861
RG 9/3522, CEB Rossington 1861
RG 9/3524, CEB Fishlake and Stainforth 1861
RG 10/4714, CEB Braithwell 1871
RG 10/4715, CEB Warmsworth 1871
RG 10/4716, CEB Sprotbrough 1871
RG 10/4724, CEB Rossington 1871
RG 10/4726, CEB Fishlake and Stainforth 1871

Primary sources, printed parliamentary papers

PP 1817, VI, *Report from the Select Committee on the Poor Laws*.
PP 1834, III, *Poor law amendment bill*.
PP 1835, *Education enquiry: abstract of answers and returns*, Vol. 1.
PP 1843, XII, *Reports of Special Assistant Poor Law Commissioner on the employment of women and children in agriculture*, 1843.
PP 1845, XV, *Report of the commissioner appointed to inquire into the condition of the framework knitters*.
PP 1847, XI, *First to eighth report from the Select Committee on Settlement and Poor Removal*.
PP 1850, XXVII, *Reports to the Poor Law Board, on the laws of settlement, and the removal of the poor*.
PP 1852–53, LXXXV, *Census of Great Britain, 1851. Population tables*, vol. I.
PP 1852–53, LXXXVIII, *Census of Great Britain, 1851. Population tables: ages, civil condition, occupations, and birthplace of the people*, vol. II.
PP 1860, XVII, *Select Committee on the Irremovable Poor*.
PP 1861, L, *Return of the average rate of weekly earnings of agricultural labourers*, part 1, 1860.
PP 1861, L, *Return of the average rate of weekly earnings of agricultural labourers*, part 2, 1861.
PP 1863, LIII, *Census of England and Wales, 1861*.
PP 1864, XXVIII, *The Medical Officer of the Privy Council: Seventh Report 1863*.
PP 1865, XXVI, *Seventh report of the medical officer of the Privy Council*, Appendix.
PP 1867–8, XVII, *First report of the Commission on the Employment of Children, Young Persons, and Women in Agriculture 1867*.
PP 1868, *Schools Inquiry Commission*, Vol. IX, General Reports of Assistant Commissioners, Northern Counties.
PP 1868–9, L, *Return of the average rate of weekly earnings of agricultural labourers*, 1868.
PP 1869, *Schools Inquiry Commission*, Vol. XVIII, Yorkshire.
PP 1871, LVI, *Return of the average rate of weekly earnings of agricultural labourers*, 1871.
PP 1873, LXXI, *Census of England and Wales, 1871: population abstracts, ages, civil condition, occupations, and birth places of the people*, vol. III.

Primary sources, printed

Appendix to the first report of the commissioners appointed to inquire into municipal corporations: part III northern and north midland circuits (London, 1835).

Ordnance Survey, 1854, first edition county series, 6 inch map, Yorkshire (West Riding), surveyed 1850.

West Riding election: the poll for the 2 knights of the shire for the West Riding of Yorkshire (Wakefield, 1841).

Newspapers and magazines

Barnsley Chronicle
Bristol Mercury
Doncaster Chronicle
Doncaster Gazette
Hull Advertiser and Exchange Gazette
Journal of the Royal Agricultural Society of England
Leeds Intelligencer
London Standard
New York Farmer and American Gardener's Magazine
Sheffield Daily Telegraph
Sheffield Independent
Stamford Mercury
The Farmers' Magazine
The Morning Chronicle
The Saturday Magazine
The York Herald and General Advertiser
Woolmer's Exeter and Plymouth Gazette
Yorkshire Gazette

Directories

Baines, E., *Directory of Yorkshire, 1822* (Leeds, 1822).
Baines, E. and Newsome, R., *General and commercial directory of Leeds 1834* (Leeds, 1834).
Kelly, E.R., *Post Office directory of the West Riding of Yorkshire, 1861* (London, 1861).
Kelly, E.R., *Post Office directory of the West Riding of Yorkshire, 1867* (London, 1867).
Kelly, E.R., *Post Office directory of the West Riding of Yorkshire, 1877* (London, 1877).
Pigot, J., *National commercial directory, 1834* (London, 1834).
White, W., *Gazetteer and general directory of Sheffield, 1852* (Sheffield, 1852).
White, W., *History, gazetteer and directory of the West Riding, 1837* (Sheffield, 1837).

Secondary sources: pre-1900 printed books, articles and pamphlets

Acland, H.W., *Health in the village* (London, 1884).
Andrews, W., *Curious epitaphs* (London, 1883).
The assembled common, or parliamentary biographer (London, 1838).
Caird, J., *English agriculture in 1850–51* (London, 1852).

Bibliography

Caird, J., *High farming, under liberal covenants, the best substitute for protection* (Edinburgh, 1849).

Caird, J., *The landed interest and the supply of food* (London, 1878).

Charnock, J.H., 'On the farming of the West Riding of Yorkshire: prize report', *Journal of the Royal Agricultural Society of England*, 9/21 (1848), pp. 284–9.

Dent, J., 'The present condition of the English agricultural labourer', *Journal of the Royal Agricultural Society of England*, 2nd series, 7/2 (1871), pp. 343–65.

Denton, J.B., *The farm homesteads of England: a collection of plans of English homesteads existing in different parts of the country* (London, 1864).

Dibdin, T.F., *Bibliographical, Antiquarian and Picturesque Tour in the Northern Countries of England and Scotland* (London, 1838).

Fardell, J.G., *Sprotbrough: or, a few passing notes for a morning's ramble* (Doncaster, 1850).

Grey, J., 'On the building of cottages for farm-labourers', *Journal of the Royal Agricultural Society of England*, 5 (1845), pp. 237–44.

Hatfield, C.W., *Hints for pedestrians* (Doncaster, 1850).

Hunter, J., *South Yorkshire: the history and topography of the Deanery of Doncaster*, Vol. 1 (London, 1828).

Kebbel, T.E., *The agricultural labourer: a short summary of his position* (London, 1887).

Knyff, L. and Kip, J., *Britannia illustrata, or views of several of the queen's palaces, also of the principal seats of the nobility and gentry of Great Britain* (London, 1707).

Loudon, J.C., *An encyclopedia of cottage, farm and villa architecture* (London, 1833).

Low, D., *On landed property and the economy of estates* (London, 1884).

Miller, E., *The history and antiquities of Doncaster and its vicinity* (first published 1804, reprinted Howden, 1984).

Morton, J.L., *The resources of estates* (London, 1858).

Parsons, E., *The civil, ecclesiastical, literary, commercial and miscellaneous history of Leeds, Halifax, Huddersfield, Bradford, Wakefield, Dewsbury, Otley, and the manufacturing district of Yorkshire*, Vol. I (Leeds, 1834).

Partington, C.F., *The British cyclopedia of natural history* (London, 1837).

Roberts, H., *The Dwellings of the Labouring Classes, Their Arrangement and Construction* (London, 1851).

Robinson, P.F., *Designs for farm buildings* (London, 1830).

Robinson, P.F., *Designs for farm buildings* (London, 1837).

Robinson, P.F., *Rural architecture: being a series of designs for ornamental cottages* (London, 1828).

Robinson, P.F., *Village architecture: being a series of designs for the inn, the schoolhouse, almshouses, markethouse, shambles, workhouse, parsonage, town hall and church* (London, 1828).

Sheardown, W., *Doncaster in 1863* (Doncaster, 1863).

Sheardown, W., *Doncaster in 1865* (Doncaster, 1865).

Sheardown, W., *Doncaster in 1867* (Doncaster, 1867).

Sheardown, W., *Doncaster in 1868* (Doncaster, 1868).

Sheardown, W., *Doncaster in 1869* (Doncaster, 1869).

Sheardown, W., *The marts and markets of Doncaster: their rise, progress and sources of supply* (Doncaster, 1872).

Skinner, Revd. J., *Facts and opinions concerning statute hirings, respectively addressed to the landowner, clergy, farmers and tradespeople of the East Riding* (London, 1861).

Stephens, H., *The book of the farm, detailing the labours of the farmers, farm-steward, ploughman, shepherd, hedger, cattle-man, fieldworker, and dairy-maid* (London, 1844).

Stephens, H., *The farmer's guide to scientific and practical agriculture*, Vol. 2 (New York, 1862).

Stephens, H. and Burns, R.S., *The book of farm buildings, their arrangement and construction* (London, 1861).

Wainwright, J., *Yorkshire: an historical and topographical introduction to a knowledge of the ancient state of the wapentake of Strafford and Tickhill* (Sheffield, 1829).

Wilson, J.M., *The imperial gazetteer of England and Wales* (6 vols, London, 1870–75).

Secondary sources: post-1900 printed books, articles and theses

Afton, B. and Turner, M., 'Wages', in E.J.T. Collins (ed.), *The Agrarian History of England and Wales*, Vol. VII, 1850–1914, Part 2 (Cambridge, 2000), pp. 1993–2019.

Allen, D., 'England's golden age: imperial cricket and late Victorian society', *Sport in Society: Cultures, Commerce, Media, Politics*, 15/2 (2012), pp. 209–26.

Armstrong, W.A., *Farmworkers: a social and economic history 1770–1980* (London, 1988).

Bailey, P., *Leisure and class in Victorian England: rational recreation and the contest for control, 1830–1885* (London, 1978).

Bailey, P., '"Rational recreation": the social control of leisure and popular culture in Victorian England, 1830–1885', PhD thesis (University of British Columbia, 1974).

Bamford, T.W., *The evolution of rural education 1850–1964* (Hull, 1965).

Banks, S., 'Nineteenth century scandal or twentieth century model? A new look at "open" and "close" parishes', *Economic History Review*, 41/1 (1988), pp. 51–73.

Banks, S., 'Open and close parishes in nineteenth century England', PhD thesis (University of Reading, 1982).

Barber, B., 'The landed gentry of the Doncaster district', in B. Elliott (ed.), *Aspects of Doncaster: discovering local history*, Vol. 1 (Barnsley, 1997), pp. 49–74.

Barnett, A.L., *The railways of the South Yorkshire coalfield from 1880* (Bampton, 1984).

Beckett, J.V., 'Agricultural landownership and estate management', in E.J.T. Collins (ed.), *The agrarian history of England and Wales*, Vol. VII, 1850–1914, Part 1 (Cambridge, 2000) pp. 693–758.

Beckett, J.V., 'The debate over farm sizes in eighteenth and nineteenth century England', *Agricultural History*, 57/3 (1983), pp. 308–25.

Beckett, J.V., 'Landownership and estate management', in G.E. Mingay (ed.), *The agrarian history of England and Wales*, Vol. VI, 1750–1850, (Cambridge, 1989), pp. 545–640.

Beckett, J.V., 'Local history in its comparative international context', *The Local Historian*, 41/2 (2011), pp. 90–104.

Beckett, J.V., 'Rethinking the English village', *The Local Historian*, 42/4 (2012), pp. 301–11.

Beckett, J.V., *Writing local history* (Manchester, 2007).

Best, G., *Mid-Victorian Britain 1851–1875* (London, 1971).

Bird, P., 'Landownership and settlement change in south-west Cheshire from 1750–2000', PhD thesis (University of Chester, 2007).

Brassley, P., 'Arable systems', in E.J.T. Collins (ed.), *The agrarian history of England and Wales*, Vol. VII, 1850–1914, Part 1 (Cambridge, 2000), pp. 456–64.

Brassley, P., 'Pastoral farming systems', in E.J.T. Collins (ed.), *The agrarian history of England and Wales*, Vol. VII, 1850–1914, Part 1 (Cambridge, 2000), pp. 465–71.

Brigden, R., 'Equipment and motive power', in E.J.T. Collins (ed.), *The agrarian history of England and Wales*, Vol. VII, 1850–1914, Part 1 (Cambridge, 2000), pp. 505–13.

Brigden, R., 'Farm buildings', in E.J.T. Collins (ed.), *The agrarian history of England and Wales*, Vol. VII, 1850–1914, Part 1 (Cambridge, 2000), pp. 497–504.

Brown, D., 'The rise of industrial society and the end of the village, 1760–1900?', in C. Dyer (ed.), *The self-contained village? the social history of rural communities 1250–1900* (Hatfield, 2007), pp. 114–37.

Bibliography

Brown, J., *The English market town: a social and economic history 1750–1914* (Ramsbury, 1986).

Brown, J., 'Malting', in E.J.T. Collins (ed.), *The agrarian history of England and Wales*, Vol. VII, 1850–1914, Part 2 (Cambridge, 2000), pp. 1076–84.

Brown, J. and Beecham, H.A., 'Implements and machines', in G.E. Mingay (ed.), *The agrarian history of England and Wales*, Vol. VI 1750-1850 (Cambridge, 1989: 2011 edition), pp. 305–10.

Burchardt, J., 'Agricultural history, rural history, or countryside history?', *The Historical Journal*, 50/2 (2007), pp. 465–81.

Caunce, S., *Amongst farm horses: the horse lads of East Yorkshire* (Stroud, 1991).

Caunce, S., 'Farm servants and the development of capitalism in English agriculture', *Agricultural History Review*, 45/1 (1997), pp. 49–60.

Caunce, S., 'The hiring fairs of northern England, 1890–1930: a regional analysis of commercial and social networking in agriculture', *Past and Present*, 217 (2012), pp. 213–46.

Caunce, S., 'Regional identity in Lancashire and Yorkshire: hunting the snark', *The Journal of Regional and Local History*, 20/1 (1999), pp. 25–50.

Chalklin, C.W., 'Country towns', in G.E. Mingay (ed.), *The Victorian countryside* (London, 1981), pp. 275–87.

Chambers, J.D. and Mingay, G.E., *The agricultural revolution 1750–1880* (London, 1966).

Chartres, J.A., 'County tradesmen', in G.E. Mingay (ed.), *The Victorian countryside* (London, 1981), pp. 300–13.

Chartres, J.A., 'The retail trades and agricultural service', in E.J.T. Collins (ed.), *The agrarian history of England and Wales*, Vol. VII, 1850–1914, Part 2 (Cambridge, 2000), pp. 1150–212.

Chartres, J.A., 'Rural industry and manufacturing', in E.J.T. Collins (ed.), *The agrarian history of England and Wales*, Vol. VII, 1850–1914, Part 2 (Cambridge, 2000), pp. 1101–49.

Chartres, J.A. and Perren, R., 'Trade, commerce and industry: introduction', in E.J.T. Collins (ed.), *The agrarian history of England and Wales*, Vol. VII, 1850–1914, Part 2 (Cambridge, 2000), pp. 947–52.

Chartres, J.A., and Turnbull, G.L., 'Country craftsmen', in G.E. Mingay (ed.), *The Victorian countryside* (London, 1981), pp. 314–28.

Cherry, G.E. and Sheail, J., 'Rural housing', in E.J.T. Collins (ed.), *The agrarian history of England and Wales*, Vol. VII, 1850–1914, Part 2 (Cambridge, 2000), pp. 1551–6.

Chisholm, M., *Rural settlement and land use* (London, 1970).

Clarke, B.F.L., *Church builders of the nineteenth century, a study of the gothic revival in England* (2nd edn, Newton Abbot, 1969).

Clarke, F.A., *Rossington: glimpses into the past* (Rossington, 1986).

Clarke, F.A., *Rossington: more glimpses into the past* (Rossington, 1990).

Collins, E.J.T. (ed.), *The agrarian history of England and Wales*, Vol. VII, 1850–1914 (Cambridge, 2000).

Collins, E.J.T., 'Dietary change and cereal consumption in Britain in the nineteenth century', *Agricultural History Review*, 13/2 (1975), pp. 97–115.

Collins, E.J.T., 'Introduction', in E.J.T. Collins (ed.), *The agrarian history of England and Wales*, Vol. VII, 1850–1914, Part 1 (Cambridge, 2000), pp. 1–29.

Collins, E.J.T., 'Migrant labour in British agriculture in the nineteenth century', *Economic History Review*, 35 (1976), pp. 38–59.

Constantine, S., 'Amateur gardening and popular recreation in the nineteenth and twentieth centuries', *Journal of Social History*, 14/3 (1981), pp. 387–406.

Crompton, C.A., 'Changes in rural service occupations during the nineteenth century: an evaluation of two sources for Hertfordshire, England', *Rural History*, 6/2 (1995), pp. 193–203.

Cunningham, H., *Leisure in the industrial revolution, c.1780–c.1880* (London, 1980).
Darley, G., *Villages of vision* (London, 1975).
Drake, M. and Finnegan, R. (eds), *Studying family and community history – 19th and 20th centuries, vol. 4: sources and methods: a handbook* (Cambridge, 1994).
Dunbabin, J.P.D., 'The "revolt of the field": the agricultural labourers' movement in the 1870s', *Past and Present*, 26/1 (1963), pp. 68–97.
Dyer, C., *The self-contained village? the social history of rural communities 1250–1890* (Hatfield, 2007).
Dyer, C., Hopper, A., Lord, E. and Tringham, N. (eds), *New directions in local history since Hoskins* (Hatfield, 2011).
Eastwood, D., 'Contesting the politics of deference: the rural electorate, 1820–1860', in J. Lawrence and M. Taylor (eds), *Party, state and society: electoral behaviour since 1820* (Aldershot, 1997), pp. 27–49.
Edgar, M.J.D., 'Occupational diversity in seven rural parishes in Dorset, 1851', *Local Population Studies*, 52 (1994), pp. 48–54.
Everitt, A., *The community of Kent and the Great Rebellion, 1640–60* (Leicester, 1966).
Everitt, A., *The patterns of rural dissent: the nineteenth century* (Leicester, 1972).
Finberg, J., *Exploring villages* (Stroud, 1998).
Fisher, J.R., 'The limits of deference: agricultural communities in a mid nineteenth century election campaign', *Journal of British Studies*, 21 (1981), pp. 98–103.
Flynn, A., Lowe, P. and Winter, M., 'The political power of farmers: an English perspective', *Rural History*, 7/1 (1996), pp. 15–32.
Fraser, D., *A history of modern Leeds* (Manchester, 1980).
Freeman, M. (ed.), *The English rural poor* (London, 2005).
Freeman, M., *Social investigation and rural England, 1870–1914* (Woodbridge, 2003).
Gaskell, M. (ed.), *Slums* (Leicester, 1990).
Gilbert, A.D., 'The land and the church', in G.E. Mingay, *The Victorian countryside*, (London, 1981).
Gilbert, A.D., *Religion and society in industrial England: church, chapel and social change, 1740–1914* (London, 1976).
Girouard, M., *The English town* (London, 1990).
Goddard, N., 'Agricultural institutions: societies, associations and the press', in E.J.T. Collins (ed.), *The agrarian history of England and Wales*, Vol. VII, 1850–1914, Part 1 (Cambridge, 2000), pp. 650–92.
Goddard, N., 'Agricultural societies', in G.E. Mingay (ed.), *The Victorian countryside* (London, 1981), pp. 245–59.
Goddard, N., 'The development and influence of agricultural periodicals and newspapers, 1780–1880', *Agricultural History Review*, 31/2 (1983), pp. 116–31.
Goddard, N., *Harvests of change: the Royal Agricultural Society of England 1838–1988* (London, 1988).
Goose, N., 'Farm service in southern England in the mid-nineteenth century', *Local Population Studies*, 72 (2003), pp. 77–82.
Goose, N., 'Farm service, seasonal unemployment and casual labour in mid nineteenth-century England', *Agricultural History Review*, 54/2 (2006), pp. 274–303.
Grace, D., 'The agricultural engineering industry', in E.J.T. Collins (ed.), *The agrarian history of England and Wales*, Vol. VII, 1850–1914, Part 2 (Cambridge, 2000), pp. 1000–18.
Griffin, C., *Protest, politics and work in rural England* (Basingstoke, 2014).
Grigg, D., 'Farm size in England and Wales, from early Victorian times to the present', *Agricultural History Review*, 35/2 (1987), pp. 179–89.

Hallas, C., 'Craft occupations in the late nineteenth century: some local considerations', *Local Population Studies*, 44 (1990), pp. 18–29.

Hallas, C., 'The northern region', in E.J.T. Collins (ed.), *The agrarian history of England and Wales*, Vol. VII, 1850–1914, Part 1 (Cambridge, 2000), pp. 402–10.

Hammond, M. and Sloan, B. (eds), *Rural–urban relationships in the nineteenth century: uneasy neighbours?* (Abingdon, 2016).

Harrison, B., *Drink and the Victorians: the temperance question in England 1815–1872* (London, 1971).

Harrison, J.F.C., *The early Victorians 1832–1851* (London, 1971).

Hawker, N. and Pugh, L.A., *A goodly heritage being a history of the parish of Braithwell and Micklebring through the millennium* (Doncaster, 2000).

Helsinger, E.K., *Rural scenes and national representation: Britain, 1815–1850* (Princeton, 1997).

Hey, D., *The grass roots of English history: societies in England before the industrial revolution* (London, 2016).

Hey, D., *Journeys in family history: the National Archives guide to exploring your past – finding your ancestors* (Richmond, 2004).

Hey, D., *The making of South Yorkshire* (Newton Abbot, 1979).

Hey, D., *Medieval South Yorkshire* (Ashbourne, 2003).

Hey, D.G., 'The pattern of non-conformity in South Yorkshire 1660–1851', *Northern History*, 8 (1973), pp. 86–118.

Hey, D., 'Reflections on the local and regional history of the north', *Northern History*, 50/2 (2013), pp. 155–69.

Hey, D., *Yorkshire from AD 1000* (London, 1986).

Higgs, E., *A clearer sense of the census* (London, 1996).

Higgs, E., 'Occupational censuses and the agricultural workforce in Victorian England and Wales', *Economic History Review*, 48/4 (1995), pp. 700–16.

Higgs, E., 'Women, occupations and work in nineteenth century censuses', *History Workshop Journal*, 23/1 (1987), pp. 59–80.

Holderness, B.A., 'Agriculture and industrialization in the Victorian economy', in G.E. Mingay (ed.), *The Victorian countryside* (London, 1981), pp. 179–99.

Holderness, B.A., 'Farming regions', in E.J.T. Collins (ed.), *The agrarian history of England and Wales*, Vol. VII, 1850–1914, Part 1 (Cambridge, 2000), pp. 361–6.

Holderness, B.A., 'Intensive livestock keeping', in E.J.T. Collins (ed.), *The agrarian history of England and Wales*, Vol. VII, 1850–1914, Part 1 (Cambridge, 2000), pp. 487–94.

Holderness, B.A., '"Open" and "close" parishes in England in the eighteenth and nineteenth centuries', *Agricultural History Review*, 20/2 (1972), pp. 126–39.

Holderness, B.A., 'The Victorian farmer', in G.E. Mingay (ed.), *The Victorian countryside* (London, 1981), pp. 227–44.

Holland, D., *Changing landscapes in South Yorkshire* (Doncaster, 1980).

Holland, D. (ed.), *Sprotbrough in history*, part two (Rotherham, 1969).

Holland, D., *Warmsworth in the eighteenth century: population change, agriculture and quarrying in a rural South Yorkshire community* (Doncaster, 1965).

Holland, D. and Holland, E.M., *A Yorkshire town: the making of Doncaster* (iBook edition, 2012).

Holland, S., 'Contrasting rural communities: the experience of South Yorkshire in the mid nineteenth century', PhD thesis (Sheffield Hallam University, 2013).

Holland, S., 'Doncaster and its environs: town and countryside – a reciprocal relationship?', in M. Hammond and B. Sloan (eds), *Rural–urban relationships in the nineteenth century: uneasy neighbours?* (Abingdon, 2016), pp. 77–89.

Holland, S., 'The evolution of a northern corn market: Doncaster, 1843–1873', *Northern History*, 52/2 (2015), pp. 233–49.

Holland, S., 'Farm service and hiring practices in mid-nineteenth-century England: the Doncaster region in the West Riding of Yorkshire', in J. Whittle (ed.), *Servants in rural Europe 1400–1900* (Woodbridge, 2017), pp. 183–202.

Holland, S., 'Knowledge networks in mid nineteenth century England: a case study of the Doncaster district, South Yorkshire, England', in Y. Segers and L. Van Molle (eds), *Knowledge networks in rural Europe since 1700* (forthcoming).

Holland, S. and Robinson, L.E., 'The fluidity of the "farming ladder": the experience of the Duffin family, Yorkshire, 1870–1950', *Journal of Community and Family History*, 19/2 (2016), pp. 106–28.

Horn, P., *Joseph Arch 1826–1919: the farm workers' leader* (Kineton, 1971).

Horn, P., *Labouring life in the countryside* (Stroud, 1987).

Horn, P., *Ladies of the manor: wives and daughters in country-house society 1830–1918* (Stroud, 1991).

Hoskins, W.G., *Local history in England* (London, 1959).

Howe, A., *Free trade and liberal England 1846–1946* (Oxford, 1997).

Howkins, A., *Poor labouring men: rural radicalism in Norfolk, 1870–1923* (London, 1985).

Howkins, A., *Reshaping rural England: a social history 1850–1925* (London, 1991).

Howkins, A., 'Rurality and English identity', in D. Morley and K. Robbins (eds), *British cultural studies* (Oxford, 2001), pp. 145–56.

Howkins, A., 'Social, cultural and domestic life', in E.J.T. Collins (ed.), *The agrarian history of England and Wales*, Vol. VII, 1850–1914, Part II (Cambridge, 2000), pp. 1354–424.

Howkins, A., 'Types of rural communities', in E.J.T. Collins (ed.), *The agrarian history of England and Wales*, Vol. VII, 1850–1914, Part 1 (Cambridge, 2000), pp. 1297–353.

Howkins, A. and Verdon, N., 'Adaptable and sustainable? Male farm service and the agricultural labour force in midland and southern England, c.1850–1925', *Economic History Review*, 61/2 (2008), pp. 467–95.

Hudson, P., 'Regional and local history: globalisation, post-modernism, and the future', *Journal of Regional and Local Studies*, 20/1 (1999), pp. 5–24.

Hunt, E.H., 'Industrialisation and regional wage inequality: wages in Britain, 1760–1914', *Economic History Review*, 46/4 (1986), pp. 935–66.

Hunt, E.H., 'Labour productivity in English agriculture, 1850–1914', *Economic History Review*, 20/2 (1967), pp. 280–92.

Jackson, A.J.H., 'The "open–closed" settlement model and the interdisciplinary formulations of Dennis Mills: conceptualising local rural change', *Rural History*, 23/2 (2012), pp. 121–36.

Johnson, J.H., 'Harvest migration from nineteenth century Ireland', *Transactions of the Institute of British Geographers*, 41 (1967), pp. 97–112.

Jones, M., *The making of the South Yorkshire landscape* (Barnsley, 2000).

Khun Song, B., 'Parish typology and the operation of the poor laws in early nineteenth century Oxfordshire', *Agricultural History Review*, 50/2 (2002), pp. 203–24.

Kussmaul, A., *Servants in husbandry in early modern England* (Cambridge, 1981).

Lane, J., *Apprenticeship in England 1600–1914* (London, 1996).

Larsen, R. and Royle, E. (eds), *Archbishop Thomson's visitation returns for the diocese of York, 1865* (York, 2006).

Lloyd-Jones, R. and Lewis, M.J., *British industrial capitalism since the industrial revolution* (London, 1998).

Lyle, M., 'Regional agricultural wage variation in early nineteenth century England', *Agricultural History Review*, 55/1 (2007), pp. 95–106.

McDonagh, B., *Elite women and the agricultural landscape, 1700–1830* (Abingdon, 2017).

Bibliography

MacDonald, S., 'Model farms', in G.E. Mingay (ed.), *The Victorian countryside* (London, 1981), pp. 214–26.

Mills, D.R., 'Canwick (Lincolnshire) and Melbourn (Cambridgeshire) in comparative perspective within the open–closed village model', *Rural History*, 17/1 (2006), pp. 1–22.

Mills, D.R., 'The development of rural settlement around Lincoln, with special reference to the eighteenth and nineteenth centuries', *East Midland Geographer*, 11 (1959), pp. 3–15.

Mills, D.R., 'English villages in the eighteenth and nineteenth centuries: a sociological approach', *Amateur Historian*, 6/8 (1965), pp. 271–8.

Mills, D.R., 'The geographical effects of the laws of settlement in Nottinghamshire: an analysis of Francis Howell's report, 1848', in D.R. Mills (ed.), *English rural communities: the impact of a specialised economy* (London, 1978).

Mills, D.R., 'Landownership and rural population, with special reference to Leicestershire in the Mid nineteenth century', PhD thesis (University of Leicester, 1963).

Mills, D.R., *Lord and peasant in nineteenth century Britain* (London, 1980).

Mills, D.R., 'The poor laws and the distribution of population c. 1600–1860, with special reference to Lincolnshire', *Transactions of the Institute of British Geographers*, 26 (1959), pp. 185–95.

Mills, D., *Rural community history from trade directories* (Aldenham, 2001).

Mills, D., 'Trouble with farms at the census office: an evaluation of farm statistics from the censuses of 1851–1881 in England and Wales', *Agricultural History Review*, 47/1 (1999), pp. 58–77.

Mills, D. and Mills, J., 'Farms, farmers and farm workers in the nineteenth century census enumerators' books: a Lincolnshire case study', *The Local Historian*, 27 (1997), pp. 130–43.

Mills, D.R. and Schürer, K. (eds), *Local communities in the Victorian census enumerators' books* (Oxford, 1996).

Mills, D.R. and Short, B.M., 'Social change and social conflict in nineteenth century England: the use of the open-closed village model', *The Journal of Peasant Studies*, 10/4 (1983), pp. 253–62.

Mingay, G.E. (ed.), *The agrarian history of England and Wales*, Vol. VI, 1750–1850 (Cambridge, 1989).

Mingay, G.E., *Land and society in England 1750–1980* (London, 1994).

Mingay, G.E., *Rural life in Victorian England* (London, 1976).

Mingay, G.E., 'The rural slum', in M. Gaskell (ed.), *Slums* (Leicester, 1990), pp. 92–143.

Mingay, G.E. (ed.), *The Victorian countryside* (London, 1981).

Mingay, G.E., 'The Farmer', in E.J.T. Collins (ed), *The agrarian history of England and Wales*, Vol. VII, 1850–1914 (Cambridge, 2000), pp. 759–809.

Miskell, L., '"Putting on a show": the Royal Agricultural Society of England and the market town c. 1840–1876', *Agricultural History Review*, 60/1 (2012), pp. 37–59.

Moore, D.C., *The politics of deference* (New York, 1976).

Moore, J.R., *Religion in Victorian Britain: sources* (Manchester, 1988).

Moses, G., '"Rude and rustic": hiring fairs and their critics in East Yorkshire, c.1850–75', *Rural History*, 7/2 (1996), pp. 151–75.

Moses, G., *Rural reform in nineteenth century England: the crusade against adolescent farm servants and hiring fairs* (Lampeter, 2007).

Mutch, A., 'The "farming ladder" in north Lancashire, 1840–1914: myth or reality?', *Northern History*, 27 (1991), pp. 162–83.

Nicholas, T., 'Businessmen and land ownership in the late nineteenth century', *Economic History Review*, 52/1 (1999), pp. 27–44.

Nunn, P.J., 'The management of some South Yorkshire landed estates in the eighteenth and nineteenth centuries, linked with the central economic development of the area, 1700–1850', PhD thesis (University of Sheffield, 1985).

Obelkevich, J., *Religion and rural society, South Lindsey 1825–1875* (Oxford, 1976).
O'Leary, J.G. (ed.), *The autobiography of Joseph Arch* (London, 1966).
Overton, M., *Agricultural revolution in England: the transformation of the agrarian economy 1500–1850* (Cambridge, 1996).
Overton, M., 'Re-establishing the English agricultural revolution', *Agricultural History Review*, 44/1 (1996), pp. 1–20.
Palmer, M., *Framework knitting* (Aylesbury, 2002).
Paz, D.G., 'William Aldam, backbench MP for Leeds 1841–1847: national issues versus local interests', *Transactions of the Thoresby Society*, 2nd series, 8 (1998).
Perren, R., 'The marketing of agricultural products: farm gate to retail store', in E.J.T. Collins (ed.), *The agrarian history of England and Wales*, Vol. VII, 1850–1914, Part 2 (Cambridge, 2000), pp. 953–98.
Perren, R., 'Markets and marketing', in G.E. Mingay (ed.), *The agrarian history of England and Wales*, Vol. VI, 1750–1850 (Cambridge, 1989: 2011 edition), pp. 190–274.
Perren, R., 'Milling', in E.J.T. Collins (ed.), *The agrarian history of England and Wales*, Vol. VII, 1850–1914, Part 2 (Cambridge, 2000), pp. 1062–75.
Perry, P.J., 'High farming in Victorian Britain: the financial foundations', *Agricultural History*, 52/3 (1978), pp. 364–79.
Perry, P.J., 'High farming in Victorian Britain: prospect and retrospect', *Agricultural History*, 55/2 (1981), pp. 156–66.
Phythian-Adams, C., 'Local history and national history: the quest for the peoples of England', *Rural History*, 2/1 (1991), pp. 1–23.
Phythian-Adams, C., 'Local history and societal history', *Local Population Studies*, 51 (1993), pp. 30–45.
Phythian-Adams, C., *Rethinking English local history* (Leicester, 1987).
Phythian-Adams, C. (ed.), *Societies, cultures, and kinship, 1580–1850: cultural provinces and English local history* (Leicester, 1996).
Pickering, P.A. and Tyrrell, A., *The people's bread: a history of the Anti-Corn Law League* (London, 2000).
Pierson, W., *Methodism in Sprotbrough* (Sprotbrough, 1980).
Pollard, S. and Holmes, C. (eds), *Essays in the economic and social history of South Yorkshire* (Sheffield, 1976).
Rawding, C., 'Village type and employment structure: an analysis in the nineteenth century Lincolnshire wolds', *Local Population Studies*, 53/2 (1994), pp. 53–68.
Reay, B., *The last rising of the agricultural labourers: rural life and protest in nineteenth-century England* (London, 2010).
Reay, B., *Microhistories: demography, society and culture in rural England, 1800–1930* (Cambridge, 2004).
Reay, B., *Rural Englands: labouring lives in the nineteenth century* (Basingstoke, 2004).
Richardson, R.C. (ed.), *The changing face of English local history* (Aldershot, 2000).
Richardson, S., 'Independence and deference: a study of the West Riding electorate, 1832–1841', PhD thesis (University of Leeds, 1995).
Roberts, B.K., *Rural settlement in Britain* (London, 1977).
Rodgers, A., *Approaches to local history* (London, 1977).
Royle, E., *Modern Britain, a social history 1750–2011* (3rd edition, London, 2012).
Rubinstein, W.D., 'New men of wealth and the purchase of land in nineteenth century Britain', *Past and Present*, 92 (1981), pp. 125–47.

Bibliography

Salmon, P., *Electoral reform at work: local politics and national parties, 1832–1841* (Woodbridge, 2002).

Sayer, K., *Country cottages: a cultural history* (Manchester, 2000).

Sayer, K., 'Field-faring women: the resistance of women who worked in the fields of nineteenth-century England', *Women's History Review*, 2/1 (1993), pp. 185–98.

Schonhardt-Bailey, C., *From the corn laws to free trade, interest, ideas and institutions in historical perspective* (Cambridge, MA, 2006).

Schonhardt-Bailey, C., 'Specific factors, capital markets, portfolio diversification, and free trade: domestic determinants of the repeal of the corn laws', *World Politics*, 43 (1991), pp. 545–69.

Scowcroft, P.L., *Cricket in Doncaster and district: an outline history* (Doncaster, 1985).

Seaborne, M.V.J.S., *The English schools: its architecture and organisation 1370–1870* (London, 1971).

Shaw-Taylor, L., 'Family farms and capitalist farms in mid nineteenth century England', *Agricultural History Review*, 53/2 (2005), pp. 158–91.

Short, B., 'The evolution of contrasting communities within rural England', in B. Short (ed.), *The English rural community: image and analysis* (Cambridge, 1992), pp. 19–43.

Sigsworth, E.M., *The brewing trade in the industrial revolution: the case of Yorkshire* (York, 1967).

Smith, G., *Cusworth Hall and the Battie-Wrightson family* (Doncaster, 1990).

Smith, G., *Sprotbrough Hall* (Doncaster, 1966).

Smith, J.A., 'Landownership and social change in late nineteenth century Britain', *Economic History Review*, 53/4 (November, 2000), pp. 767–76.

Snell, K.D.M., *Annals of the labouring poor: social change and agrarian England 1660–1900* (Cambridge, 1985).

Snell, K.D.M., 'Gravestones, belonging and local attachment in England 1700–2000', *Past and Present*, 179 (2003), pp. 97–134.

Snell, K.D.M., 'Settlement, poor law and the rural historian: new approaches and opportunities', *Rural History*, 3/2 (1992), pp. 145–72.

Snell, K.D.M. and Ell, P.S., *Rival Jerusalems: the geography of Victorian religion* (Cambridge, 2000).

Spencer, D., 'Reformulating the "closed" parish thesis: associations, interests, and interaction', *Journal of Historical Geography*, 26/11 (2000), pp. 83–98.

Spring, D., 'English landowners and nineteenth-century industrialism', in J.T. Ward and R.G. Wilson (eds), *Land and industry: the landed estate and the industrial revolution* (Newton Abbot, 1971), pp. 16–62.

Spufford, M., *Contrasting communities: English villagers in the sixteenth and seventeenth centuries* (Cambridge, 1974).

Stead, D.R., 'The mobility of English tenant farmers, c. 1700–1850', *Agricultural History Review*, 51/2 (2003), pp. 173–89.

Stobart, J., 'Food retailers and rural communities: Cheshire butchers in the long eighteenth century', *Local Population Studies*, 79 (2007), pp. 23–37.

Tann, J., 'Corn milling', in G.E. Mingay (ed.), *The agrarian history of England and Wales*, Vol. VI, 1750–1850 (Cambridge, 1989: 2011 edition), pp. 397–415.

Taylor, C., *Villages and farmstead. a history of rural settlement in England* (London, 1983).

Thompson, F.M.L., *English landed society in the nineteenth century* (London, 1963).

Thompson, F.M.L., *Gentrification and the enterprise culture, Britain 1780–1980* (Oxford, 2001).

Thompson, F.M.L., 'Landowners and the rural community', in G.E. Mingay (ed.), *The Victorian countryside* (London, 1981), pp. 491–505.

Tiller, K., *English local history: an introduction* (Stroud, 1992).

Tiller, K. and Dymond, D., 'Local History at the Crossroads', *The Local Historian*, 37/4 (2007), pp. 250–58.

Turner, M.E., Beckett, J.V. and Afton, B., *Agricultural rent in England, 1690–1914* (Cambridge, 1997).

Turner, M.E., Beckett, J.V. and Afton, B., *Farm production in England 1700–1914* (Oxford, 2001).

Various authors, 'Food processing industries', in E.J.T. Collins (ed.), *The agrarian history of England and Wales*, Vol. VII, 1850–1914, Part 2 (Cambridge, 2000), pp. 1060–100.

Verdon, N., 'Changing patterns of female employment in rural England, c. 1789–1890', PhD thesis (University of Leicester, 1999).

Verdon, N., 'The employment of women and children in agriculture: a reassessment of agricultural gangs in nineteenth century Norfolk', *Agricultural History Review*, 49/1 (2001), pp. 41–55.

Verdon, N., 'The "lady farmer": gender, widowhood and farming in Victorian England', in R. Hoyle (ed.), *The farmer in England, 1650–1980* (Farnham, 2013), p. 241–62.

Verdon, N., *Rural women workers in nineteenth-century England: gender, work and wages* (Woodbridge, 2002).

Verdon, N., '"… subjects deserving of the highest praise": farmers' wives and the farm economy in England, c. 1700–1850', *Agricultural History Review*, 51/1 (2003), pp. 23–39.

Verdon, N., *Working the land: a history of the farmworker in England from 1850 to the present day* (London, 2017).

Waddington, K., '"It might not be a nuisance in a country cottage": sanitary conditions and images of health in Victorian rural Wales', *Rural History*, 23/2 (2012), pp. 185–204.

Wade-Martins, S., *The English model farm: building the agricultural ideal* (Macclesfield, 2002).

Wade-Martins, S., *Farmers, landlords and landscapes: rural Britain 1720–1870* (Macclesfield, 2004).

Walton, J.R., 'Pedigree and the national cattle herd c. 1750–1950', *Agricultural History Review*, 34/2 (1986), pp. 149–70.

Ward, J.T., 'The squire as businessman: William Aldam of Frickley Hall (1813–1890)', *Transactions of the Hunter Archaeological Society*, 8/4 (1962).

Ward, J.T., 'West Riding landowners and mining in the nineteenth century in Yorkshire', *Yorkshire Bulletin of Economic and Social Research*, (1963).

Ward, J.T. and Wilson, R.G., *Land and industry: the landed estate and the industrial revolution* (Newton Abbot, 1971).

Watts, M., *Corn milling* (Aylesbury, 1983).

Webster, S.A., 'Agents and professionalism: improvement on the Egremont estates c.1770 to c.1860', PhD thesis (University of Nottingham, 2010).

Webster, S.A., 'Estate improvement and the professionalisation of land agents on the Egremont estates in Sussex and Yorkshire, 1770–1835', *Rural History*, 18/1 (2007), pp. 47–69.

Wells, R. and Reed, M. (eds), *Class, Conflict and Protest in the English Countryside 1700–1880* (London, 1990).

Wiener, M.J., *English culture and the decline of the industrial spirit, 1850–1980* (2nd edn, Cambridge, 2004).

Williams, S., *Poverty, gender and life cycle under the English poor law 1760–1834* (Woodbridge, 2011).

Williamson, T. and Bellamy, L., *Property and landscape: a social history of landownership and the English countryside* (London, 1987).

Wilson, R.G., *Gentlemen merchants: the merchant community in Leeds 1700–1830* (Manchester, 1971).

Wolffe, J. (ed.), *Yorkshire returns of the 1851 census of religious worship, vol. 3: West Riding (Yorkshire)* (York, 2005).

Wrathmell, S., *Leeds* (London, 2005).

Wright, G.N., *Discovering epitaphs* (Aylesbury, 1972).

Wrightson, K., 'Villages, villagers and village studies', *Historical Journal*, 18/3 (1975), pp. 632–9.

Wrigley, E.A., *Continuity, chance and change: the character of the industrial revolution in England* (Cambridge, 1988).
Yamamoto, C., 'Two labour markets in nineteenth century English agriculture: the Trentham Home Farm, Staffordshire', *Rural History*, 15/1 (2004), pp. 89–116.
Yasumoto, M., 'Industrialisation and demographic change in a Yorkshire parish', *Local Population Studies*, 27 (1981), pp. 10–25.

Index

Agricultural engineering 62, 67
Agricultural machinery 42–4, 59
Agricultural workers
    agricultural labourers 32, 46–7, 71–3, 97–9,
        106, 115–18
    children 24, 74, 76–8, 100, 103, 106–9
    cottages 71, 79–5
    farm servants 24, 26, 32, 74–6, 85, 107
    Hodge stereotype 15, 32
    wages 32, 47, 72–6, 78, 84–6
    women 74, 76–9, 82
Aldam (family) 11–12, 18–19, 22–5, 82–4, 103,
    108
Amory, Mary 20–1
Anglican *see also* Church of England 4, 24,
    87–92, 95–101
Anti-Corn Law League 22, 27
Apprenticeships and apprentices 60, 68
Arable crops 36–7, 39–40
    barley 36–7, 39, 55
    peas 36–7
    potatoes 36, 78
    turnips 18, 30, 36–8, 40, 46, 77–8
    wheat 18, 36–8, 46, 49, 51, 55
Arch, Joseph 95
Askern 121–2

Balby 8, 35, 64, 82, 100, 118
Barnby Dun 55, 83
Battie-Wrightson family 11–12, 18, 24–6, 54,
    65, 93
Blacksmith 53, 57–61, 70, 123
Bladworth, John (Stainforth) 48, 78, 83, 109
Boat building 65, 68–9
Boot and shoe maker 58
Braithwell
    agriculture 38
    cottages 83–4
    education 101–3, 106, 108
    farms and farmers 42, 47, 50, 108, 122

Farmers' Club 20, 46–7
    landownership 20–1
    multi-freeholder village 11–12
    quarrying
    recreation 115
    religion 89–90, 100
    trades and crafts 54–9, 69
Brewers/brewing 55, 85
Brickmakers/brickmaking 53, 57, 63–4
British and Foreign School Society 101
Brown family 11–12, 19–22, 63–4, 80–2, 94, 101

Cadeby 28, 46, 91–2, 96, 103–4, 108
Caird, James 15, 29, 40, 124
Cattle plague 18
Charnock, J.H. 37–41, 45, 72–3, 78, 80
Church of England *see also* Anglican 23
Clarkson family 69
Clergy 23–4, 71–2, 75, 81, 97, 111–13
    Bower, Revd 95
    Fardell, Revd 45, 80, 105, 112–13, 120
    Hodgson, Revd 103
    Jennings, Revd 104
    Ornsby, Revd 24, 98, 102, 105, 113, 116
    Skinner, Revd 24
    Surtees, Revd 77–8, 82, 85, 91, 97, 105
    Thomas, Revd 23–4, 75, 77, 82–4, 94–8,
        108–9
    Vaughan, Revd 75, 98
Coal mining 65
Contrasting communities *see* village
    differentiation
Copley family 9–11, 17–18, 45, 91–2, 103–4,
    114–16
Corn Laws 20, 22–3, 27–9
Cottages 64, 77, 79–84
Cusworth 18, 84, 91, 93, 121

Darley's Brewery (Thorne) 55
Denton, J.B. 44

Domestic servants 107, 115
Don Foundry 62, 67
Don Pottery (Swinton) 67–8
Don Valley 119–121
Doncaster 29, 32, 35, 49–52, 73–4, 118–19
    Agricultural Society 20, 26, 31, 40, 47–8, 50
    Anti-Corn Law Association 27
    Board of Education 103
    Choral Union Festival 112
    Corporation 11–12, 19, 30–1, 43, 49–52, 124–5
    Doncaster Chronicle 31, 47, 76, 84, 99, 116–19
    Doncaster Gazette 27, 31, 49–51, 76, 117, 121
    Farmers' Club 20
    Horticultural Society 116
    Races 98
    Statutes 75–6, 119
Dyson, Thomas 12, 20–1, 46–7, 50, 122

Edlington 47, 121
Education 101, 104
    attendance 106–9
    clergy 24, 102, 105
    curriculum 104–5
    Doncaster Board of Education 103
    Education Act (1870) 100, 103–4
    landowners 21
    Royal Commissions on Education 101–2, 106
    teachers
    village schools 101–4

Farm size 19, 41–3, 50, 69, 123
Farmers
    tenant farmer 17, 21, 24–7, 29, 41–2, 44–7
    Birks, Thomas and Joseph (Fishlake) 55
    Blagden, George (Warmsworth) 29, 50, 65
    Bradford family (Rossington) 42, 122
    Butterill family (Rossington) 44
    Crawshaw family (Warmsworth) 25–6
    Ellis family (Rossington) 44
    Hanson, Mr (Rossington) 44
    Hickson, Richard (Sprotbrough) 46, 48, 50
    Hudson family (Rossington) 44
    Innocent family (Rossington) 25–6, 44, 50
    Jenning family (Rossington) 25, 50
    Kay, George and Charles, 21, 55
    Piggott family (Rossington) 44, 48
    Thompson family (Braithwell) 47, 50, 54, 60, 122
    Vickers, Mr 26
    Wainwright family (Rossington) 25, 122
    Walker family (Warmsworth) 25, 48, 50
    Walker, Mr (Rossington) 48, 50
    Wilkinson, Thomas (Fishlake) 55
    Webster, Mr (Sprotbrough) 48
    Wood, John (Sprotbrough) 25
    Wood, Thomas (Sprotbrough) 18, 25–6, 29–30, 48, 50, 82
Fishlake
    agriculture 36, 38–9
    cottages
    education 101–2, 104–7, 109
    farms and farmers 42, 122
    landownership 20
    multi-freeholder village 11–12, 28
    recreation 112–13, 115–16, 118
    religion 24, 89–90, 98–9
    trades, crafts and industry 54–5, 57, 59–60, 64
Flint grinding 67
Food processing 53–5, 125–6
Fox, Edward (Braithwell) 21
Framework knitting 69
Frickley 18–19, 22–3, 82

Gardens 79–80, 83–5, 116–17
Geology 11, 35–7, 46, 48, 53
Great Northern Railway 8, 11, 35, 51

Hanley's flourmill 54
Harvest 74, 77, 108
Haymaking 74
    Hatfield 13, 99
Hexthorpe 8, 35
High Farming 41–2
Hiring Fairs *see also* Doncaster Statutes 23–4, 74–6, 125
Hiring Practices 20, 23–4, 32, 75, 85–6, 119

Innkeeper *see* publican

Index

Knowledge network(s) 26, 30, 45–7, 68, 70, 124–6

Land agent 17–18, 26–30, 124
Levitt Hagg 12, 18, 62, 65–7, 97, 121
Lime 38, 65–7, 121, 124
Livestock 26, 38–40, 48, 51, 98
    cattle including cattle breeding 18, 38–40, 43, 51
    sheep 38, 40, 48

Maltsters/malting 39, 55–6
Manure 37, 42, 46, 48
Market (Doncaster) 9, 31, 47–9, 70, 98, 118
    butter 51
    cattle 39, 51
    corn 31, 49–50
    corn exchange 51–2
    fruit 51
    hall 31, 51
    meat 51
    poultry 51
    wool 51
Marshalls, Sons and Co 44
Micklebring 47
Micro-commerce 13, 35, 53, 58, 69–70
Mills, Dennis R.
    application of theories to village case studies 41, 53, 73, 80, 88, 96
    theories 2–6, 123–5
Millers/milling/mills 52, 54–5, 67–8, 96, 106, 120–1
Model farms 19, 43–4, 124
Models of village typology *see* village differentiation

Nassau, George 58–9
National Society for Promoting the Education of the Poor in the Principles of the Established Church 100–1, 104
National Schools 100–4
Non-conformity 88, 91–2, 95–100

Politics 4, 21, 27
Poor law 3–5, 7, 60, 71, 81
Poverty 4, 71, 82, 125
Public house 59–61, 113–14, 120
Publican 55, 57, 61

Quarrying 12, 64–7, 96–7
    Levitt Hagg 18, 62, 65–7, 90, 97, 121
    Lockwood, Kemp and Blagden (later Lockwood, Blagden and Crawshaw) 65

Reciprocal relationship *see also* town and country (relationship between) 7, 9, 30–1, 49–50, 70, 125
Recreation 17, 21, 24, 111–22
Religious Census (1851) 88–92, 95, 98
River Don 10–13, 17, 35, 67–8, 120–1
Rossington
    agriculture 36, 38–40
    cottages 80–2, 84
    education 101–102, 107, 109
    estate village 1, 11–13
    farms and farmers 25–6, 28, 42–4, 48, 50, 122
    landownership 19, 61, 63, 124
    recreation 115–116
    religion 89–90, 92–6, 99
    trades and crafts 57, 59–60, 64
Royal Agricultural Society of England 19, 26, 32, 37, 79
Rural Idyll 71, 79, 119

Sail making 69
Scawsby 46
    self-contained community *see* village differentiation
Shop keeper 57, 59, 61, 84, 117
South Yorkshire Railway 11, 35, 51, 62
Spheres of influence 7, 21, 29, 67, 98, 125
Sport 100, 111, 115–116, 118
Sprotbrough
    agriculture 36–8
    Annual Subscription Ball 114
    cottages 80–2, 84–5
    education 103–6
    estate village 9–11, 28
    Farmers' Club 30, 45–6, 48
    farms and farmers 25–6, 42, 48, 50, 52
    landownership 17–18, 25, 62
    recreation 112–116, 118, 120–1
    religion 89, 91, 95–7
    trades and crafts 54, 56–9
Stainforth
    agriculture 36, 38

    cottages 83
    education 103–4, 106
    farms and farmers 42, 44, 48, 78, 109
    landownership 20, 78
    multi-freeholder village 11, 13
    recreation 112, 122
    religion 89–90, 99
    Stainforth and Keadby canal 68
    trades and crafts 54–7, 61, 68
Stainton 47
Steam threshing 74
Stone picking 77
Swinton 67–8, 121

Tailor 57, 59
Thorne 47, 55, 68, 99, 104, 113
Town and country (relationship between) *see also* reciprocal relationship 6–9, 22, 47–52, 70, 119, 124–6

Village differentiation *see also* Mills, Dennis R.
    Banks, Sarah 5, 124–5
    Beckett, John 3
    Brown, David 2
    continuum 6, 124–5
    contrasting communities 1, 3, 5–6, 124

    Howkins, Alun 5–6, 111, 124–5
    open-close model 2–6, 73, 124–5
    Reay, Barry 2, 125
    self-contained community 3, 7, 30, 56, 58
    Short, Brian 5–6, 124
    Spencer, D. 6, 125
    Spufford, Margaret 3
    village typology 1–2, 15, 41, 62, 71–3, 123

Wadworth 104, 121
Warmsworth 11
    agriculture 36–8
    Cottagers' Horticultural show 84, 116–17
    cottages 82–3
    education 103, 105–8
    estate village 1, 11–13
    farms and farmers 25–6, 29, 42, 48, 50
    landownership 18–19
    quarrying 62–7
    recreation 112, 115, 118
    religion 89–90, 93–4, 97–8
    trades and crafts 57–61

Wheelwright 53, 57–9
Wood, Thomas 17–18, 26, 29–30, 48, 82, 109